DISTRIBUTIONAL ARCHAEOLOGY

DISTRIBUTIONAL ARCHAEOLOGY

-- -- -- -- -- -- -- -- -- -- -- -- --
-- -- -- -- -- -- -- -- -- -- -- -- --
-- -- -- -- -- -- -- -- -- -- -- -- --

JAMES I. EBERT

UNIVERSITY OF NEW MEXICO PRESS

-- -- -- -- -- -- -- -- -- -- -- -- --

ALBUQUERQUE

Library of Congress Cataloging–in–Publication Data

Ebert, James I.
Distributional archaeology/James I. Ebert.—1st ed.
    p.   cm.
Includes bibliographical references and index.
ISBN 0–8263–1350–7
1. Archaeology—Methodology.
2. Distributional archaeology.
3. Antiquities—Analysis.
I. Title.
CC75.7.E38   1992
931.1'01—dc20
91–46078
    CIP

First edition

This book is dedicated to my father,
IAN OLERIA EBERT,
who taught me that being a scientist entails questioning previous science, and to my mother,
DORIS FULLER EBERT,
who tried to teach me that one should be considerate and polite when questioning others.
I hope I fulfill their expectations.

CONTENTS

-- -- -- -- -- -- -- -- -- -- -- --

FIGURES

-- -- -- -- -- -- -- -- -- -- -- -- --

TABLES

-- -- -- -- -- -- -- -- -- -- -- -- --

PREFACE

-- -- -- -- -- -- -- -- -- -- -- -- --

This book discusses a number of topics: the philosophy of science; human settlement and mobility on a systemic level; subsistence and technological strategies; ethnoarchaeology; the archaeology, ethnography, and ethnohistory of the Great Basin; field survey methods and techniques; cultural and natural "formation processes"; and statistical and spatial analytical methods. But let there be no mistake: this is *not* a book about hunter-gatherers, Wyoming, archaeological survey, post-depositional processes, or statistics. Rather, I bring all of these areas of explanation and argument to bear on what I believe is the most critical question in archaeology today: whether we can continue to think in terms of *sites*, or whether this most basic unit of archaeological discussion rests upon so many untenable, unarticulated, in fact unarticulable assumptions as to be a liability to the advancement and credibility of our field.

It may sound as if I am advocating a completely different archaeology. I am not. Simply put, this is archaeology minus sites as units of discovery, "analytical units," or in fact operational or conceptual units of any sort. Although I illustrate that the site concept is flawed and unworkable on virtually all theoretical and methodological levels, this need not mean that an archaeology built largely upon the site must be wholly discarded. What it does mean is that archaeologists must work actively to exclude the conceptual baggage that accompanies sites from the methodological and theoretical aspects of their work.

We must stop trying to see instants in the past, since we cannot. We must begin to understand that the archaeological record is a composite of distributions at many spatial and temporal scales superimposed one upon another. This realization will free us to characterize the archaeological record as the unitary and inseparable product of many millions of human events upon the landscape.

ACKNOWLEDGMENTS

-- -- -- -- -- -- -- -- -- -- -- -- --

Many people have encouraged and helped me in this work. Foremost, I thank Dr. Lewis R. Binford, who is directly responsible, whether he likes it or not, for much of what appears here. He has not always agreed completely with all of my perceptions and interpretations of the archaeological record, and I am not sure he does now, but he has always been a source of inspirational approaches, most important of which is the constant questioning of one's own assumptions.

I would also like to thank the many colleagues who have participated with me in innumerable discussions and some of whom were directly involved in the work upon which this book is based. These people include but not limited to Eileen Camilli, Gregory Camilli, LuAnn Wandsnider, Robert Foley, Glynn Isaac, Robert Dunnell, Chris Carr, David Hurst Thomas, John Pfeiffer, Lawrence Straus, Sarah Schlanger, Signa Larralde, Galen Brown, Alberto Gutierrez, Eric Ingbar, Thomas R. Lyons, Francis McManamon, Jack Bennett, Bryan Marozas, Jeffrey Reid, Bill Rathje, Michael Schiffer, Jeremy Sabloff, Jim Hester, Jackie Rossignol, Michael Berman, Robert Hitchcock, Henry Harpending, Ed Wilmsen, Robert Santley, Janet Santley, Anna Backer, Nancy Stone, Michael Shott, Tim White, Robert Blumenschine, Fidelis Masao, Audax Mabullah, Lee Heinsch, Garth Sampson, Charlie King, Shelley King, Homer Campbell, Karen Campbell, Bill Gossett, and Cye Gossett (not necessarily in that order). Without their encouragement and help, I might not have chosen to proceed in this archaeologically rather unconventional direction.

None of these people necessarily agrees with anything you will read here. But they were always willing to listen and talk to me about these things, or read and comment on what I have written during the last fifteen years. Some of them participated in arriving at the many assertions I advance here. All of them are to be thanked, and none should be faulted for what you will read in this book. Some of them will probably argue with it eloquently. I certainly hope so.

DISTRIBUTIONAL ARCHAEOLOGY

1

MANY ARCHAEOLOGIES,

TWO ARCHAEOLOGICAL RECORDS

-- -- -- -- -- -- -- -- -- -- -- -- --

In 1967, as a sophomore physics major at Michigan State University, I made a terrible mistake and took an introductory class in archaeology. I enjoyed it enormously, intrigued that artifacts left behind by people long dead could help one learn about things that are difficult to define even when studying living groups: social systems, politics, subsistence, and interaction with the environment. Archaeology as anthropology was a new direction that had only very recently been proclaimed by Lewis Binford. I was immediately enthralled by the implication that archaeologists, largely due to the lack of verbal or historical biases in their data, might become better anthropologists than ethnologists themselves.

Charles Cleland, my teacher, offered me inspiration and encouragement. The following semester I decided to take another of his courses. Shortly after registration, my advisor called me to his office. The entire curriculum to be taken by physics majors, he told me, was predetermined, class by class. There was no room for "soft elective courses." I would have to drop my archaeology class and take something more appropriate for a scientist.

Many college students in 1967 were making drastic decisions that would change their lives forever. Mine was to forget about being a physicist. Instead of dropping my archaeology seminar, I dropped all my physics classes. With a full anthropology class load, my grade point average plummeted. I was used to problems that could be solved and answers that could be calculated, and there were none of these in my newly chosen field. Deciding that *real* archaeology—field archaeology— might be less equivocal, I applied for and received a National Science Foundation traineeship to work with a Michigan State University Museum crew along the shore of Lake Michigan the following summer.

We walked many miles of Lake Michigan beach, became suntanned, and found dozens of those most basic entities in archaeological dis- covery and analysis, sites. I remember one site in particular. It was located on a tiny stream emptying into the lake, Wycamp Creek, and in the damp and easy-to-excavate dune sand were hundreds of stone flakes and tools, ceramic sherds, and stains defining pits and post molds. They were distributed in a bewildering array of clusters and layers. One feature in the site interested everyone. It was a large, flat rock, around which five or six small clusters of chert flakes seemed to be piled. Careful inspection and measurement of the flakes in the sepa- rate piles suggested that they might be different from one another.

"Look, that just has to be where he sat, and he sorted the flakes into piles as he made them," we repeatedly told one another and many visitors to the site. Privately, however, I was disturbed. Was this what we wanted to know about the past—what some individual did in a specific place and time? Later, as I lay in my sleeping bag feeling just a bit cheated, I decided that my disillusionment would probably soon fade. This was the first time I had been in the field, I was young, and there was undoubtedly something I was missing.

Unfortunately, my frustration with the dominant focus of archae- ology—reconstructing anecdotal scenes from the past—has not faded. Over the years, however, I have found that many other archaeologists are similarly frustrated, and thus there may be hope for change.

Archaeology has, in fact, undergone some very profound changes since my undergraduate days. Spectacular innovations have been made in analytical technologies: materials analysis, remote sensing, dating techniques, and particularly the use of computers for recoding and stor- ing data, statistical analysis, mapping, drafting, and writing.

A brief florescence in ethnoarchaeological studies has now largely subsided. While archaeologists ascribed great promise to the study of "primitive" peoples, especially hunter-gatherers, a number of factors may have dulled their passion. In particular it soon became apparent that direct translations between the observed behavior of living peo- ple and the archaeological record resulted in tautological or trivial conclusions. Yet few archaeologists were energetic or courageous enough to go beyond geographic and temporal affinity as criteria for equating ethnography and archaeology. It is largely through the efforts of archaeologists "as anthropologists," too—concentrating on material culture and subsistence, rather than kinship or mythology—that it has been realized that all of those primitive hunter-gatherers really aren't. They are parts of contemporary, far more inclusive cultural systems and their behavior is no closer to that of past people than anyone else's.

The twenty-five years since the mid-sixties have also witnessed the beginning and possibly the end of the "New Archaeology." Almost everyone attributes the beginning of the New Archaeology to Lew Binford, although when I came to the University of New Mexico to study with him in 1973 I found that it was less apparent from close up just what the New Archaeology might be. The heady atmosphere in the department of anthropology was permeated with discussions of deductive versus inductive reasoning, archaeology as anthropology, archaeological statics and cultural dynamics linked by middle-range theory, processual studies, and the like. For the most part, however, the New Archaeology seemed to be Lew himself: an immensely insightful, dynamic, and charismatic man dedicated to teaching new ways (which changed almost daily) of looking at the world. Binford invested hundreds or perhaps even thousands of exciting ideas in his students (and sometimes we even reciprocated). But the most important one, and the only one that really stuck, was that to be scientists, archaeologists must think carefully about and question, explicitly and loudly, everything and everyone, every pronouncement and every assumption.

If this message was its kernel, perhaps the New Archaeology will never really end. There are some archaeologists today, however, who would tell you that it has. They promote other archaeologies or ways of thinking about the archaeological record and its origins that, it is implied, go beyond the indefinable New Archaeology.

New ways of thinking about anything are welcome, of course. Behavioral archaeology stresses the minute and cumulative interactions between artifacts and the environment that distort or transform the appearance and associations of archaeological materials, but which may be allowed for or filtered out through the exhaustive enumeration of those processes and their effects. Some of the tenets of behavioral archaeology will be examined later in this book. Postprocessual archaeology (in several guises) is essentially an antiscientific approach that questions our very ability to know and evaluate knowledge, instead of evaluating the validity of specific claims. Postprocessualism will not be evaluated in this book, for, realistically, it cannot be. Some other recent archaeologies stress common-sense reasoning swathed in almost overwhelming erudition, or the complex organization of tasks and technological components as reflected in discarded materials and faunal remains at settlements or special-use places or nodes. Most archaeologists, however, still focus unabashedly on reconstructing events and episodes at camps, pueblos, villages, and hamlets.

And on a very basic level, the foundation upon which nearly all past and present archaeologies are built is the same. They are all based on one overarching concept. The critical evaluation of this concept, and how it determines not only what we know but the very questions we can ask as archaeologists, is the subject of this book.

The concept to which I refer is that of the site. The idea of sites is so basic to archaeology that it is in essence a primitive term, not only undefined but perhaps undefinable. One needs to attempt a definition, however, in order to evaluate it.

In the remainder of this chapter I shall define the site concept, its major correlates, and its implications for archaeological thought and science. I shall do this by contrasting the two kinds of archaeological record that the site concept mandates: sealed sites and the surface archaeological record. These are not terms that all archaeologists would use, but almost all archaeologists would make equivalent verbal and conceptual distinctions.

Sealed sites consist of sealed deposits, and they have integrity. Things within the site (to a greater or lesser extent, but at least at site-sized spatial scales) remain where they were during or after they were abandoned by their users at specific times. Sites thus present a scene, or window, in space and time. They are composed of a layer or layers, stratigraphy the archaeologist can "read" to distinguish discrete, nonassociated events and times.

Surface archaeological deposits do not have integrity. They present interesting objects to the archaeologist, and are thought by many to embody some information, but the things that comprise the surface archaeological record are mixed, blended, and cannot be associated with one another reliably. No archaeologist discounts the surface archaeological record as useless, but one cannot really tell much about it because it does not have the spatial and temporal integrity that a site has. Environmental processes move things around on the surface, and the surface record has no time content, no chronological resolution, because things are not associated in sedimentary layers.

This book questions such a distinction, asking whether the surface or landscape archaeological record may not have more to tell us, and the site record less to tell us, than most archaeologists or archaeologies insist. It wonders about many of the assumptions upon which the site concept and much archaeology is implicitly founded. It offers suggestions about how data collection and analysis that is explicitly nonsite might be utilized to arrive at an archaeology based not upon sites but upon the scales and distributions of the actual, definable physical items occurring in the surface archaeological record across large, contiguous landscapes.

First, however, let us accept for a moment that there are two different sorts of archaeological record. Let us consider what and where they are, how we find them, and how conclusions about the nature of things in the past and the archaeological record follow naturally from a focus on each.

PHYSICAL REALITY

Sealed sites are rare. There is but a narrow range of circumstances within which discarded materials reflecting short behavioral episodes can be encapsulated in sediments and left undisturbed, until found by an archaeologist. Three sets of conditions must intersect in order to form a sealed site:

1. A short, relatively simple behavioral episode is prerequisite. Long occupations, many activities, and overlapping activity areas result in the overlap of debris from events, and thus their "blurring."

2. Geomorphic events must encapsulate artifacts and features shortly after the artifacts are discarded, enough to prevent disturbance by cultural or environmental processes and to preserve them in their discarded arrangement without destroying integrity.

3. An archaeologist must find the site while it still retains integrity. This is perhaps the most precarious condition of all, since a sealed site is by nature buried and invisible; sites with visible components invite environmental disturbances, artifact

hunters, and other archaeologists. When sites are discovered as a result of erosion or during construction some of their integrity is already destroyed. Only sealed sites that are discovered purposely by archaeologists retain all of their integrity, which then disappears as they are excavated. There are undoubtedly many more sites in existence than are known and have been studied—but they are hidden. We can never know how many remain, or what sorts they are.

The **surface archaeological record**, on the other hand, is ubiquitous in many types of geomorphic environments, although in some places it is difficult to detect because of ground cover. In arid regions, where the land surface can be seen, there are vast expanses covered by a detectable, continuous archaeological record of varying density and composition. Environmental processes, such as the movement of sediments by wind and water, act upon such surfaces constantly. While some archaeological materials on the surface have always been on the surface, others may have been buried and exposed many times, and in either case levels of episodic discard can be expected to be collapsed upon one another. There is no reason to suspect that in areas with heavy ground cover a surface archaeological record does not also exist, but it cannot be found easily.

It should also be borne in mind that all sealed archaeological materials were once on the surface. While they remained on the surface, they too were subjected to all of the cultural and environmental disturbance processes that affect the present surface. Unless they met the quick and gentle burial conditions discussed above, they became simply a sealed surface record. I know of no convincing or noncircular method to determine whether a stratum or floor in a sealed site deposit is (or is not) a sealed surface record. It seems likely, however, that there are far more sealed surface records than there are sealed sites, although their excavation and recovery might be very difficult.

SITES AND CONSERVATION

The rarity of sites, as opposed to the abundance of surface archaeological landscapes, has implications on various realistic as well as more theoretical planes. Quite obviously, the site record is a limited resource, although we do not know how limited. Certainly more sealed sites will be discovered, but at any moment one has access only to those already known. There really are not enough of them to go around, and when one is excavated it is gone as surely as if it had been eroded, vandalized, or bulldozed. Site-oriented archaeologists must compete for sites to excavate, and there is always the possiblity that there will be no more sites.

The surface archaeological record, however, can quite literally be expected to cover the earth's inhabitable surface. In many places it cannot be discovered easily, and in other local circumstances it has been obliterated. In many areas the density of this surface archaeological record is very low, but that fact conveys information too.

Until methods are developed to recover reliably what might be termed "sealed subsurface surface archaeological materials," however, there is enough exposed and available surface archaeological record in a few arid Western states alone to keep thousands of archaeologists busy. What is more, it is inconceivable that much of this surface archaeological record will be destroyed, although in some rare instances such activities as surface mining and reservoir digging may alter it considerably.

EXPENSE OF DATA RECOVERY

Every archaeologist knows that it is almost prohibitively expensive to excavate. As costs of excavation have continued to rise astronomically in recent years, interest in site conservation as an alternative to excavation has surged, particularly in the cultural resource management sector. In the last thirty years the excavation of large, complex sites has almost ended, and few contemporary archaeologists will ever be fortunate enough to be funded to excavate any but the smallest sealed sites.

The surface archaeological record, on the other hand, is exposed over entire regions "for free" and requires no excavation. Surface artifacts are simply sitting there, waiting to be mapped and characterized. A possible economic drawback to this process is that across large areas of the surface there are large numbers of artifacts and features, larger numbers than would be encountered during the course of most excavations. Archaeologists working with surface materials usually counter this problem by defining sites (clusters of archaeological materials) on the surface, and recording them rather than artifacts as entities, or by sampling portions of the surface record within or outside of sites. Later in this book I will suggest that an approach focusing on all discoverable surface items, rather than sites or samples, can in fact be put into operation and is far less expensive per item and per unit of information recovered than any excavation.

SEALED SITES AND IDIOSYNCRATIC BEHAVIOR

Sealed sites with integrity are by definition the product of the behavior of a small number of individuals carrying out activities and discarding materials within a short period of time. The information that such a site contains, then, informs the archaeologist about the unique, idiosyncratic behavior of individuals during a virtual instant. Such information is anecdotal in the truest sense of the word. Some archaeologists even memorialize the highly personal nature of such information by seeking to identify individual potters' decorative styles or determine whether certain inhabitants of a site were right- or left-handed.

There is nothing wrong with the anecdotal information yielded by the study of a sealed site, once it is acknowledged that it is more properly viewed as historical than anthropological or behavioral. Even individuals undertake the same task in different ways from day to day, depending on circumstances as well as properties that only individuals exhibit, such as whim or fancy.

The surface archaeological record is also, of course, the product of individuals in a simple sense. But there is no basis to assume that the artifacts found on the surface of a landscape are associated with the activities of only a single person or group—an assumption that is often made (perhaps with just as little basis) when studying sealed sites. Instead, the items comprising the surface archaeological record have probably been exposed and available over long periods. Both their forms and their distributions are likely the product of extensive reuse and recycling by many individuals, possibly from many groups or cultures.

Some archaeologists contend that this property of the surface archaeological record makes it impossible to interpret. If by interpretation they mean solely the reconstruction of single-individual, instantaneous events, then they may be right. Another way of thinking about this, however, is that when using the surface archaeological record we are relieved of even the possibility of being anecdotal historians, and that we can instead focus our attention on such anthropological questions as mobility, procurement of materials, and the use of landscapes by human systems rather than by Ayla or Broud. Analyses based on the surface archaeological record unify rather than separate people, groups, cultures, and the environment itself from the beginnings of the human career.

From the perspective of the surface archaeological record, people, artifacts, mobility, groups, and the environment are continually interacting components of a single system. There is no need to separate systemic contexts from archaeological contexts, nor to postulate truistic transformations to translate between the two. In the same way, it is unnecessary and misleading to separate cultures or cultural processes from the environment. In the surface archaeological record, cultural materials such as discarded stone tools are part of the environment since they are available as raw materials to at least as great an extent as unmodified stone, and perhaps even more. Environmental materials such as native cobbles are no more native than stone tools that were recycled and used by people as raw materials. There is no logical distinction between the two. There are no boundaries. Things that are there are there, to be used, and many of them were. The archaeological record is a fascinating chronicle of what may be mankind's greatest asset—the ability to recycle what others have left behind.

SPATIAL BOUNDARIES AND COMPARABILITY

Sealed sites are bounded in space, and thus one site is not part of another site. They are separate spatial entities with no physically demonstrable connections between them. Thus their relationship is not directly determinable. Perhaps the bulk of the thought, research, inference, and writing of archaeologists since the beginnings of the science has been devoted to linking separate sites and what is found in them through recourse to similarities in artifact form or style. The only such formulations that are not without serious question, however, are refitting studies, and the number of circumstances in which these can be used successfully to link sites is vanishingly small.

The surface archaeological record is not bounded. It is a single entity, within which the nature and locations of physical artifacts and features must be assumed to be potentially related. Again, the archaeologist dealing with the surface archaeological record is relieved—this time of having to try to link one bounded place to another.

TEMPORAL BOUNDARIES AND COMPARABILITY

There is an adamant contention within site-oriented archaeology that establishing a chronology—placing sites in time by dating materials within them—is one of the most important and basic of components of our field. The strongest objection to any study that focuses on the surface archaeological record is that it "cannot be dated," and therefore that it yields inferior information when compared with sealed sites.

Why are archaeologists interested in dating sites and materials? When this question is posed the answer is nearly always that dating sites allows us to detect changes in how things were done through time, and that the reason we want to know about this is that we are interested in cultural evolution. A logical step has been skipped early in this argument. The hopeful goal of dating sites, rarely realized unfortunately, is not to place them or relate them in time but to freeze them in time. It is an attempt to prove that one's sealed site is sealed not only in space but during a short temporal period as well.

One problem with attempting to freeze one's site in an instant in time stems from the fact that we have virtually no generally applicable dating methods precise enough to ensure that a site has any very meaningful temporal integrity at all. Radiocarbon determinations are replicable only to within a few decades at best, and often hundreds of years, a period far too long for materials to have retained their behavioral integrity had they lain on the surface of the ground. Some geological studies may ascertain the temporal integrity of sediments, but not necessarily or knowably that of the archaeological materials contained within them. In addition, even very accurate dates obtained from one item (for instance, a cutting date derived through dendrochronological methods) do not date another item, even if the two are found next to one another.

Neither does chronology allow one to order or put in sequence separate sites and thus their contents, the patterns within them, and the anecdotes derived from this evidence. Two sites with the same radiocarbon date may have been occupied hundreds of years apart; conversely, those with dates hundreds of years apart may have existed almost simultaneously.

One need not even attempt to date materials found in the surface archaeological record, for even relative chronology is not a component of that record—at least through any current technology or analytical method. The surface archaeological record is instead a reflection of the repetitive repositioning of human systems and their activities and materials across the landscape over long periods. It is also the record of the interaction of many individuals, groups, and systems, the physical materials and the places they used, and the environment.

SAMPLING ERROR

If a small group of items with a small number of varying characteristics is chosen from a large population, and these items are assigned places (spuriously or not) in either a spatial or a temporal sequence, changes in the characteristics of those items can appear to be directional when in fact they are not. Discovered and investigated sealed sites are rare, and the characteristics of sites that are taken to represent adaptive or cultural change are small in number (generally the form of "diagnostic" artifacts, or proportions thereof).

Significance tests performed on data pertaining to changes in artifact composition through time are imprecise, as the size and nature of the population which the known sample of sites is taken to represent is not known. Presumably the total population of sealed sites is large, although those that have yet to be discovered are of course hidden and unknown to us.

These problems are unfortunate for those involved in studying what they believe to be sealed sites. Other than reconstructing idiosyncratic behavior during supposed temporal instants, the only additional avenue by which sealed site data can be exploited is by attempting to use sequences of changes to define culture histories. Because of sampling error and an undefined universe, such sequences are to an unknowable degree determined by chance rather than any supportable directionality in technology or other components of human behavior.

SCALES OF ANALYSIS

One of the most promising approaches to measuring archaeological patterning, whether in sites or on the surface, is the analysis of varying scales of variability within a study area. The largest spatial scales of variation in artifacts and their associations that can be measured and analyzed across a study area vary with the mathematical methods employed. With the variance-to-mean-ratio (VMR) measures I use later in this book, the largest examinable scale is half the size of the study area; other spatial analytical methods may detect variation in scales of distributions up to nearly the maximum dimension of the study area (but not quite, due primarily to edge effects).

Sealed sites, being bounded, have a finite size. Although some very large sites have been excavated, site integrity must to some degree be dependent upon small site size, as very large sites have been occupied by many people (probably doing many things at once), or for a long period of time, or both. In addition, the longer a site is occupied the more likely organized cleaning and refuse disposal become, further overlapping discard events. Some credible ethnoarchaeological studies, discussed in greater length below, suggest that realistic sizes for sites that might be expected to retain high behavioral integrity are on the order of 250 to 300 square meters, or (if circular) about 16 to 20m in diameter.

The range of spatial scales that can be examined in the surface archaeological record, which is bounded only by the constraints of archaeological economics, is continuous and virtually limitless.

THE FALLACY OF SITES

Even given this relatively brief discussion of the analytical and informational possibilities offered by the two types of archaeological record that are mandated by the application of the site concept, it should be clear that what we can learn from sealed sites is seriously limited. Essentially, they can offer us a collection of stories about what a few people did at instants in the past. These stories cannot be used convincingly to tell us anything more.

If archaeology insists that true and reliable information can be derived only from sealed sites and not from the surface archaeological record, then we will forever be stalled where we are today. We will be able to determine only where the individual at Wycamp Creek sat, and what piles he sorted stones into.

Archaeology has far more than this to offer, to itself and to everyone else. I like to think that archaeologists are some of the most inventive and insightful people, and archaeology one of the most exciting fields. We study an obscure body of data and use it to arrive at information and ideas that should be directly applicable to what every person does each day. It is incumbent upon us to fulfill the promise of our profession. We cannot do this if we continue to believe that the only reliable data we can measure and analyze comes from "sealed sites," or in fact from "sites" at all.

2

EXPLANATORY FRAMEWORKS
IN CONTEMPORARY ARCHAEOLOGY
-- -- -- -- -- -- -- -- -- -- -- -- --

In 1973, David Clarke announced what he saw as a painful but laud-able "loss of innocence" (1973:6) accompanying a shift from a state of "self-consciousness" to the "critical self-consciousness" of the New Archaeology. The self-conscious state in any science, he went on to say, entails the attempt to gain knowledge from a large body of data. It involves the rigorous definition of concepts, classifications, proce-dures, and methods, and the rise of alternative models and paradigms argued from positions of authority. Sciences in the self-conscious stage partition themselves into subfields, often on the basis of new tech-niques of measurement and analysis. In archaeology, techniques de-veloped during this stage are exemplified by statistics, sampling, mathematical methods in general, dating methods, the concept of seriation, and aerial reconnaissance.

The new state of critical self-consciousness, Clarke felt, was the result of a philosophical or metaphysical transition rather than a technologi-cal one. Explanation, interpretation, and theory became central top-ics, underlining archaeology's new "need to know about knowing" (Clarke 1973:7). The impetus within this new stage was from students who challenged and questioned untested, authority-dictated tradi-tional precepts.

Nearly two decades later, although the questioning and challenging that characterized the New Archaeology for Clarke have certainly continued at an ever-increasing pace, it appears that much of archaeology still may be ignoring the "critical" part of "critical self-consciousness." Lewis Binford, in a plenary address before the Society for American Archaeology in 1985, identified two dominant reactions to the New Archaeology: reconstructionism and contextual-structuralism. Neither of these reactions constitutes a critically self-conscious archaeology, but adherents of each may view the other as being the "new archaeology," creating a "double bind" (Binford 1985:15) that could forestall further development of the profession.

Briefly, reconstructionism follows the legacy of strict empiricism, holding that we can see the archaeological record objectively, and that it can speak for itself or reflect the past. It advocates "laws" or transformations by which the archaeological record can be translated into glimpses of past instants from the participant's perspective, a kind of archaeology as ethnography. In seeking to see the archaeological record most objectively, reconstructionists continue to call for more rigorous observation strategies and complex discovery and measurement technologies. If we cannot see the truth by looking at an ever-growing body of archaeological data, it is because various processes acting on it through time have distorted it, blurring the reflection that we see. What Binford has called "reconstructionism" (1985:14) is clearly the approach that dominates most archaeology today, particularly "dirt archaeology" and virtually all phases of government and contract cultural resource management and conservation archaeology.

Contextual-structural archaeology recognizes the importance of our own culture, which stands between us and our interpretations of the archaeological record, a necessary concept in critical self-consciousness. Unfortunately, this realization has grown into a cynicism that denies that we can ever ultimately see "reality" because we cannot divest ourselves of our culture. Explanation is not possible, only a personal (and personally unique) "understanding." While not as numerous as reconstructionists, contextual-structural archaeologists are intellectually active, and have considerable influence within the educational system of archaeology and anthropology.

The solution to current archaeology's double bind, according to Binford, is a more explicit dedication to the "concept that our ideas directly condition how we meaningfully organize and assimilate experience at the very point of observation," that "we cannot think thoughts that we do not have or use knowledge that is unavailable to us" (Binford 1985:13–14, 18). A corollary of this, of course, is that we can only think thoughts and use knowledge that is available to us. We must constantly inquire as to the effects of our conceptual tools on the meaning we give to the archaeological record. While on the surface this might sound like an invocation to think about theory more carefully, I shall begin here with the assertion that one of our most basic conceptual tools is instead embodied in method, which determines the basic nature of our data. Method and theory are inextricably part of one another within the explanatory framework of archaeology.

The most basic component of archaeological method is the specification of units of discovery and measurement. Consistent with the continued dominance of noncritical self-consciousness in archaeology today, our basic unit of discovery and analysis—the site—is enforced by arguments of authority. I shall attempt to show that the site as an analytical unit is inappropriate in terms of both the nature of the archaeological record and what we want to know about the past. The concept of the site is a methodological remnant, the product of an archaeological paradigm that is certainly not dead, but needs to die. A transition to a critical self-consciousness in the profession requires not only a theoretical transition, but a methodological one as well.

THE SITE CONCEPT IN HISTORICAL PERSPECTIVE

Methodological and theoretical concepts are inextricably interrelated. The concept of the site as the unit of archaeological discovery, measurement, and analysis can be seen as a component of the archaeological approach characterized by Binford and Sabloff as guiding much European archaeology. This paradigm emphasizes the "continuity . . . demonstrable among the materials left at different archaeological sites by representatives of the same 'people'" (Binford and Sabloff 1982:142). Assemblages that are similar are grouped and named for a typical site; when new assemblages are found they are grouped with known ones on the basis of similar forms and proportions of artifacts.

Such a normative approach is native not only to Europe, but in fact has dominated most American archaeology, too. The normative approach is based on the assumption that certain traits, the reflections of which archaeologists see in technological remains, were popular shared ideas within groups of people over relatively large spans of time. European archaeology attributes such popularity almost exclusively to ethnicity, while American archaeologists tend at least partly toward arguments of technical efficiency, usually with the caveat that there are more ways than one to do a specific job. Whatever the underlying reason, different peoples did things differently.

Of course they also did these things differently at different places, or if at the same places then at different times. Under the normative paradigm, one does not expect "blended or mixed 'traditions,' since each people manifests its essential characteristics, its 'spirit,' in its products" (Binford and Sabloff 1982:142). In order to use the archaeological record to demonstrate the truth or workability of a normative paradigm, it must be perceived as representing or "reflecting" separate episodes of the activity of specific groups of people at circumscribed places. It must be seen as "sites." Sites are necessary in order to operationalize a normative approach.

I suggest that sites are not necessary, and in fact are antithetical to, an archaeological approach directed toward understanding the operation of past adaptational systems. To this end, it is necessary to consider the relationship between the operation of ongoing systems and their components—some of which might be thought of as "ethnographic sites"—and the archaeological record.

Obviously, behavioral episodes in the living world are circumscribed in space and time. These kinds of sites are real—they can be seen, and we all experience them every day. Nonetheless, it can be argued that ethnographic activity loci are not the actual units in the framework within which people do things, either. The units of organization of human behavior are greater than occupations or locations, and include not only places but physical objects as well as many less tangible things, such as mobility, planning, strategies, and ideology. In short, the units of human organization have to do not just with the physical world (the reconstructionist stance), or just with culture (contextual-structuralism), but with both. The units of human organization, those we are interested in interpreting and reconstructing, are systems: "In cultural systems, people, things, and places are components in a field that consists of environmental and sociocultural subsystems, and the locus of cultural process is in the dynamic articulations of these subsystems" (Binford 1965:205).

Three decades later, I am not sure that we can offer a more complete statement about the nature of human systems. "System" is a primitive term in archaeological science at the present. Nonetheless, I shall venture some statements about what systems are not. They are not purely physical entities, but are composed of processes and articulations between physical actors (people, places, things) as well. They are not what some specific group of people or culture does, either, as might be implied in some discussions of "settlement systems" or seasonal rounds. Human organizational systems might better be viewed as kinds of adaptations.

It is important to adopt a nonparticularistic view of systems, because only then can what we want to know about be congruent with the nature of the archaeological record. The archaeological record is qualitatively different from specific episodes of human behavior. If systems are defined as being what a specific group does, then we will never see all of a system in the archaeological record. Unanswerable questions, such as, "how much area do we have to look at to see a whole system?" will arise. Rather than showing us all of the parts of one group's seasonal round (or whatever else), the archaeological record instead provides windows through which we can view the overlapping results of the positioning of components of adaptations.

SURFACE SURVEY AS A FOCUS OF THIS INQUIRY

By its very nature archaeological survey is far more dependent on the site concept than excavation projects are. Surface survey directed toward discovering sites, coupled with sampling, was one of the most important of the new techniques accompanying Clarke's noncritical self-consciousness phase.

What is more, regional survey coupled with probability sampling is necessary for the study of human systems. This point was made explicitly by Binford (1964); according to Dunnell and Dancey (1983), however, more archaeologists took the concept of sampling to heart than those who realized the central importance of a regional perspective on systems. Concentrating on sampling methods, the site reconstructionists tend to think of their sampling universe not as areas of the landscape searched, but rather as a sample of sites, a "map of the archaeological manifestations discovered" (Dunnell and Dancey 1983:268). If complex sites are the units of focus, only a small percentage can be excavated; unfortunately, one has to look at more than just a small portion of a region to answer questions of land use, settlement, ecological adaptations, and resource procurement—parts of the systems we need to understand (Dunnell and Dancey 1983:269).

Surface survey may yield much more useful data than excavation because of the cost-effectiveness of its discovery. In fact, data derived through surface survey may already "have begun—in the scope of their contribution—to outpace excavation" (Ammerman 1981:64). Systematic surface surveys have been a part of American archaeology since the 1916 effort by Spier at Zuni Pueblo (Ammerman 1981:65).

Although survey in the past was often regarded simply as a means to locate subsurface sites with excavation potential, these roles are now reversed in most funded archaeology in the United States. Today, excavation is used to test sites interpreted within the framework of site survey. There are data that can be discovered only through excavation, of course, but the reverse is also true—some data can be recovered only through surface survey. The places where sealed, nonsurface deposits can be found (for instance riverbanks and caves) are probably rare compared to those where a surface archaeological record is formed. Different components of systems might occur in these two places, as well. Both sorts of record are different and complementary: *"the surficial distribution of artifacts constitutes an appropriate source of archaeological data independent of subsurface remains"* (Dunnell and Dancey 1983:270; emphasis theirs).

According to Lewarch and O'Brien (1981:312), "much of the rationale behind the invocation of post-depositional disturbance is based on assumptions that subsurface materials are 'fossilized' records of the past," clearly a reconstructionist hope. The refutation of that possibility requires only a cursory consideration of the fact that almost all assemblages, presently buried or on the surface, have been subjected to the same disarranging processes while originally on the surface.

Finally, incorporating methodological changes into surface survey may be the best way to bring about changes in archaeological science as a whole in the United States today. Surface survey is virtually the only archaeological activity funded by most government land management agencies today that lends itself to both conservation and the collection of data that could have research value. The data upon which the research reported here is based were derived through fieldwork funded by the National Park Service and the Bureau of Reclamation, agencies that, while not necessarily aware of it at the time, may have helped to change some of the methodological directions of archaeology. Before discussing some of those possible new directions in Chapter 3, however, I intend to examine the relationship between the archaeological record and the operation of past systems within the explanatory framework of archaeology.

THE EXPLANATORY FRAMEWORK OF ARCHAEOLOGY AND THE DIRECTIONALITY OF METHOD AND THEORY

Although many taxonomies that describe the logical structure of archaeology have been envisioned, I advance one more for the purposes of this discussion (after Ebert and Kohler 1986). This taxonomy illustrates a progression of processes that can be thought of as responsible for the formation of the archaeological record and for what we, as archaeologists, make of it. In general, these include:

1. The systemic processes of organized life, particularly mobility, labor scheduling, technological and subsistence planning, and other activities that affect the differential placement of human activities;

2. The behavioral events of aggregation of natural materials, their modification, and their discard, loss, and abandonment that structure the archaeological consequences of activities, creating an entrophic archaeological record, rather than one that is the sum of all human activities;

3. The interaction of behavioral and depositional events, separated by time and tempo differences that result in the overlap of multiple discard events within single depositional units, causing the archaeological record to differ from human behavioral events in the time scale and phase of its representation;

4. Postdepositional natural and cultural processes that affect the preservation, integrity, and visibility of the archaeological record;

5. Archaeological methodology—that is, the ways we discover, measure, and analyze our data and the biases that these methods introduce into our interpretations of their meaning.

The explanatory framework presented here (Fig. 2.1) begins with "higher-range" theory, ideas about the organization of subsistence, settlement, and mobility, and proceeds through more "middle-range" concepts of technological organization and discard behavior, natural depositional and postdepositional processes, to the methodological domains of archaeological discovery, attribute coding, data analysis, and pattern recognition, and finally to the interpretation of data itself. The major point that this figure is intended to illustrate is that there

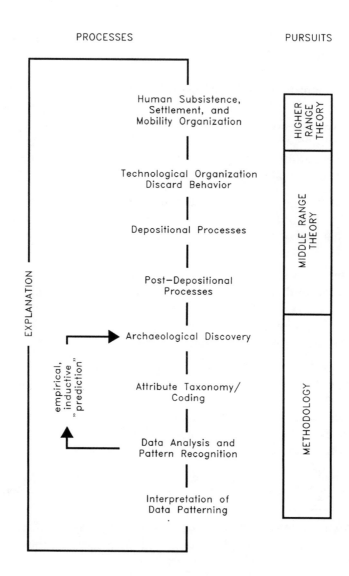

PROCESSES   PURSUITS

Figure 2.1. A taxonomy of processes and pursuits that make up the tactical framework of archaeological science.

are many factors intervening between theory and method, and that these form a continuous and necessary progression of thought, and of the tactical integration of archaeology.

Explanation is probably best thought of as a two-way, feedback process, for not only does the examination of data engender ideas about its meaning, but ideas about these data—the archaeologist's paradigms— have a direct relationship not only to the interpretation of data, but, more fundamentally, to the ways in which data are collected and measured. Thus, while our paradigms might be seen by some "contextual-structuralists" (Binford 1985) as distorting our interpretation of data, it is just as true that our paradigms affect the data we collect.

The intellectual double bind confronting archaeology today may be the result of following a path that results in problems of theoretical concern being influenced by arbitrary or historically determined methods, rather than vice versa (Dunnell 1985). To better illustrate what I mean by this, I shall examine the effects of each of these "directions of influence," abstracting from them two ways in which archaeology might be approached: one in which method dictates theory, and one in which theory dictates method.

From Method to Theory

Most American archaeology today proceeds from method to theory. The method that has been adopted looks for and interprets archaeological sites. A survey crew walks around systematically, and when artifacts are discovered the boundaries of their distributions are sought. The densest distributions of artifacts and features are "sites," and densities fall off toward their edges, where boundaries are drawn.

Sites are where people in the past did things, and when we look at their boundaries we have vivid mental pictures of such scenes as Indians sitting around a hearth. Of course this is what our own cultural experience indicates: people focus their activities in space and time. Sites are very real in the ethnographic present. Translating behavioral reality directly into a methodology for discovering and measuring the archaeological record, however, assures that our data will look like the stylized representation illustrated in Figure 2.2 (Ebert 1985). We cannot help but discover an archaeological record consisting of peaks of activity surrounded by areas that contain no significant archaeological record. There are things between the sites, called isolated occurrences or some similar term, but we simply cannot deal with

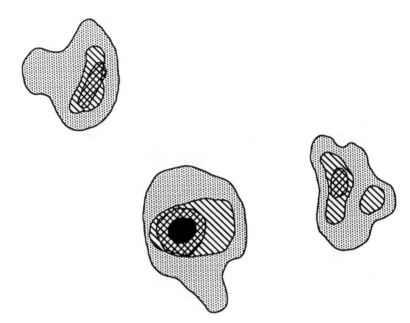

Figure 2.2. Sites, as often conceived by archaeologists, have simple or complex concentric density gradations. This "bullseye" or "fried egg" site model is a direct extension of the assumption that clusters of artifacts and features found in the archaeological record correspond to discrete behavioral episodes.

everything. The densest areas, the sites, are the bases upon which we interpret the past.

Such an instantaneous, reconstructionist view of how people do things, based on the product of the site survey methodology, also determines how we treat and interpret the archaeological record. A site is seen as the result of one or a relatively small number of coinciding activities or occupations. As sites are where activities took place, they are important; the areas beyond the sites are not. If funding or management choices are to be made, sites will be preserved or studied rather than nonsite areas.

Under this approach, how does one decide what exactly was going on at a site? Starting with the site and its contents, the archaeologist "works up" from data to ideas. But what about the things that lie between data and higher-level theory—particularly postdepositional and depositional processes? Under such a method-to-theory framework these processes can be regarded only as introducing distortions into the archaeological record, preserving some evidence and destroying or disarranging the rest, coming between us and a full understanding of past activities. Explanation, under this method-to-theory framework, becomes a series of anecdotes about specific natural and cultural events that occurred to produce the unique patterning found at the site, and thus the differences among sites in an area. As unique distortions have been introduced, there is no way to test any aspect of the anecdotes independently.

From Theory to Method

Thinking from theory to method, on the other hand, one must begin by considering how the organization of human systems is responsible for the archaeological record. From a systems perspective, the archaeological record is the sum of the accretion of materials lost to the system in the course of the repetitive patterning of the placement of different parts of those systems. This repetitive placement has generally happened over long time spans and large regional areas.

This idea is not the result of just looking at data, either archaeological or ethnographic. Nonetheless, both of these, and especially ethnographic observations and reasoning, can help us imagine what such an archaeological record might look like, given some understanding of systems dynamics. Some of the characteristics of systems behavior indicated by ethnographic studies conducted among living hunter-gatherer and pastoralist groups are relatively low rates of artifact discard even at residential bases, continuous discard of materials throughout a foraging radius, and relocation of residential bases near but not directly on top of previously used sites. It is important to remember that the archaeological record is the result of patterns of ongoing systems entropy taking place over very long periods. The archaeological record is the product of a qualitatively different set of time scales than is living human behavior. The translation between the two, even given our most sophisticated chronological controls, is not automatic or simple.

An interesting reconstruction of artifact accumulation over time, based on ethnographically-suggested home range sizes, mobility, discard, and artifact-life rates has been expounded by Foley (1981a), who estimates that over a period of a thousand years one might conservatively expect

163 million artifacts to accumulate within a home range with a 10km radius, with a resulting artifact density across the landscape of less than 0.5 artifacts per square meter. Both the low average density and the incredibly large total number of artifacts are surprising. Apparently, artifacts accumulate slowly over long time periods. But if residential bases are reoccupied again and again, then where are the billions of artifacts that should have accumulated there over thousands of years? If only, say, a quarter of a group's artifacts—about 40 million in 1,000 years—were discarded within the confines of even a large residential camp (let us say 500 square meters), then artifact densities of about 80,000 per square meter should be found over that area. Even if one is willing to consider past reuse or recycling to have been intensive (as I shall suggest later), and each artifact to have been reused, say, 16 times, densities of "only" 5,000 per square meter might be expected. Realistically, there is not enough physical space within a square meter to contain so many artifacts. If each artifact measured 3mm on a side, they would literally pave the surface. Such densities are never found by archaeologists. If they were found by prehistoric people during the search for a campsite, they would be avoided because they would make activity there physically impossible. If reconstructions like this hold any validity, it is clear that only a very small fraction of a prehistoric group's lithic discards ever took place within base camps located at specific, often reoccupied places. Rather, they must be spread relatively evenly across the landscape, largely undiscovered by archaeologists.

As ethnographically directed archaeologists, we intuit that people reuse the same place again and again resulting in concentrated sites in the archaeological record. This may have more to do with how we define sites than with archaeological reality. There is also a great difference between ethnographic and archaeological time spans. How would people even know they were reoccupying the same place over thousands of years?

If resources at a site are an important factor in site placement and the activities that took place at these sites, humanly relevant distances to resources must be determined. Assuming that people might be willing to walk as much as 1km from the center of a base camp to gather resources (this is ethnographically supportable) and that an average base camp is 250 square meters in size (after Foley 1981a), there are more than 12,000 places within a 1km radius that could be used as base camps before any overlap occurred. Total lack of overlap in occupational episodes, of course, is probably as unlikely as total overlap.

Instead, one would expect partial overlap over time in most cases, except where severe topographic constraints are present (caves, for instance).

Following the logical progression from theory down to the data collection stage completes this short example. How would one go about collecting data informed by the arguments made here about the character of the archaeological record? Certainly one would not draw boundaries around density peaks, call them sites, and forget the rest of the continuous archaeological record. The continuous archaeological record can be discovered and recorded only by an archaeology that, methodologically, has nothing to do with sites. Individual artifacts and features, or their attributes, must be the primary units of discovery and measurement. More importantly, however, our methodology must make no *a priori* assumptions about boundaries and the integrity of clusters, or what clusters may mean behaviorally. I have called this archaeological approach "distributional archaeology" elsewhere (Ebert 1983, 1985; Ebert et al. 1983) and shall use that term here as well. I hope to illustrate why such an approach is not only desirable but perhaps necessary at this juncture in archaeological science, as well as illustrating by way of example how distributional analysis might be done in a practical way.

HUMAN SYSTEMS, THE ARCHAEOLOGICAL RECORD, AND SOME THINGS THAT SEPARATE THE TWO

The following discussion is general, and the models used are intended to be illustrative rather than immediately applicable to any specific archaeological explanations. My intent is to emphasize some of the factors that make the archaeological record and the operation of past systems qualitatively different things. In the course of these illustrations, I hope to show that a distributional approach may better link the two than contemporary site survey methods.

Systemic Mobility and Settlement Organization

"Inherent in cultural products is the systematics of the people who produced them" (Taylor 1948:128)—that is, the patterning of materials is related to the organization of the cultural system that produced them. A cultural system is not the combination of the actions of individuals, but rather of components in an organizational framework under which actions are structured, and the patterning of cultural materials embodies aspects of this framework rather than providing any sort of "instant" view of a frozen ethnographic moment (Binford 1981). In other words, the systematics that result in the archaeological record exist on an extrasomatic level very different from single behavioral episodes. One of the reasons for this is that systems have multiple, complexly interconnected components: "In cultural systems, people, things, and places are components in a field that consists of environmental and sociocultural subsystems, and the locus of cultural process is in the dynamic articulations of these subsystems" (Binford 1965:205). The actors in a cultural system are not only people, but places, artifacts, strategies, scheduling, landscapes, climate, environment, resources, and many more.

The organization of past human systems is related to the archaeological record through a complex series of stages, the first of which is the interaction between places within systems and what has happened at those places over long time periods. The processes that cause patterning in the archaeological record are not individual preferences or the decisions of prehistoric bands about where to stay for the night. Instead, site patterning is due to long-term, repetitive patterning (or lack thereof) in the "positioning of adaptive systems in geographic space" (Binford 1982:6).

What is more, the use of space is not uniform but differentiated within even a single system. Some activities occur again and again within circumscribed areas, and some do not. The resulting concentrated locations of some activities, compared to the dispersed nature of others, has been discussed in terms of "ranges" of various types (Foley 1977, 1978, 1981b, 1981c, 1981d; Jochim 1976), settlements as opposed to activity "nodes" (Isaac 1981:134), and catchments (Vita-Finzi and Higgs 1970).

The nature of the events that occur at any place during an occupation will of course have a relationship to the resources available there. This relationship in itself may not be a simple one, and it has been suggested that such environmental characteristics as the distribution or diversity of resources (Harpending and Davis 1977) or the annual range of temperatures requiring, enabling, or restricting storage of foodstuffs (Binford 1980) may be more important than simple distance to resources. But subsistence or other resources are not the only actors in human organizational systems, and they are not the only determinants of where different events occur in the system's space. What a group does at one place may have as much to do with what they plan to do at the next place they visit, or what they did at the last place they visited, as it does with what resources are there.

The patterning of the archaeological record is better viewed as being conditioned by "repetition, or lack thereof, in the spatial positioning of systems," arising from the interaction between economic resources and mobility, which is the way that "a given place may be economically modified relative to the human system" (Binford 1982:6, 8). An examination of one taxonomy of differential mobility patterns will help illustrate the interlocking nature of the parts of a human organizational system.

Binford (1982) has distinguished types of ranges or mobility zones that can be used to characterize the ways that people use the space around their **residential base.** A residential base is where a group lives and is universal among all ethnographically known people. At the residential base, food consumption, child rearing, and technological maintenance generally take place. Outside the radius occupied by the residential base is the **foraging radius**; this is where resources are exploited in the course of trips lasting a day or less, after which both resources and people return to camp. Within this area **locations** accumulate, places where resources have been extracted and limited processing has been carried out. Little if any tool maintenance occurs at locations. Still beyond the foraging radius is a **logistical radius** exploited by special-purpose task groups of producers traveling separately from consumers, who stay away from the residential base for at least one night and sometimes much longer. Occupations taking place within the logistical radius may have maintenance functions as well as special-purpose functions.

Not all groups use or "develop" (after Binford 1982:8) these different radii to the same extent. Instead, there are distinct relationships between the ways people use the radii around their residential base and the frequency with which their residence is moved. This, in turn, is conditioned by environmental and in some cases social factors. In highly diverse environments, almost all resources can be found within a group's foraging radius, and people in equatorial jungles and possibly some other environments such as the Kalahari Desert acquire nearly all resources using a generalist "encounter" strategy during daily walkabouts. Intensive use of the foraging radius, however, leads to quick depletion of resources there, and when this happens the residential camp is moved. It need be moved only to one edge of the old foraging

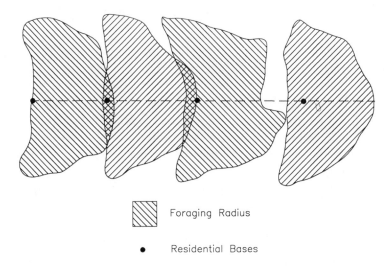

Foraging Radius

●   Residential Bases

Figure 2.3. An idealized map of a half-radius continuous pattern of residential mobility and landscape use (after Binford 1982). This pattern is typical of generalist foragers and should result in an archaeological record characterized by low and even densities of materials across the landscape.

radius, however, where another foraging radius is established—or rather half of a new radius, as the old one is depleted (Fig. 2.3). This sort of mobility strategy results in what Binford (1982:10) calls a **half-radius continuous pattern.**

In more differentiated yet still high-biomass environments, a **complete radius leapfrog pattern** of residential mobility is more often found ethnographically. This consists of residential moves that result in little or no overlap between successive foraging radii, but having logistic radii that do overlap (Fig. 2.4). In this situation, logistical camps are often relocated at old residential bases because there are materials to reuse there and because the specialized task-group members are familiar with the old residences and their surroundings. A variation of the complete radius leapfrog pattern common in lower-biomass settings is the **point-to-point** pattern, with no overlap of logistic zones. Residential camps under this mobility pattern represent an adjustment to incongruent known resource distributions, which are exploited through logistic mobility.

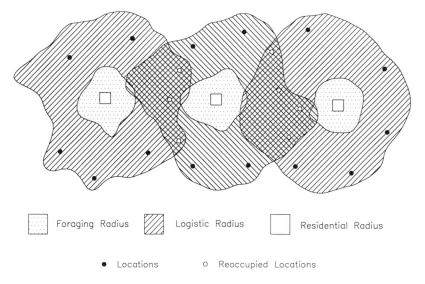

Figure 2.4. An idealized map of a complete-radius leapfrog pattern of residential mobility and landscape use (after Binford 1982). Logistically organized collectors following such a pattern use some nodes in the landscape in a concentrated way, in addition to relatively even exploitation of a large radius. When residential bases are relocated, some activity nodes in the overlapping portions of logistic radii are reused, often for different purposes.

Ethnographic Examples of Differentiated Settlement Pattern and Mobility within Systems: the Reuse of Places within Systems

A brief survey of ethnographic accounts of variations in mobility and settlement patterning can be drawn from the ethnographic and ethnoarchaeological literature. These illustrate that the differential reuse of places by groups operating under different mobility and settlement patterns has important implications concerning the complexity of the archaeological record.

An obvious consequence of Binford's mobility zone models is an expectation that the same places that served as old residential bases would be reused for different, special-purpose logistic functions under the complete-radius leapfrog pattern. Under such a mobility organization, then, "sites" should occur at definite points within the landscape where different functions overlap. In addition, as residential bases represent compromises among the dispersed locations of resources exploited through logistic mobility, residential locations should be reused repeatedly. This should not be the case in the half-radius foraging pattern, in which there are no logistic camps and in which resources are relatively evenly distributed; residential camp foraging radii would more likely be depleted of critical resources for some time. Foraging radius locations—places where resources are encountered and perhaps minimally processed—should occur at many places within the foraging radius, and should eventually lead to a low-visibility but continuous archaeological record.

Living hunter-gatherer and pastoralist groups that pursue a predominantly generalist strategy and fall towards the foraging end of the mobility/settlement scale utilize their foraging radii more or less continuously, and population densities among such groups are characteristically low. An annual average density of 0.03 persons per square kilometer among the /Kade area Bushmen has been recorded (Tanaka 1976; Harako 1978), and even among the relatively dense population of the Ituri Forest Pygmy only 0.2 to 0.6 persons per square kilometer is typical. These people characteristically exploit their sparsely populated ranges relatively evenly. As Foley (1981b:12) observes: "The focal points to which the energy having been harnessed may be transported—and which later go to constitute archaeological sites—are secondary. Studies of human activities through these focal points alone is indirect."

Foley cites very low densities of artifacts even on residential bases resulting from single occupations among such groups in Africa: 0.163 artifacts per square meter discarded per month for Namaqua settlements, and 2.22 artifacts per square meter for Dassenatch. What is more, a large percentage of artifacts among such groups is discarded at what he calls "secondary home range foci" (Foley 1981b:21), which are equivalent to Binford's "locations" within the foraging radius. These locations are usually used only once (during ethnographic time), and their occurrence throughout the environmentally diverse home range should (over archaeological time) reinforce an even distribution of discarded items. Gould (1980) reports that Australian aborigines discard only about one percent of lithic manufacturing debris and implements at their residential base camps. The greater part of the rest is discarded elsewhere within the home range or foraging radius. The product of widely distributed, low-density discard over the length of time monitored by ethnographers is almost invisible, but over archaeological time it could result in impressive densities of discarded materials. One significant implication of this sort of archaeological record formation in terms of intersite variability is that in much of the record discrete sites should not be apparent. The archaeological record in many situations should instead be continuous, in the sense of not exhibiting discrete or definable boundaries.

Of course, few human groups pursue a pure foraging subsistence strategy resulting in a completely continuous archaeological record. With groups that incorporate more logistically organized collecting strategies there are also definite nodes or foci in the landscape that are used repeatedly for the same or different purposes. Even among the "foraging" Bushmen described by Yellen (1976), almost universally cited when the intrasite structure of foraging camps is discussed, some camps are resettled even in ethnographic time. Yellen's Dobe group occupied 27 camps for an average of 3.1 days each during the January—July 1968 rainy season; two were reoccupied once and one reoccupied twice. Yellen reports that if Bushmen find huts in good repair at old sites they use them, and if not, they select a "new site in the same general area" (Yellen 1976:58). Among 10 occupations in 7 months observed by Tanaka (1976) among /Kade area Bushmen, 3 were reoccupations of the same camps. On the basis of ethnographic as well as archaeological observations, Wills (1980) reports that the Wikmunkan of the Cape York Peninsula reinhabited wet season and early and late dry season camp sites repeatedly, but for different functions—which is to be expected under a logistically organized mobility strategy.

Reuse of places calls into question the equation of clusters of materials with "sites" that we can interpret conventionally and label as organizational entities, such as residences, hunting camps, or tool manufacturing locations ("chipping stations," and so forth). Site size as a functionally discriminating factor, for instance, may be skewed by the reuse or lack of structures or their construction on or near past structures. In the residential camps of the Northern Ute, for instance, menstruating women were required to build a new menstrual hut each month; these were similar to family shelters in size and functional characteristics, having internal hearths and activity areas. By proscription they were not built on areas occupied by past menstrual huts (Smith 1974). Hypothetically, if a residential camp were occupied by an extended family with eight women, half of whom were pregnant during the year, there would be about sixty new menstrual huts constructed each year. If each old hut structure lasted (was visible) for fifty years, as some taphonomic studies indicate might be possible, this Ute camp would accrue three thousand menstrual hut locations with continuous occupation during this time.

Thus the nature of site patterning—and what those sites look like and how easily they are found by archaeologists—is determined in many cases not solely by activities during a single occupational episode. The archaeological record is instead created by the repetitive superimposition of materials resulting from adjustments of human systems to their landscape through mobility and the differential organization of labor, residence, and activity.

TECHNOLOGICAL AND DISCARD ORGANIZATION

A consideration of intersite and intrasite assemblage variability (differences in artifact content between and within clusters of associated materials) is a possible starting point for separating overlapping activity sets. Some expectations for different sorts of assemblage variability can be arrived at through reference to the general model of subsistence, settlement, and mobility outlined above.

Curated versus Expedient Technology

One middle-range concept with great potential for tying together the dynamic organization of past human systems and the static archaeological record is that of the difference between curated and expedient implements. Expedient tools are manufactured in the immediate context of their use when circumstances that require them arise. Generally, the overall use of expedient technology should be greatest in foraging systems geared toward an encounter strategy. In the environments that favor such a strategy there is an equal chance of coming across a variety of resources, and in fact there is no need for the participants in such a system even to attempt to predict what they will find. Other things (such as material availability) being equal, it might well be most efficient for these people to manufacture tools on the spot in response to their immediate situation.

Curated technologies differ in that the tools employed are planned to fit specific uses that have been anticipated (Binford 1976). This is an efficient strategy when the occurrence of resources is predictable, and for systems that focus on specific resources. Collecting strategies that feature a logistic organization of mobility—special producer task groups that are mobile for previously planned purposes—are those in which curated technologies should be most dominant.

As in any model, of course, these two polar types of technology are ideal, analytical constructs. Actual technologies employed within a system are organized integrations of these two types. The technological strategies employed by a group at any time differ with their immediate context and as a function of the other parts of their overall, systemic technology.

Bamforth (1986) argues that it is not the subsistence strategies of a group that determine whether its technology is curated or expedient, asserting that curation is instead a response to raw material shortages. This is tantamount to thinking that someone will not use a pocket knife for cutting if there is a source of steel nearby with which an expedient blade could be fashioned. A far more convincing argument can be made that a curated technology is the result of the necessity for carefully planning the need for tools for specific tasks, and for scheduling the performance of toolmaking activities. Identifying staged manufacturing strategies, which will be dealt with in later chapters, may be one of the most efficient approaches to deriving indicators of curated technologies in the archaeological record. Staged manufacturing should occur in systems that emphasize special-purpose, stringently planned mobility (that is, collecting systems).

In addition, it must be recognized that the concepts of foraging and collecting are analytical constructs, as are curation and expediency. Foraging people may produce and use curated tools of a general-purpose nature in addition to manufacturing situational tools. It is not only likely but probable that the participants in logistically organized systems or system components encounter unplanned situations that require the fabrication of expedient tools, or the modification of tools with planned uses into tools with new ones. It may be that the use of highly specialized, curated tools is always likely to occur in conjunction with the use of more expedient ones. In the archaeological record, then, indications of the curated technologies of the logistically organized activities of collecting groups may be associated regularly with indications of expedient tool use, while the activities of foraging groups may show the less expedient use of more generalized tool kits.

Expedient and curated technical strategies leave an archaeological record with different meanings, primarily due to differences in the contexts of tool use and discard. Expedient tools are by definition manufactured where they are needed, and they are also discarded there. They occur in direct association with the activities in which they were used. As expedient tools are made to be used and discarded almost immediately, the energy put into shaping the objects is low: they exhibit little in the way of formalization or style. Most expedient tools are probably exempted from analysis by archaeologists, or lumped under the category of debitage.

Curated tools, on the other hand, are neither manufactured nor discarded in the context of their immediate use. Tools intended for use during the mobile activities of special-task groups are most likely to be manufactured at residential base camps (Binford 1980) for anticipated uses away from those camps. Curated tools, designed to be used over some time period, are more durable than those made expediently for immediate discard. Often, curated tools are compound (Allchin 1966; Oswalt 1973), having hafted components or multiple parts. All of these characteristics help ensure that a curated tool will not end its useful life at the locus of use but will be brought back to the residential base for maintenance. Both manufacturing debris and broken portions of curated tools are likely to be found at the residential site and not at the places in which they were utilized.

Some general implications for the nature of the archaeological record, consisting of discarded tools and the debris associated with their manufacture or maintenance, can be generated from the above assumptions. Under a foraging strategy, there are two situations in which discard should take place: the residential base camp and the location. Manufacture and discard of expedient tools should take place at both of these loci, with the implements discarded at places indicative of the activities that took place there. There should be major variations in the size, mobility, and composition of groups with a foraging strategy during the year or from year to year, in response to short-term variations in the environment (Binford 1980), leading to the expectation that the activities performed at various times at foraging sites of either type could be quite diverse. In addition, as camps are not necessarily relocated relative to previous camps or locations, this diverse archaeological record—at least partly representative of the activities that occur at the places it is found—should in time become relatively continuous over the landscape. Variability in the contents of residential sites of foraging people is the result of differences in seasonal scheduling of activities, the differential duration of occupation, and occupational history (Camilli 1983a).

This variability could be expected to lead to a pattern of increasing assemblage diversity (with respect both to increased numbers of types, and more even proportions among them) with increasing site size, as noted by Yellen (1976), whose study is often taken by archaeologists as a model to be applied to all hunter-gatherers. Forager residential sites are essentially of the same type: as their contents increase, they contain more and more of everything. The nonsite archaeological remains left by foragers are more important for archaeologists attempting to elucidate the operation of past systems of this type, as they contain information concerning variability in activities over space. It is quite likely that some components of all human systems leave continuous archaeological remains with little visibility, and these remains must be studied and understood before the mechanisms behind the placement of activities in systems can be explained. In addition, because it is sparser and simpler, the record left by expedient activities may be understood far more easily than that of the more complex and superimposed portions of past systems.

With a logistically organized system, intra- and interassemblage variability can be expected to be very different from that produced by a foraging system. Collectors use specially organized, highly mobile task groups to cope with situations in which consumers are near one or more critical food resources but distant from others. In addition to residential base camps, these groups also use field camps, stations, caches, and other places for specific functions. Reasoning on the basis of Palaeoindian data, Judge (1973) estimates that field camps in such systems may outnumber residential camps by as much as four to one. Data from a contemporary Nunamiut Eskimo system at Anaktuvuk Pass, Alaska (Binford 1978: 173) indicate that the proportion may in fact be far higher, as much as thirteen to one. Nonresidential camps may be occupied for long durations and (or alternatively) may be sites of intensive processing, thus becoming as large and visible as residential bases (Binford 1980). As noted above, groups organized under a collecting strategy are likely to employ a curated technology to at least some extent, as well as high levels of mobility and activity planning. Discard of curated tools rarely takes place at the locus of their use. This means that in situations in which the archaeological record looks most like bounded sites, assemblages are least likely to reflect the activities that took place there.

Intra-assemblage Variability and the Occupational History of Places

Reconstructing the activities that took place at the traditionally defined sites of a collecting system is further complicated by the fact that places are reused for different purposes through the course of a year or over longer periods. Many different combinations of activities are possible at each place. For instance, a place might be used as a residential base for several months and contain domestic tool-manufacturing and maintenance-related debris. Six months later the same place might be used as a field camp, with discarded debris from staged down-time manufacture that would not be expected to represent activities that actually occurred there. A wide range of technological variability—but of specific and easily differentiated types—might occur in the discarded archaeological record, resulting from a collecting-based systemic organization. Investment in facilities such as structures for shelter or storage, caching of items to be used later at the site, and other cultural "improvements" of a place might also occur at such reused places. This means that differential function under a logistically organized collecting system might not be obvious on the basis of either site size or site contents.

Interassemblage Variability and Mobility

Variability between assemblages at different sites resulting from the operation of a system is the result of the overlay of an organized series of events, differences in which have been discussed in terms of "grain size" by Binford (1980:17). Coarse-grained assemblages are the cumulative product of events spanning relatively long periods, for instance several months or a year. Fine-grained assemblages accumulate over short periods. The finer-grained the assemblage, the greater the probable content variability between assemblages, because there is less chance that the total range of activities occurring within that system will be found there. The main factor responsible for grain size is mobility (assuming organizational factors to be constant), but this relationship is far from simple or linear. In a foraging group, residential mobility would be expected to be highest in the least diverse, least seasonal, and least predictable environments, resulting in an increase in interassemblage variability. But under logistic strategies, residential mobility is lower, so coarser-grained assemblages would be expected in residential sites; the more mobile logistic sites under such a system would also be more differentiated from one another.

The Explanation of Intra- and Interassemblage Variability

We have seen two major implications arise from the modes of technological organization that can accompany varying residential and logistic mobility. One of these lies in the realm of intra-assemblage variability. It grows from the assumption that with increasing logistic mobility the effects of curation and the reuse of places make it difficult to identify the functions of sites and predict their occurrence in terms of repetitive association with resources. The other implication is that with increasing logistic mobility there is greater differentiation between assemblages at residential base camps and those at special-task locations, as well as between those at different special-task locations.

The archaeological record in the latter case (other things such as depositional processes being equal) should appear as a series of sites relatively uniform in size, visibility, and contents in terms of structures or facilities, but which should contain assemblages that can appear strikingly different in terms of the formal attributes of their constituents, or at least some of their constituents.

One of the obvious ways of explaining an archaeological record like that described above is in terms of separate technical or cultural traditions, an approach that has been dominant in most archaeological explanation since the science's beginnings (Willey and Sabloff 1974). This approach, which has been referred to as the "Kriegerian" method (Binford and Sabloff 1982:143), will be discussed and illustrated in Chapter 4 through a review of the archaeology of southwestern Wyoming and related areas. One hallmark of the Kriegerian method important to this illustration is the grouping of sites into cultures or traditions on the basis of the formal similarity of selected diagnostic artifacts.

A systems perspective on the archaeological record suggests the likelihood that under certain types of mobility and technological organization, contemporaneous technological traditions are actually functionally different parts of the same system. Without chronological control for all components of the system, which is rarely available, most of the archaeological record in any place may consist of different portions of essentially similar adaptations over very long periods of time, and not the birth, blending, alternation, evolution, or collapse of cultures or traditions. The archaeological record is not directly referable to episodic behavior; instead, "a detailed consideration of the factors that differentially condition long-term range occupancy or positioning in macro-geographical terms is needed before we can realistically begin to develop a comprehension of . . . subsistence-settlement behavior. The latter is of course necessary to an understanding of archaeological site patterning" (Binford 1980:19).

NATURAL FORMATION PROCESSES AND THE ARCHAEOLOGICAL RECORD

Human mobility, the patterning of different economic activities in space, the redundancy in economic activities across the landscape, and differences between the loci of artifact discard and use all result in a complex spatial patterning of cultural materials. This patterning reflects the organization of a system but is in no way directly referable to episodes or events occurring within this organization. What is more, at the point of discard this patterning still has a long way to go before it is discovered and interpreted by the archaeologist. Processes affecting the deposition, accumulation, preservation, disturbance, and exposure of the materials that make up the archaeological record have been investigated, largely due to the influence of interdisciplinary studies, such as the taphonomy of culturally utilized or culturally modified organic and inorganic materials (Brain 1967a, 1967b, 1969, 1981; Behrensmeyer and Hill 1980; Gifford 1977a, 1977b, 1980, 1981; Gifford and Behrensmeyer 1977) and "geoarchaeology" (Butzer 1977, 1982; Gladfelter 1977).

Deposition and the Coincidence of Natural and Cultural Events

Cultural materials enter the archaeological record as a result of taphonomic processes, during which they are buried, stabilized on a surface, or otherwise disturbed or preserved. Taphonomic processes may be cultural; in most cases, however, they are natural, consisting of aeolian, fluvial, lacustrine, or residual aggradation. These natural processes of deposition may or may not coincide with episodes of cultural discard.

Materials discarded as the result of an occupation or activity may lie on the surface for long periods without being buried, or may be buried as quickly as they are lost to a cultural system. Materials buried in layers or levels have often been assumed to be the result of single occupational episodes (for instance, see Conkey 1980), but this is not necessarily the case. The nature of the deposited archaeological record is controlled by the periodicity or "tempo" (Binford 1982:16) of occupation or use of a place and its relationship with the periodicity of taphonomic processes. If the discard of artifacts occurs with the same regular periodicity as natural forces—for instance, floods—that incorporate these materials into sediments, a regularly stratified archaeological record will result. If discard occurs more often than natural encapsulating events, however, cultural materials resulting from multiple behavioral episodes—multiple "activity sets," in Carr's terms (1984: 113)—will be incorporated into the same geomorphic stratum. In situations such as the complete radius leapfrog pattern of residential mobility, for instance, in which certain logistic sites may be reoccupied or reused for different activities within a short period following the move of a residential camp, one might expect that episodes of discard would occur more frequently than episodes of natural deposition. This would result in single-layer assemblages or depositional sets (Carr 1984:114) composed of materials from more than one occupation or function. It is not simply the organization of a cultural system that conditions differences in the appearance of the deposited archaeological record, but interactions between the organizational system and taphonomic processes. The interactions pose another set of problems for the archaeologist that did not exist in the "discarded record" prior to deposition: "demonstrably associated things may never have occurred together as an organized body of material during any given occupation" (Binford 1982:17–18).

Postdepositional Processes

Another set of processes affecting the nature of the archaeological record are postdepositional, occurring after the stabilization of cultural materials, although it must also be kept in mind that natural processes can disturb, reorder, or act to destroy or preserve the form of material prior to actual burial in the ground as well. Generally, almost any process that disturbs or acts upon the surface of the earth and subsurface deposits also acts upon archaeological materials. Biological processes such as "faunalturbation" and "floralturbation" (Wood and Johnson 1978) caused by burrowing, trampling, and root heaving can modify the original deposition of cultural materials. Chemical and physical processes that affect the archaeological record include freezing and thawing cycles, mass wasting (and subsequent gravitational effects), the growth and wasting of salt crystalline structures, the swelling and shrinking of clays, volcanism and tectonism, disturbances caused by the action of gas, air, wind and water, and pedogenesis.

A somewhat different taxonomy of the postdepositional processes acting on the archaeological record is advanced by Foley (1981b), who presents five sets of processes responsible for burial, movement, destruction, exposure, and "small scale oscillation" (Foley 1981a:167) of archaeological materials. Discarded artifacts enter the archaeological record through burial by cultural or natural agencies; once assemblages are buried they may remain in place, or they may be moved through stream action, sediment movement, faulting, or mass wasting. At the same time, certain materials may or may not be destroyed by physical and chemical agencies while in or on the ground. Small-scale oscillation processes include animal burrowing, human disturbances, root action, and water or wind action, which may alter the position of components of the archaeological record slightly but presumably do not totally disarrange it. Exposure of the archaeological record by water or aeolian erosion, tectonic activity, or human disturbance may also disturb the archaeological record, but these forces also expose materials and make them visible.

Just as variations in the coincidence of episodes of discard and episodes of deposition or burial can create either fine-grained or coarse-grained (palimpsest) assemblages, exposure and reburial can also introduce further complexities in patterned archaeological materials. These processes are rarely simply gravitational but also usually contain some lateral component, and are therefore influenced by small variations in topography. Exposure and redeposition in many places are highly localized for this reason, and portions of the material record resulting from, say, two occupations may be mixed, while a few feet away other portions may be separately stratified. Controlling for the complexities caused by differential deposition, exposure, and reburial of artifacts may be one of the most difficult and yet necessary tasks facing the archaeologist.

The Scale of Depositional and Postdepositional Processes

Natural depositional and postdepositional processes are not necessarily or even often conditioned by the same factors that cause people to visit and use an area. Depositional and postdepositional processes are localized and patterned on a small scale. Rarely, then, will the actions and results of these natural processes be spatially congruent with specific activity areas or the actual distributions of cultural events. Instead, their effects serve to remove the archaeological record yet another level from past behavior and the organization of human systems.

It is common in contemporary archaeology to view postdepositional processes as somewhat evil, as distorting the archeological record and diminishing its research potential. This probably springs from the seemingly popular belief that natural postdepositional processes are random in their operation (Bowers et al. 1983; Kirkby and Kirkby 1976). Almost all modern survey forms have a space for the assessment of a site's integrity—and if the site is disturbed, it is obviously of limited utility to science, and is therefore of diminished significance. Archaeologists can ignore it and move on to undisturbed sites. The problem with this strategy is that all archeological materials, whether they are found in sealed sites or lying on the surface, have been affected by natural processes. Taphonomic processes are not random in nature; in order to allow for their effects on archaeological data, however, these processes must be studied and understood in terms of the scale at which they distort the past.

This is doubly necessary because the effects of postdepositional processes on what we see as the archeological record may be far greater than we recognize intuitively. They not only disarrange artifacts and features, but in fact may be almost totally responsible for most of what archaeologists discover during surface survey. If the physical dimensions of behavioral events that produce discarded materials are of the same spatial scale as depositional and postdepositional processes, there is some chance that entire sites will be exposed to the archaeologist's view. This will probably rarely be the case, however. The material record will almost certainly be acted upon by a series of partially overlapping depositional and postdepositional processes of widely varying scales, combining the products of behavioral episodes, blurring or sharpening (and in fact probably often creating) their apparent boundaries, and differentially affecting the placement of artifacts depending on their sizes and shapes. These effects are all-important, for they determine where archaeologists may see sites and what they look like, and may even be responsible for the fact that we think we see sites at all.

THE KRIEGERIAN PARADIGM AND HUMAN SYSTEMS

Since the later 1970s, archaeology seems to have been predisposed to two major theoretical directions that still seem prevalent today: (1) reconstructionism, a continuation of most empirical, traditional archaeological approaches; and (2) what has been defined as contextual-structuralism, holding that our understanding of the past is determined entirely by our own cultural milieu. My perspective is that archaeology can be neither wholly empirical nor a self-serving, internalized social pursuit. Rather, it must be a process of linking the physical world, including the archaeological record, with the meaning we give it through a constant explanatory procedure. A possible schematic representation of such a procedure is presented in Figure 2.1.

The framework of archaeological research presented here consists of recognizing a series of processual steps or stages, processes that separate the archaeological record from our conventional interpretations of what it means. In seeking explanations we must proceed from one processual link to another. This is not necessarily easy, for one stage is not necessarily automatically translatable into the next. Each must instead be linked through warranting arguments. While each stage is qualitatively different, the stages can be divided into two broad domains, those of theory and method.

Through a step-by-step consideration of each theoretical explanatory stage, undertaken with respect to anthropologically and archaeologically relevant reasoning, I have shown that the processes that result in the formation of the archaeological record are complex, and that attempting to reconstruct the past by starting with sites as arbitrary discovery units can only result in the creation of untestable anecdotes about instantaneous past scenes. The synthesis of many such recreated scenes, approached again on an empirical basis by contrasting the form of diagnostic artifacts, is the basis of the Kriegerian paradigm. This paradigm is antithetical to comprehending the interaction between the parts or components of human systems.

3

TOWARD A DISTRIBUTIONAL

ARCHAEOLOGICAL METHOD

-- -- -- -- -- -- -- -- -- -- -- -- --

Higher- and middle-range theory involve thinking about what it is we want to know, and deciding how these dynamic, essentially abstract, and unmeasurable things may be manifest in the static contemporary archaeological record. In the preceding chapter I used abstract concepts about the nature of dynamic human systems to illustrate that the archaeological record may not result from the simple translation of living camps and activity locations into archaeological sites. In this chapter I shall continue that discussion from a methodological standpoint, dealing with contemporary archaeological discovery methods—many of which are not consistent with the examination of the organizations of systems and their components—as well as a few promising approaches that are.

CONTEMPORARY ARCHAEOLOGICAL SURVEY METHODS

Archaeological discovery consists of those methods employed to find archaeological facts. The archaeological discovery methods discussed here are those that take place during surface survey. Probability sampling methods are usually among the first discussed whenever the subject of archaeological discovery arises. The frequency of sampling discussions in the literature has accelerated without abatement since

Binford (1964) suggested the use of probability sampling as part of regional research designs directed toward understanding the different parts of past systems. In this regard, Binford's primary research objective was "the isolation and definition of the *content*, the *structure*, and the *range* of a cultural system" (1964:427). Ideally, probability sampling methods would insure that a representative sample of systems components was chosen.

Unfortunately, probability sampling was almost immediately translated by many archaeologists into a method for collecting information to use as the basis of inductive statistics: projecting characteristics of the sampled archaeological record to a population of archaeological records in a larger study area. The sampling literature has increased manyfold since this time, another typical aspect of Clarke's (1973) uncritical self-consciousness period in archaeology.

Predicting, Modeling and Sampling

Predictive modeling is a popular subject for discussion in archaeology today. Approached inductively, as it almost always is, it is essentially a reconstructionist activity in that it proceeds from method to theory, with the attendant logical dangers (Fig. 2.1). Yet unlike a complete reconstructionist strategy, predictive modeling as defined and attempted by many archaeologists does not utilize or result in the refinement of theory at any level. It is solely concerned with projecting, on the basis of the archaeological record, expectations about additional archaeological observations that could be made in the same or a similar area. Projection is almost always made on the basis of "independent" environmental variables—the assumption that one will find certain types of sites in certain types of areas.

I have argued elsewhere (Ebert 1985; Ebert and Kohler 1986; Ebert et al. 1983, 1984) that without knowing the systemic mechanisms behind the placement of activities across the landscape—that is, without knowing about the articulation of systems components—there can be no generally applicable predictions. Understanding the articulation of systems components requires recourse to theory, among other things. It cannot be simply an exercise in empirical projection from a specific sample to other uninvestigated areas. To be generally successful, predictive modeling must allow us to connect the processes that take place in one area, through explanation, to those in other areas.

Sampling Consistency

Most discussions of the best choices of units, stratifications, and designs in archaeological sampling stress accuracy and precision. These are criteria important to the determination of how efficient a sample is at predicting characteristics of the population from which it is drawn. In order that these characteristics can be compared in a general way from place to place, however, an even more important consideration must be consistency.

There are two general levels of consistency that must be considered. The first of these has to do with consistency of the sample as integrated with the theoretical portion of the investigatory framework. Our data must be consistent with the things we want to explain, because these shape our perception of what we see as appropriate data. There are compelling reasons for believing that, on a physical level, the archaeological record may not often consist of discrete sites, the locations of which can be interpreted on the basis of simple behavioral reasons. The archaeological record is more complex than a simple, unarticulated collection of past events. Methods of discovery, including choices of units to be sought and ways to sample these units, must instead be consistent with the perception of a continuous, overlapping record resulting from the repetitive positioning of components of systems in space and time. Later in this chapter I shall review and discuss some approaches that are more or less consistent with this sort of archaeological record.

The other sort of consistency is simpler, lying within the methodological domain. There is no way to compare data generated by survey or any other data collection strategy if these strategies do not employ consistent methods and units; unfortunately, they hardly ever do. An often-repeated theme in the literature dealing with sampling and survey is that, ultimately, every archaeological situation (and every archaeologist) is unique and this in turn justifies unique data collection procedures.

Sites as Units of Discovery

One illustration of the lack of methodological consistency in archaeology is the use of variably defined sites as the units of discovery. It is difficult to find examples of sample survey in which the site is not implicitly or explicitly the unit of discovery (Dunnell and Dancey 1983:271). Sites have been defined both as loci of past behavior and as the locations of archaeological materials found by archaeologists, although the latter definition is generally the one used in survey archaeology (Brooks and Yellen 1987; Dunnell and Dancey 1983; Schiffer and Gumerman 1977). The ways these definitions are made operational in the field are nearly always arbitrary. The SARG research program (Plog and Hill 1971:8), for instance, defines a site as the locus of artifacts, features, or facilities with an artifact density of at least five per square meter. Many other researchers define sites differently, and even more never do so explicitly. Even an explicit definition such as the SARG statement would require relatively meticulous measurement and calculation of artifact densities in the field, and it is difficult to imagine how such a definition could be practically operationalized.

Some authors face the difficulty of operationalizing site definitions by leaving it up to the individual surveyor in the field to translate from qualitative to quantitative, from subjective to objective:

> The decision as to what empirical manifestation constitutes a site often must be made in the field using multiple criteria. Clearly, crews need to have considerable expertise and the ability to account for their decisions **quantitatively** (Schiffer, Sullivan and Klinger 1978:14).

> One of the most critical decisions we must face if we are to develop survey data with an iota of comparability is the question of what is and what is not a site. Upon the discovery of artifacts, a surveyor must make a "yes" or "no" decision concerning site status. . . . The adequacy of a survey, then, depends in part on the surveyor's perception of the importance of certain classes of archaeological data (Plog, Plog, and Wait 1978:385–86).

The same authors, however, also note that archaeological materials are not always clustered and easily boundable. Plog, Plog, and Wait (1978), drawing on their experience in the arid Southwest, reveal that they have rarely encountered sites with densities as high as the minimum five artifacts per square meter suggested by SARG, and feel that sparse, diffuse archaeological remains are as useful as sites. Although sites and "isolates" are apparently not the same thing, the major difference is their density:

> A **site** is a discrete and potentially interpretable locus of cultural materials. By discrete we mean spatially bounded with those boundaries

marked by at least relative changes in artifact densities. By interpretable we mean that materials of sufficiently great quality and quantity are present for at least attempting and usually sustaining inferences about the behavior occurring at the locus. A nonsite area is a potentially interpretable but not spatially discrete locus of cultural materials (Plog, Plog, and Wait 1978:389).

Schiffer and Wells (1982) also recognize this distinction, and "recommend that all archaeological occurrences—including isolated finds—be recorded as 'field loci.' For administrative (and research) purposes, criteria can then be consistently applied in the laboratory to designate sites. If all field lòci are reported, then other investigators can use the same data to define a different set of sites" (1982:376). It is difficult to tell just what these writers mean by field loci; virtually the only meaning that would allow the flexibility to reconstitute sites in different ways would be the individual recording of all of the artifacts comprising both sites and isolated occurrences. One wonders why the methodological concept of the site is even necessary if this is the case.

Sample and Survey Design

Another broad area of institutionalized inconsistency in archaeological discovery methods is illustrated by attempts to determine or specify appropriate sample unit shapes and sizes and design optimal surveys using these units.

Possibilities for sample unit shapes include squares, rectangles, circles, and irregular shapes. While all of these have been used by archaeologists, and several will be mentioned in a review of nonsite archaeological approaches below, squares and rectangles are easiest to locate and most likely to provide the equal probability of choice necessary for probability samples. An important property of any sample unit is occasioned by the "edge effect" (Plog, Plog, and Wait 1978). The edge effect occurs because archaeological materials are discovered within a sample unit if even a portion intrudes within the sample unit boundary. Thus, if sites represented by circles 10m in radius are found in an area, the effective discovery boundaries of a sample unit are extended 10m outward from each of its edges. Sample units can therefore be expected to overestimate the density of archaeological materials in an area. The effects are obviously greatest when the archaeological materials being discovered are large and the ratio of edge length to area of a sample unit are greatest. It is just as obvious that it is sites, rather than physical objects, that are being sought.

Because of the edge effect, according to Plog, Plog, and Wait (1978), long, thin transects are the most efficient way to survey an area. During surface collection (within sites), however, square sample units are superior because they reveal the association of materials more faithfully.

Sample unit sizes, they go on to say, should be variably determined on the basis of site size and the artifact density on each site. For instance, in the Black Mesa area, where the average site size was 650 square meters and the average artifact density about 2 per square meter, these researchers employed 4-by-4m sample units. They disagree with Redman (1974) who specified that such sample units should be of such a size that they contain at least 100 artifacts per unit.

Another property of sites and materials that is important to consider when determining appropriate survey methods is "obtrusiveness" (Schiffer and Wells 1982:347):

> Every archaeological phenomenon . . . generates a specific surface which, when intruded, results in discovery. . . . The discovery probability is 1.0 when obtrusiveness is equal to or greater than the crew spacing interval [in transect surveys, this is equivalent to intensity]. Thus, in order to consistently discover phenomena with low obtrusiveness, one would have to survey at impractically high intensities (ca. 1000–1500 crew members/square mile).

This amounts to a restatement of the edge effect contention, one in which artifacts or features are being considered as minute sites and (apparently) a huge army of crew members is surveying laser-thin lines. In most instances, it should not be impractical for a surveyor to scan a reasonable swath on each side of his path (widths of 2 to 5m have been suggested by "nonsite" authors) for the presence of artifacts. In reality, it is always artifacts or other discrete material occurrences that surveyors discover, and not sites. Very few artifacts are obtrusive in this sense given realistic sample unit sizes or transect widths. The sites that are obtrusive enough to cause overestimation due to edge effects are abstractions that have been created during the discovery process. What is more, if surveyors are staying within their sample unit boundaries (which they must to insure consistency), then "sites" are abstractions made on the basis of seeing only a small part of their supposed constituents.

The intensity of coverage of transect surveys is another property of surveys that shows a marked lack of consistency. Intensity in transect coverage is simply the distance between transects or some other measure derived from crew spacing (Schiffer et al. 1978), and is in at least a general way proportional to survey time and costs. "Since it is seldom practical to conduct an entire survey at 2m spacing—thus ensuring high discovery probabilities for all phenomena within survey units—compromises in intensity are in order. Commonly, intermediate spacing intervals of 10–75m are employed" (Schiffer et al. 1978:13). In a table exemplifying some typical crew spacing in projects over the last ten years in Arizona, Schiffer and Wells (1982) list the following spacings (in meters): 4, 10, 10–20, 12, 17, 20–25, 20–30, 25–30, 32–40, 35, and two at 50.

It been suggested that there are optimally cost-effective survey intensities, and that these are specific to the study area and the phenomena being studied, "including target parameters, range of obtrusiveness, available support and, of course, visibility and accessibility. Abstract prescriptions for intensity, made without reference to project-specific information, should be discounted" (Schiffer et al. 1978:14).

Nonetheless, other authors have suggested that optimal transect intervals can be determined and that there is a point of diminishing returns at which decreases in transect spacing have little effect on survey yields (for instance, Judge 1981). This is an intuitively appealing idea, but could hold true generally only if we limit the size or obtrusiveness of the archaeological phenomena or the abstracted archaeological phenomena (sites) we are interested in seeing or willing to accept as possible or relevant.

Of course, one can find some isolated occurrences along transects with any spacing, but "parameter estimates for material of low obtrusiveness may be sacrificed because it is difficult to standardize the sample size" (Schiffer et al. 1978:13).

Multistage Surveys

Schiffer et al. (1978) contend, however, that most research problems require the location of rare, clustered things (meaning sites) rather than common, unclustered ones (isolated items), for they feel that the most important aspects of archaeological materials are abundance and clustering. When abundance decreases and clustering increases, unfortunately, the sample size for maintaining specific levels of accuracy and prediction rises dramatically (following Asch 1975; Read 1975). Probability sampling is therefore inappropriate for dealing with clustered items, including most sites; "purposive" (Schiffer et al. 1978:5) sampling methods are often required. While these can include anything from making educated guesses to talking to pothunters, one of the more systematic purposive methods for these and other authors is multistage sampling (Schiffer and House 1977a, 1977b; Doelle 1976, 1977).

A multistage survey design appropriate for southern Arizona, according to Schiffer and Wells (1982), would consist of three phases, each of increasing survey intensity. Phase 1 would be undertaken at a crew spacing of ".25 mile, to improve the chances of discovering site clusters. . . . In the event that field workers object to walking alone, some adjustments to the transect design will be necessary. Regardless of how the logistics are resolved, the crew spacing must remain large (at least 100m)" (Schiffer and Wells 1982:376). Phase 2, employing a higher transect intensity, would be directed toward identifying "priority areas" of high site density or with rare kinds of sites. Phase 3 is an "intensive survey of nonsite phenomena and testing" in areas where phases 1 and 2 disclose a "rich and varied nonsite resource base in a study unit" (Schiffer and Wells 1982:380).

Considered in the light of the expectation of a continuous, overlapping archaeological record, some cautions might be raised about such multistage surveys. Artifact occurrences within a transect are being used as the basis for abstracting site areas—that is, areas of high artifact density or high site cluster density—and these areas are successively more intensively surveyed. Given a continuous or regular distribution of archaeological materials, however, as areas are more intensively surveyed, more things will be found there. There is a distinct chance, at least in certain archaeological situations, that multistage surveys will be definitionally self-fulfilling. Imagine an experiment with an artificial, completely even or random archaeological distribution. If there were slight perturbations occasioned by, say, surface visibility differences or sporadic crew inattention, a multistage survey design would automatically result in the recording of clustered data. Unless controls are instituted in archaeological survey to test for actual as opposed to discovered distributions of artifacts, at any rate, we have no assurance that this will not happen.

A number of authors have contended that small, simple sites or clusters may be better candidates for spatial analysis than large complex ones, given our present understanding of formation processes (Moseley and Mackey 1972; Dillehay 1973; Talmadge, Chester, and Stoff 1977). If this is the case, perhaps multistage surveys aimed at finding and accurately recording sparse distributions would be more appropriate. The lowest-density areas found in each phase could be surveyed more intensively. In implementing such a design one would immediately have difficulty with the site concept. In the commonly suggested multistage design concentrating on dense areas, sites are abstracted from the onset of survey, and their existence (or the existence of dense clusters, behavioral loci, hot spots, or some other scholarly euphemisms) continually reinforced. In a multistage survey aimed in the other direction, toward inspecting areas of lower and lower density at greater and greater intensities, sites could not be abstracted, and would in fact be meaningless.

There is an underlying problem with both of these survey strategies, however—again, one of consistency. The results of discovery procedures undertaken at different intensities are not comparable. The difference between data collected through large-interval transects and those through very small-interval survey will be qualitative, not simply quantitative.

NONSITE APPROACHES TO THE ARCHAEOLOGICAL RECORD: A SEARCH FOR SOLUTIONS

Beginning in the early 1970s a number of archaeologists began to respond to problems they perceived in reconciling the nature of the surface archaeological record with traditional techniques of discovery and their built-in guides to interpretation. The impetus to these attempts was from two directions.

The Empirical Impetus to Nonsite Archaeology

Some of the earliest nonsite approaches were sparked by difficulties in bounding and recognizing sites encountered when applying traditional methods in the course of survey. In most American archaeology, calls for nonsite discovery and analysis are still based upon the empirical recognition that the archaeological record is not clustered in all places and therefore cannot be dealt with everywhere as discrete sites (Dunnell 1971; Dancey 1973; Doelle 1976; Klinger 1976; Morenon et al. 1976; Wait 1977; Wilke and Thompson 1977). Two consistent characteristics mark these approaches. The first of these is that the archaeological record is perceived by these authors (see particularly Rodgers 1974; Morenon et al. 1976; Wait 1977) as composed of sites and nonsites. Nonsites are areas where, for reasons of density, extent, or some other properties of the archaeological record, archaeologists are unwilling or unable to assign cluster boundaries. These areas are intensively surveyed through various sampling strategies, usually in the hope of producing data from which sites can be abstracted.

For instance, Rodgers (1974), in a survey in Arizona, sampled a study area using 146 circles 45m in radius, which were surveyed at transects 4m apart. Densities of artifact types within quadrants of the circles were recorded, and clustered materials bagged together. In northwestern New Mexico, Wait (1977) surveyed larger areas intensively at an approximately 15m transect spacing, flagging all artifacts discovered. In a second stage, surveyors went back to perceived clusters of artifacts and systematically searched those areas more intensively to identify sites. In Maryland, Wilke and Thompson (1977) mapped lithic scatters found within randomly placed 30-by-30m grid squares, confirming their feeling that a low-density scatter existed between sites. Recently, there has been a resurgence of "site versus nonsite" approaches initiated because of empirical perceptions of the nature of the archaeological record, particularly in the context of cultural resource management survey (Jones 1984).

One might imagine that in arid regions with sparse plant cover the continuous nature of the archaeological record would most obviously call for nonsite approaches. In the Priest Rapids area in Washington state, Dancey (1974) noted that the continuous distribution of artifacts in arid areas required precise discovery and mapping of artifact locations so that sites could be analytically separated from "out of site" materials in the laboratory. Interestingly, a major impetus to nonsite archaeology has been provided by the frustrations of survey archaeology in wetter and densely vegetated areas, as well. In such places archaeological materials usually can be found only in circumscribed places where the vegetation has been removed or altered: blowouts, eroded places along streams or rivers, plowed fields, and shovel test pits. The systematic digging of test pits at intervals has been employed to find sites (Lovis 1976; Wilke and Thompson 1977), but other authors contend that all such strategies yield nonsite samples (Nance 1980; McManamon 1981, 1984).

Another essentially nonsite strategy has grown from the consideration of survey in plowed fields. Initially, the intent of "plowzone archaeology" (O'Brien and Lewarch 1981) was to demonstrate that agricultural practices do not totally destroy patterning in the archaeological record (Trubowitz 1978). Through controlled resurvey of field areas (Ammerman and Feldman 1978; Riordan 1982; Dunnell 1985), it has been demonstrated that while the archaeological record of plowed areas is biased in certain ways, it is nonetheless useful even at small scales of spatial analysis. While earlier "plowzone" replication experiments asked whether surface archaeology reflected the subsurface, the usefulness of such questions has recently been called in question by Robert Dunnell (1985:3–4):

> The validity of surface distributions was somehow to be assessed by its correspondence with the location and content of subsurface deposits. There is, of course, no **a priori** reason why this should be the case any more than an expectation that the contents and distributions of two different stratigraphic units would be synonymous. That such a view could be so widely held can only be interpreted as the dominance of a static rather than dynamic view of the nature of the record itself and an inherent priority assigned to buried materials.

Nonsite Discovery and Analysis: Theoretically Based Studies

Other authors' approaches to nonsite archaeology seem to have been based primarily on theoretical expectations or problems rather than simply empirical observations about the archaeological record. One of the earliest of these approaches was that of Davis (1975), who felt that tool kits defined in the California desert and ascribed by some to different cultures might actually be two components of the same adaptive system. On many desert surfaces, she reasoned, erosion had collapsed the archaeological record to a wholly surface manifestation. A number of 305-by-305m survey squares near China Lake were surveyed at 4- to 5-ft. intervals, and all artifacts flagged and mapped using a plane table and alidade. Two types of tool kits were found through analysis to be spatially coexistent, which Davis interpreted as confirming that they were used by the same people.

At about the same time, Albert Goodyear (1975) initiated his Hecla survey on the Papago reservation in Arizona. This study was directed toward both prehistoric and historic archaeology; from an ethnographic perspective, it was clear that most of the study area was probably used continuously at a low rate. Some of the sites surveyed measured more than a mile on a side. Reasoning that the whole project area was essentially a site, Goodyear surveyed intensively using sample circles about 130m in diameter, recording densities of artifacts for the "reconstruction of activity subsystems" through the "identification of techno-behavioral correlates" (1975:35).

By 1976, Dancey's (1974) approach to sites as opposed to nonsites had shifted to the examination of densities of different artifact classes compared with environmental zones in his Priest Rapids study area, an obvious shift to more theoretically oriented nonsite archaeology. A similar approach is found in the work of O'Brien et al. and Mason (1979), who sought information on "occupational densities" (O'Brien et al. 1979:61) to compare with agricultural food production potential at Xoxocotlan in the Valley of Oaxaca, Mexico. This discovery strategy was termed a "zonal approach" by Mason (1979:89), concentrating on subregional zones that might include several sites, the goal being "plotting distributions of artifact densities relative to a zone or region" (Mason 1979:94) while making no *a priori* guesses about sites.

The necessity for theoretically based nonsite approaches has been reinforced in the 1980s. Basing his strategy on a regional descriptive settlement model, Nance (1980) divided a study area in the lower Cumberland River Valley of Kentucky into three landscape strata, and surveyed and tested intensively within 200-by-200m grids placed randomly in each stratum to comprehend "systems of sites" (1980:170). An artifact-directed probabilistic sampling approach was used for predicting material densities in the Tellico Reservoir project in Tennessee by Davis (1980a, 1980b). Reasoning that the archaeological materials found between sites represent a large portion of the record left by prehistoric systems in the Steens Mountain area of southeastern Oregon, Jones (1984) undertook intensive sampling of large areas for nonsite discovery there. Stafford (1985), expecting continuous archaeological remains in almost all places devoid of severe topographic constraints, advocates large-scale, nonsite regional discovery and analysis for understanding hunter-gatherer systems.

Since the early 1970s, however, it is from the work of three archaeologists that the major theoretical justification for nonsite archaeology has come. In the United States, David Hurst Thomas's work and writing provide one of the clearest statements of a developing methodology and its rationale. In Africa, Robert Foley and Glynn Isaac and colleagues also devised nonsite approaches that can serve as sources of ideas for distributional archaeology. These authors have gone beyond most of the other nonsite experimenters cited above in that they have applied their work to specific research problems that are coherently described in depth in their written works.

Thomas's Nonsite Archaeology

In the late 1960s David Hurst Thomas, then a graduate student at the University of California at Davis, initiated an approach to nonsite archaeological survey from a theoretical rather than empirical direction. He noted that Julian Steward's model of Great Basin adaptive systems, which will be discussed at length in Chapter 5, had been adopted many by archaeologists, including Flannery (1966), MacNeish (1964), Irwin-Williams (1967), and Wilmsen (1970), as exemplary of hunter-gatherers from many time periods and geographic areas. The question that directed Thomas's inquiry was whether Steward's Great Basin adaptive model actually reflects prehistoric Great Basin adaptations as we know them from the archaeological record (Thomas 1972). The necessity of verifying Steward's interpretation for prehistoric people in the Great Basin, and its connection with the validity of such pronouncements for modeling the archaeological record there or elsewhere will not be questioned here. The important point is that a general model—"not a *fact* but a *theory*" (Thomas 1972:675)—was the impetus for explanation and for strategies to discover and record the archaeological record. In order to test the validity of the model, logical congruences were to be deduced, with the eventual result of predicting artifact frequencies in different microenvironmental zones.

Thomas's study area was the Reese River Valley in central Nevada, where during the 1930s Steward studied Paiute groups, their material cultures, and their subsistence and seasonal rounds. Steward's primary ethnographic method was the use of informants, from whom answers to questions about lifeways during their youth—no later than the 1870s—were elicited. Were the stories Steward was hearing plausible accounts of prehistoric life in the Reese Valley during approximately the last 2,500 years, or had Paiute life already been irreparably modified by European contact in the late nineteenth century? To compare the ethnographic and archaeological records, Thomas (1974) felt that three requirements must be met by his data: they must represent all parts of the seasonal round, rather than single sites; they must be unbiased by sampling techniques; and they must provide negative as well as positive evidence (that is, not only what took place, but also what did not).

Previously, the sites most frequently studied by archaeologists working in the Great Basin were cave sites and a few large open sites—both of which Thomas felt were likely to have been winter habitations, representative of only the largest and longest-occupied site types expected. Winter camps were occupied for a maximum period of about six months, and perhaps considerably less in some Great Basin settings. During other times, smaller and shorter occupations by families or other small groups were more typical, which would result in a sparse and continuous archaeological record. Accordingly, "Kill sites, gathering stations and the like are of crucial importance in the seasonal round. In short, we must deal with more than the traditional 'archaeological site.' Surface scatters are vital since they may be the only remnants of some prehistoric task activities" (Thomas 1973:167). Because in many areas sparse discard during foraging activities would result in continuous scatters of materials to which it may be difficult to assign boundaries, the "inclusive regional random sample" of the archaeological record must contain "all visible remains of prehistoric subsistence activities" (1974:36).

In order to connect the implications of Steward's general Great Basin model with the archaeological record, Thomas devised a more specific, mechanistic model through which artifact frequencies in three environment zones within the Reese River Valley study area were simulated. Thomas synthesized a "subsistence-settlement system" (1974:41) from Steward's work. The resources that would have been important within each of the three environmental zones were next deduced. A computer simulation model (Thomas 1972) was employed to simulate the availability of nonconstant resources and thus predict settlement size and reuse period.

The three nonconstant resources modelled were pinyon, Indian ricegrass, and antelope, the differential availabilities of which were taken as determinants of variability in the degree and intensity of use of the three environmental zones. Next, tool kits appropriate for the exploitation of each nonconstant resource were abstracted, using a combination of Steward's material culture lists, ethnoarchaeology, and the functional suggestions of archaeologists. A number of "tool kit units" or TKUs (Thomas 1972:696) for each zone over a millenium was predicted.

The "slippery transition" (Thomas 1972:696) between abstract tool kits and observable artifacts, which embody many functional and stylistic properties, required that attributes of artifacts rather than the artifacts themselves serve as the ultimate analytical units. Attributes found in each area were taken as contributing to a number of functionally different assemblages; that is, "sets of functional attribute states of a particular mode" were used to "reduce the activities [of Steward's model] into their correlative tool assemblages" (Thomas 1973:161). Edge angles, a biface and uniface dichotomy, and functional tool types served as the major criteria for distinguishing between butchering, hunting, plant processing, and habitation group assemblages.

To assure a representative sample, the study area was divided into approximately 1400 squares 500 by 500m, and a 10 percent sample (140) was randomly selected for surface survey. A crew of 6 people covered 1 to 2 of these units per day at an unspecified (perhaps not constant?) survey intensity, collecting and labeling all tools, flakes, and other lithic artifacts. Between 25 and 45 people participated in the survey for 4 months and recovered approximately 3,500 formal tools and about 180,000 flakes (Thomas 1972, 1973). The analysis of survey data included comparison with attribute frequencies predicted by the computer simulation model and analysis of the degree of clustering of items found within survey quadrats by comparison with Poisson distributions (indicating that artifacts may have been deposited by rare and random events), and using analyses of coefficients of dispersion (useful for indicating clumped distributions). Winter village distributions were expected to be clumped, and foraging radius distributions (perhaps ricegrass collection locations) were expected to be dispersed. This expectation was realized, as were most of the rest of Thomas's predictions; other observations from the Reese River data were unexpected. Both of these will be discussed later in light of artifact and attribute distributions in my study area in southwestern Wyoming.

In an even more forceful statement of his nonsite position Thomas (1975:62, emphasis in original) argues that "it is a mistake to conclude that just because the site concept is almost universally accepted as archaeology's minimal *spatial* unit it is always *archaeology's minimal operational unit*," and calls for regional sampling procedures that take the cultural item as a minimal discovery and analytical unit and "ignore traditional sites altogether." This is clearly not a site and nonsite dichotomy, based on notions about how the archaeological record appears in different places.

In an unfortunate use of terminology not encountered in any of Thomas's subsequent writing, he refers to nonsite archaeology as "Easter egg sampling" (1975:62), in which individual eggs are the units discovered and analyzed: "This is not to deny that artifacts generally occur in well-defined sites—Easter eggs often arrive in baskets—but rather to assert that in some instances, under special research circumstances, discrete clumpings of artifacts (a) either do not occur or (b) are not relevant to the problem at hand."

Archaeological methods must be based on the things we want to know about, which are of course theory-guided, he goes on to say, and "must be helpful rather than restrictive, so I have scrapped the site concept altogether in [the Reese River] context" (Thomas 1975:63).

DISTRIBUTIONAL APPROACHES IN AN OLD WORLD CONTEXT: TWO EXAMPLES

To concentrate only on North American approaches to archaeology that question the sole use of the site as an appropriate unit of discovery and analysis would be to ignore at least two useful and informative Old World examples.

Glynn Isaac and Colleagues

Glynn Isaac's impetus for considering alternative ways of comprehending the archaeological record springs from his work with Acheulean and other late Pliocene and early Pleistocene materials in East Africa (Isaac 1966, 1967, 1978). The great time depth represented by these materials—as much as two million years or possibly more—suggests the necessity of controlling carefully for natural postdepositional processes in the context of research questions directed toward determining whether these adaptations were human strategies or rather something qualitatively different. Many African Pleistocene archaeological materials are derived from alluvial sedimentary contexts, with a high potential for disturbance both during deposition and subsequently through sorting, transport, material alteration, and reorientation. What is more, these processes can occur independently in sediments; an example would be the transport of artifacts without abrasion or other surface modification.

In order to interpret Pleistocene deposits, Isaac (1967) saw the need to discriminate between fluvial rearrangements of bone and artifact deposits and humanly determined patterns of debris, as well as the ability to account for the proportional representation of skeletal parts in bone accumulations from natural as opposed to cultural conditions.

Taphonomic experiments on the shores and minor tributaries of Lake Magadi, Kenya showed that archaeological materials may under certain circumstances be buried with little disturbance, that larger materials are often disturbed more than smaller ones, and that in certain deposits flakes have been preferentially removed by fluvial action (Isaac 1967). The latter effect gives the false impression that assemblages consist of tools manufactured elsewhere. In order to control for postdepositional processes, Isaac concluded, it is necessary to consider carefully the exact placement and orientation of each artifact over large areas.

Once natural processes are controlled for, archaeologists can proceed with the understanding of prehistoric economies and adaptations through the consideration of man-land relationships. According to Isaac, such efforts in East Africa (and elsewhere) most often proceed from the plotting of sites, "in general conspicuous concentrations of objects or features that occur within a restricted area" (Isaac 1975:1). Not all traces of prehistoric activity, however, are concentrated into clusters that "we can conveniently call sites and mark with a dot on the map" (1975:1). Some material is distributed as scatters between the "patches" (1975:1), and these may not be the same sorts of materials. In order to investigate the relationship between late Pliocene and early Pleistocene sites and scatters, Isaac and Harris developed a method for "coping with the material between the concentrated patches" (1975:1). His aim was to measure the absolute density of artifacts, as well as the proportions of types of artifacts and debitage, over 1,000 square miles in the East Lake Rudolf (now Lake Turkana) area of Kenya. A systematic stratified sample of transects of unspecified area was chosen, and these were surveyed intensively (Isaac and Harris 1975).

A later effort in the same region, at Koobi Fora, was more explicitly oriented toward investigating differences or similarities between the mobility and subsistence organization of hominids and present-day primates through the differential surface distribution of artifacts (Isaac 1978). Discrimination between natural and cultural arrangements of bone and artifacts required the very careful examination of subtle evidence, which in turn required looking at individual items and not any sort of abstraction to "sites." Over the very long time period represented by the African archaeological record, Isaac reasoned, artifact distributions are the result of many episodes of low-intensity activity overlaid atop one another, and therefore must be viewed as compound in nature.

This sort of archaeological record is best seen as a "web of pathways over a piece of terrain" (Isaac 1981:131), as the product of mobility rather than the focus of specific activity; this is quite clearly a systems approach, emphasizing relationships between places and activities at them. Even over short periods, human mobility forms a dense web consisting of lines with "nodes" at which discard is repeated. Over longer periods the nodes tend to blend together in different ways; the result is that "the archaeological record as it comes down to us is in no sense a simple 'map' of where humans discarded things, much less a map of where they used things or where they went" (Isaac 1981:134). Nonetheless, we must attempt to use it as evidence, and can if we use care. Especially in places with low-density artifact scatters, such care entails recording all surface occurrences, their characteristics, and their locations. Some scatters surveyed by Isaac had estimated densities of less than one artifact per ten thousand square meters. Although there were denser scatters and sites found against this background, which had been a major focus of archaeology previously, Isaac also estimated that there were very likely more things between these clusters than within them, and that they contain as much or more information as clusters do. In the great majority of cases, then, individual artifacts are the appropriate unit of discovery and analysis. Each artifact is seen as contributing its bit of information, in terms similar to Thomas's (1975) Easter egg metaphor: "We are fortunate that in addition to contributing their bones as markers, and sometimes footprints, early protohumans dropped bits and pieces of modified materials in many places. The spatial configuration of all of these 'visiting cards' constitutes the most powerful clue we have to the beginnings of the human condition" (Isaac 1981:152).

One of the most obvious reasons that the archaeological remains of the early Pleistocene are often misinterpreted, according to Isaac et al. (1981:102), is that they are "meager," typically sparse and simple, so archaeologists compensate by concentrating on areas where they are exceptionally dense and clustered—that is, on "sites." Interested in developing "alternative approaches to research that accept this meagerness of the record, and indeed move to recognize sparsity and simplicity as real reflections of the patterns of life and the status of mind that prevailed in remote prehistory" (Isaac et al. 1981:102), they decided instead to concentrate on the "overall scatter pattern of artifacts across ancient landscapes." With their methodological perspectives thus shifted, Isaac et al. discerned three basic levels of artifact density at Koobi Fora:

1. Low background levels in areas up to several square kilometers, with densities in 25-square-meter sample squares typically 0 to 2–3 artifacts, with 0 the most frequent observation;

2. Intermediate-density areas, up to 500m in diameter, with much higher densities, on the order of 2–3 to 10–20 artifacts per 25-square-meter sample area (within these areas smaller clusters of 30–100 artifacts were sometimes found);

3. Highly localized concentrations of 20–100 or more artifacts within a 25-square-meter unit; where these units are clustered they form classic sites with thousands of artifacts.

Their conclusion was that there are some very large areas or even regions where activity was constant but at very low rates, and other very small areas where prehistoric activity was concentrated and repeated, but was "not representative of the total artifact forming-using-discarding system" (Isaac et al. 1981:105). The most typical, most common, and most archaeologically important manifestation lies between these two extremes, and also contains the greatest number of artifacts overall: the minisite. Minisites are simple distributions, possibly the record of single events, such as tool making or finding a meal, and therefore have the greatest potential for interpretation under a paradigm directed by a belief in prehistoric simplicity. Although they are simple, minisites, if the product of single events, are also ironically difficult to compare with one another on the basis of diagnostic criteria; interpreting them requires the recording of all their contents on a nonsite basis.

Robert Foley's Off-Site Archaeology

Another nonsite approach, termed "off-site" by its author (Foley 1981d:157), is also based on research questions and fieldwork in East Africa, but focuses on later periods in the Amboseli Basin of southern Kenya. Foley prefers the term "off-site" to "nonsite" (after Thomas

1975) because it emphasizes the spatially continuous nature of the data (Foley 1980:39). The initial impetus for Foley's off-site approach was a consideration of how to compare site locations and distributions of available resources in a catchment area or home range around sites (Foley 1977). Foley proceeds from the contention that resource usage is distance-dependent, and proposes a model in which a study area is gridded into sample areas of humanly relevant size and the total relative resource productivity for each of these areas is calculated on the basis of detailed ecological field studies. Next, given the location of a site of interest, isocals or contours of consistent extractive values for that site are drawn. All those areas in which the availability-to-cost ratio for resources is positive are likely candidates for the home range of that site (Foley 1977:178).

Although some of the localities participating in cultural systems are seen in the archaeological record as clusters of materials, in most East African cases "archaeological remains are distributed ubiquitously across the landscape. In contrast to this, demonstrable primary stratified sites are extremely rare" (Foley 1980:39). What is more, archaeological materials are acted upon by a wide variety of natural processes subsequent to their deposition, which act differently in various microenvironmental settings. Given this, "It may no longer be valid to use site distribution as a direct indicator of observed prehistoric settlement patterns" (1980:39). Spatial continuity is a fundamental basis of regional studies. To study the archaeology of human adaptive systems, continuity must be stressed over clustering. In order to test his higher-range theoretical ideas about the correspondence between past activities and the distribution of resources, Foley undertook a study of the Amboseli Basin of southern Kenya to examine the relationship between settlement patterns, artifact distributions and densities, and ecological resources.

The problems of archaeologists, Foley feels, are similar to those faced by plant ecologists—they must sample small items (plants or artifacts) over large areas, paying strict attention to variations in density and frequency of different types of items. Plants and artifacts in the Amboseli region are similar in that both are ubiquitous (continuous), and both evidence enormous densities of individual occurrences. Furthermore, a major problem for the interpretation of both is determining the appropriate scale of analysis (Foley 1980:40).

To illustrate the magnitude of the potential information contained in the largely off-site archaeological record of small-scale, mobile societies, principally the lithic remains left by prehistoric hunter-gatherers and pastoralists, Foley (1981a) first models the archaeological record left by such groups in a general manner. He divides formation processes into three general sorts: behavior and discard, accumulation, and postdepositional processes.

Human subsistence behavior is distributed continuously across the landscape because the energy that man extracts from the natural environment is similarly distributed. Resources are extracted relatively continuously from the landscape, and only secondarily transported to focal points such as settlements, processing areas, and the like; a settlement-centered approach obscures the loci of resource procurement. The difference between settlements and the landscape in general is thus one of degree and not kind.

The area within which human energy-extractive activities are conducted is the home range—the area through which a group travels. Foley (1981a) distinguishes between core area, seasonal range, annual range, and lifetime ranges within the home range. Although the patterns of activity and discard of artifacts vary in home ranges on the basis of topography, environmental productivity, climate, and subsistence strategy, they can be modeled in a general way through reference to ethnographic data. Some of the assumptions, gleaned from a wide array of ethnographic data, used by Foley (1981a) in estimating the effects of discard are:

1. A hunter-gatherer band exploits a home range of 10km radius (after Yellen 1976).

2. A home base (residential base) occupies approximately 250 square meters (Wiessner 1974).

3. The band moves its base camp about every four weeks (after Woodburn's 1972 Hadza reports); some may move at least forty times a year (Yellen 1976:57–58). Home bases are "normally located on fresh ground" (Foley 1981a:9).

4. Following a period of home base occupation, the density of lithic artifacts and debris is a mean of 16.8 per square meter (Price 1979).

5. Focal points for activities (not residential bases, but hunting, fishing, trapping, and other raw material exploitation locales) occur five times as often as home bases (Wood and Johnson 1978), and cover an average area of 30 square meters (Price's

[1979] extractive camps, 27 square meters; Binford's [1978] Mask Site, 60 square meters).

6. Artifact densities at focal points (loci) are about 8.5 artifacts per square meter (Price 1979).

7. Within the home range, places used for activities increase at a rate of:
   a. gathering spots, one per day;
   b. hunting spots, one every two days (Tanaka 1976); and
   c. fuel collecting spots, one every two days.

8. An average of one artifact is discarded at each gathering spot; two at each hunting spot; and five at each fuel collecting spot.

Based on these admittedly general assumptions, Foley calculates the discarded results of one year's activity at different components of the settlement system of one human group to be:

At base camps: 12 camps x 250m^2 x 16.8 artifacts/m^2 = 50,400 artifacts per year.

At areas within 20m of the radius of these base camps: 12 camps x 2377.6m^2 x 3.36 artifacts/m^2 (20 percent of the density within the base camp radius itself) = 95,864 artifacts per year.

At nonresidential focal points: 60 focal points per year x 30m^2 x 8.5 artifacts/m^2 = 15,300 artifacts.

At resource extraction points: 1 gathering point + 1 hunting point every two days + 1 fuel collecting point each two days, with 1, 2, and 5 artifacts at each point respectively = 1639 artifacts.

On the basis of these calculations, Foley estimates that the total number of artifacts annually discarded by a single group within its home range would be 163,203, or 519.42 artifacts per square kilometer per year. Maintaining these discard rates over a period of 1,000 years would, then, result in the discard of 163 million artifacts, or 519,000 per square kilometer, or 0.5 artifacts per square meter over this period.

If there were a complete overlap of base camp locations within the 1,000-year period, 146,264,000 of these artifacts would be located within a 250-square-meter area (585,056 artifacts per square meter) and another 16,939,000 (about 11 percent of the total within the foraging radius) within a 10km radius of that camp (about 0.5 artifacts per square meter).

I know of no circumstances in which hundreds of millions of artifacts have been found within one 250-square-meter area anywhere in the archaeological record, and 585,000 artifacts per square meter seems to be a physical impossibility. A partial overlap, or even total lack of overlap, of residential bases through time is not only likely, it is the only realistic possibility given Foley's (1981a) model of discard frequency to density. Even if Foley's estimates of artifact discard rates were exaggerated 10 or even 100 times, a total overlap model of residential base locations over a 1,000-year period cannot be empirically supported as a general condition. Clearly, discard must be relatively evenly distributed over home ranges through archaeological time periods.

To play this game a bit further using Foley's estimates of discard rates, if residential bases over a 1,000-year period were relocated so that they just abutted each other, 3 million square meters of the total 314,159,000 square meters of home range (about 0.95 percent of the home range area) would contain 146,264,000 artifacts—about 48 artifacts per square meter within an area bit less than 1,800 by 1,800m. "Sites" of this magnitude are often recorded during the course of surface survey, but it is doubtful whether an overall density of 48 artifacts per square meter occurs in many of these. Another 17 million artifacts would be distributed within the home range radius of 10km. If Foley's estimates are at all accurate, it seems certain that residential bases are neither totally overlapped, nor are they even proximate in many cases. Over long periods the archaeological record is far more evenly distributed. Another conclusion that must be drawn from these calculations is that we recover only a very small proportion of artifacts discarded between home bases. An alternative possibility, that there is far more recycling and reuse over longer-than-ethnographic time periods, far longer than those Foley takes into account, will serve as the basis for further discussion later in this book.

Skewing our recovery of potentially discarded artifacts, according to Foley (1981a), are postdepositional processes. In almost all cases our recovery of the archaeological record falls far below expectations due to artifact burial, erosion, which can concentrate accumulations, large- and small-scale movements of discarded items, and, in some cases, the total destruction of artifacts.

Even more important than these natural processes, however, is the fact that "the archaeological record is not a fixed and immutable entity but a product of our own perception" (Foley 1981d:157). We tend to ignore the effects of debris-forming activity that is not focussed in centralized places. To judge from Foley's expected density estimates, this includes a large component of the total number of artifacts that can be expected to occur in any one place on the landscape. Many human activities, however, take place away from clustered sites. We must record not only what we think of as sites, but also "off-site" archaeology, or "nonsite" (Thomas 1975) occurrences, or the "scatter between the patches" (Isaac and Harris 1975:1).

This is necessary because the archaeological record is conditioned by the facts that in all places,

1. sites are nodes in a continuous distribution of archaeological materials;
2. home range behavior provides the theoretical underpinning for continuous archaeological regional distributions; and
3. postdepositional mechanics and continued but relatively non-overlapping occupancy, leading to the continuous accumulation of materials, compound the continuous distribution of archaeological materials, as well as increasing its complexity.

As a result, the artifact and not the site must serve as the basic unit of regional analysis (Foley 1981b:31).

DOING WITHOUT SITES

Although site surveys constitute the great bulk of surface discovery and recording today, particularly within the sphere of cultural resource management, it is apparent that we are on the threshold of realizing some of the problems that site-oriented methods present. While almost all archaeologists recognize some of these problems, there is still a reluctance to discard the concept of sites at a methodological level. This reluctance is shown in equivocal statements about how there really are sites in some places, or that the archaeological record consists of clusters with lower densities of material in between. While a number of new archaeological approaches espousing either a partially or wholly nonsite strategy offer promising potential, most of them are only partial answers to how we should deal with the archaeological record left by past systems.

Data collection methods must be consistent on two levels. Data collected must be consistent with the more theoretical parts of the explanatory framework—that is, with what we want to know. In Chapter 2, I suggested that a site-oriented data collection strategy is inappropriate for approaching questions about systemic organization using an expectably continuous and overlapping archaeological record that has been differentially affected by depositional and postdepositional processes. This chapter illustrates the absence of methodological consistency in most contemporary surveys. The notion that each survey is unique and therefore such survey parameters as sampling fraction, sample unit size, and survey intensity must be decided by the individual researcher can only lead to totally incomparable data. Unfortunately, as anyone who has attempted to use the compiled results of many surveys can attest, it is rare that any sort of comparability is found.

As if it is not enough that different surveys are not comparable, the even more insidious suggestion that survey parameters should be varied within a specific survey is popular in the literature today. Multistage surveys in which not only intensity and sample unit size and shape are varied, but in which the units of discovery are changed from sites to nonsites, have been advocated and experimented with. Data resulting from site discovery and artifact discovery are qualitatively different and incomparable, as sites are abstractions and as such are subject to abstract sampling problems such as edge effects and "obtrusiveness." In artifact-based discovery, edge effects and obtrusiveness are myths. Data based on site discovery and abstraction can never be compared with data based on artifact discovery. These data are not reflections of the same things, and cannot be used to test one another.

What is more, a multistage survey design based on surveying more and more limited areas of suspected higher site or artifact density at increasing survey intensities is self-fulfilling. At higher search intensities more cultural materials are found, at the same time that pragmatic and economic factors cause smaller areas to be searched. A multistage survey directed toward finding small, higher-density areas—sites, hot spots, loci, or whatever they are called—within a low-density background always does so.

The greatest impediment to methodological consistency within site-based survey, however, is the concept of the site itself. Consistency in the definition of a site can never be reached, due to the very nature of the concept. Sites are never discovered during survey; it is always artifacts, features, and other individual, physically real materials that we find. Bounded sites and statements about their contents are abstracted—that is, essentially made up—by looking at individual artifacts, and usually if not always by looking at only a portion of those making up the site abstraction. The differences between sites that we are interested in comparing—and that we can in fact compare—are differences in proportions of artifacts occurring commonly between them and the scale of spacing of these items, not the occurrence or nonoccurrence of "diagnostic" items. Comparing sites would require a complete cataloging of all of their contents.

On the borderline between site and nonsite approaches—and it might be argued that even many avowedly "nonsite" approaches sit astride this boundary—stands the idea that there are some archaeological occurrences that are sites and some that are not sites. Both sites and nonsites contain artifacts and useful information and are interpretable, but they usually differ in terms of density. Some authors do not use the term "sites," calling them loci or resorting to some other euphemism. The major point that I hope to make here is that we do not need a nonsite, or an off-site, or a site as opposed to a nonsite archaeology. What we need is an *antisite* archaeology, an archaeology that has nothing to do with sites, at least at the methodological level. It may be acceptable to use the concept of sites at an anthropological level, although we have better and more discriminating theoretical terms, and the use of the word "site" would be confusing. Rather than using the term "antisite archaeology," I introduce the term "distributional archaeology."

Two African approaches to nonsite, off-site, or distributional archaeology have been discussed as exemplary. The property of the East African archaeological record that sparked the authors of both of these approaches was the great time depth that they perceived in the archaeological record of their study areas, in one instance a million or more years and in the other at least forty thousand years and perhaps longer. Over these sorts of periods it is easy to imagine that many "meager," simple behavioral episodes overlap to yield, in some places, a dense record comprised of hundreds of episodes that are not necessarily functionally related. I feel that American archaeologists have largely ignored the time depth of the archaeological record in North America. In most places, the North American archaeological record has a potential time depth of ten thousand years or more, or at least five hundred generations.

Foley (1981b) found maximum densities in his Amboseli survey of about 100,000 artifacts per square kilometer, only about 0.1 artifacts per square meter in places where he expected a potential density over 40,000 years of accumulation of about 2 artifacts per square meter;

this was only about 5 percent of what he expected. We may easily be discovering only this proportion of our archaeological record, too. North American archaeologists seem to think that they are looking at the products of sparse and sporadic use of the landscape, of single or only a few episodes of behavior. This is an unwarranted assumption. There is no reason to believe that North American landscapes were not also utilized again and again, intensively and continuously. The North American archaeological record also is probably the product of many simple, meager episodes that did not completely overlap. We need to adopt a distributional archaeology of our own to deal with this record.

If distributional archaeology is the beginning of the solution to some major problems of archaeology, just what kind of distributional archaeology do we need? I have reviewed here number of archaeological approaches that are avowedly nonsite and employ artifacts or their characteristics as units of discovery, measurement, and analysis. A workable distributional archaeology can build upon these approaches and the lessons they teach.

One of these lessons has to do with sample areas and units. What is the scale of systems, and what is the scale of the study areas and sample units that we need to look at in order to study systems? The definition of systems that was offered in Chapter 2—systems as kinds of adaptations, rather than as sets of settlements occupied by groups of people—makes it clear that we will never actually see an entire system in the archaeological record, nor would we necessarily want or need to. The question of how big a system is, then, is a moot point; systems do not have a purely physical size. The things that we see in the archaeological record are physical components of systems—artifacts and other cultural materials, and their characteristics and spatial relationships.

Our sample units, the areas that we actually inspect to discover items and measure the information they contain, offer a "window" through which we can see these physical facts, resulting from the repetitive positioning of the nonphysical systems components in the past. Given our present understanding of what the physical components of systems and their spatial relationships may look like (which is not very well developed), it seems that the best sample units would be as large as possible. They should at least be large enough to contain a reasonable number of partially overlapping episodic activity areas of the largest size we think may have occurred in the past. Small, thin transects—used not only in site approaches but also in some artifact-oriented approaches (Foley 1981b)—are not the ideal units for distributional archaeology.

It is appropriate to ask whether we really want to sample, in the statistical sense of the term. Probability sampling is directed toward predicting or projecting from one sample to a larger universe. What are the properties of a large universe that we might want to project? Empirical predictive modeling for discovery of new site locations has been discussed. Even if predictive modeling is possible, it is simplistic. It cannot help but be unsatisfying in explanatory terms and should not occupy much of our time or energy. At our present level of understanding of the archaeological record and its formation processes, we may instead want to begin with lower-level methodological or middle-range theoretical areas of concern. I will offer my own approach to questions of this sort and developing a workable distributional archaeology in the following chapters.

We can build on the work of Thomas, Isaac, Foley, and others doing nonsite or off-site archaeology, but there are two analytical directions represented in these studies that might be best be avoided. One is simplistic environmental correlations. Correlating the archaeological record we find with static environmental properties is a possibilistic approach that at best results in stories about what people "should" have been doing during behavioral episodes. At worst it becomes an optimal foraging approach. In neither case does it admit to a systemic perspective. At any one place the overlapping archaeological record probably has been deposited during different seasons, as the result of different sorts of resource extraction or other activities. We cannot know exactly what resources were being used at any place at any time, even assuming that the environment has remained constant over the last ten or more millennia.

What is more, the things that occurred at any given place were components of a system. The resources that were there had a bearing on activities at a place, but the other components of the system also had a bearing: what happened at the last place, what was anticipated at the next place, and invisible components of the system, such as mobility, planning, and technological strategies. Finally, it may be that people did not always need or know how to follow the most optimal strategies. There may have been many alternative strategies that were just as successful. We see only components of these in the archaeological record, at any rate.

In two of the examples of non- or off-site archaeology that I consider the most useful—those of Foley and Thomas—there is another analytical direction that may be unwarranted. Both of these authors attempt to correlate static environmental variables, expressed as strat-ifications of their study area, with functional assumptions about the archaeological record found in these places based on the formal char-acteristics of artifacts. Assemblages with edge angles below a certain value are cutting tools, part of hunting assemblages, used by men, and thus part of a logistic strategy. Steeper edge angles are hide working tools, used by women in clothing manufacture, and thus are represen-tative of residential bases. This sort of functional assignment fails to recognize that tools are parts of systems. Systems are interrelated sets of things, places, and other less obvious components. Rather than guess at the specific functions of implements or their attributes, it may be more realistic to begin by looking at the trajectories or stages through which lithic implements are manufactured, curated, discarded, and otherwise used between different locations. Ultimately, it may be the scales at which technological systematics are repeated across the land-scape that are most important to understand.

4

GREAT BASIN ADAPTIVE SYSTEMS
INTERPRETED BY ARCHAEOLOGISTS
-- -- -- -- -- -- -- -- -- -- -- -- --

This chapter and the next have essentially the same goals: to examine what has been written in the archaeological and ethnographic literature about the systemic strategies of the aboriginal inhabitants of an area in southwestern Wyoming. This is not a book about Wyoming archaeology or ethnoarchaeology, but I shall use this area to illustrate my ideas. I shall suggest alternative systemic strategies, certain components of which could have been pursued by past groups in this area that would result in the archaeological record found in the course of my distributional archaeological survey there.

This chapter approaches the construction of such alternative systemic models from an archaeological standpoint. It builds on the interpretations that archaeologists have made of their observations of the archaeological record in the study area. In Chapter 5 I shall approach alternative models from a somewhat different but complementary direction, through ethnohistoric and ethnographic literature on Great Basin groups.

These two chapters do not comprise an exhaustive review of the archaeological and anthropological literature, even that concerned with the study area. They are intended, rather, to provide samples of the ways in which archaeologists and anthropologists have looked at their data and interpreted it. Before attempting to glean ideas or models of possible alternative systemic adaptations from ethnographic or archaeological interpretations it is necessary to consider the reasons that scientists have interpreted their data as they have—that is, the paradigms or culture that scientists bring to their data, which have as much to do with subsequent interpretation and the assignment of meaning to those data as the realities of past systems and behavior.

The archaeology and ethnology examined here deal with higher-level, dynamic explanatory components on a regional basis. I shall narrow the geographic focus as I discuss specific components of past adaptive systems that may have operated within the Green River Basin, and narrow it further as I examine technological strategies, taphonomic postdepositional processes, and expectations for the character of the overlapping archaeological record.

CHOOSING A STUDY AREA

Before reviewing the archaeological literature relevant to the Green River Basin, it is appropriate to describe this area, why it was chosen for a test of distributional archaeology, and some of its general characteristics. This latter subject, especially, sets the stage for a more complete understanding of how archaeologists and anthropologists have interpreted data from this area.

I have not discussed from an environmental point of view the area of the fieldwork I have chosen to illustrate and test the methodological precepts outlined in previous chapters. This is because one major thrust of distributional archaeology is that it does not matter where an archaeologist gathers data as long as his methods are consistent with and appropriate to the nature of the archaeological record and the questions asked of it. Obviously, however, data has to be found and examined somewhere if the investigatory framework of distributional archaeology is to be reconciled or tested.

In order to examine the method and implications of distributional archaeology, I wanted to choose a field situation in which there was at least some measure of archaeological visibility. In most places the archaeological record can be considered continuous and overlapping. This is likely to be less obvious in areas with discontinuous surface visibility caused by depositional and postdepositional processes, however. The archaeological record is more continuously visible in arid areas with little vegetation cover and relatively slow rates of geomorphic activity. The arid West, particularly its desert or basin settings, is ideal in terms of archaeological surface visibility.

It is also advantageous to begin a study such as this with some knowledge about past possibilities in an area, that is, in some area where archaeological or ethnological work has been done and where different ideas can be compared and contrasted. Great ethnographic emphasis was placed on the desert West by anthropologists beginning in the late nineteenth century, at which time the density of nonnative populations, if not their influence, was slight.

Finally, it is desirable to choose an area in which a variety of alternative systems could be expected. One could choose a marginal or frontier area that has accommodated a large number of different peoples or cultures. Or one could choose a place characterized by abrupt topographic variation that has a resource structure that might be influenced by the environmental simplicity or clumping found at northern latitudes.

The final choice of a study area in which to explore a distributional archaeological methodology, however, was pragmatic, as indeed archaeologists' final decisions almost always are. In 1983, while I was employed at the National Park Service's Remote Sensing Division in Albuquerque, I was given the opportunity to help direct an archaeological survey in and around the Seedskadee National Wildlife Refuge and the Fontenelle Reservoir in the Green River Basin of southwestern Wyoming. The survey, carried out by my office for the Bureau of Reclamation, was to involve a relatively small "sample fraction" of a large area, and this sample was to be designed through the use of environmental data derived from remote sensing. Funding for the project was relatively low, particularly the amount set aside for fieldwork, but support was sufficient for a field crew of about ten for two months. This short field time meant that data collection had to be well planned, organized, and efficient, which may prove to be great advantages of an artifact-oriented, distributional approach. The sampling design and field methods used in this survey are detailed in Chapter 6.

I jumped at the opportunity to test a distributional approach in the Seedskadee area. Southwestern Wyoming, despite its remoteness, has been the scene of an impressive amount of archaeological work since the 1930s, accelerating through the 1970s and 1980s with mineral exploration. Ethnographic research and recording in this area and surrounding regions includes some of the classic North American aboriginal studies. Geographers, archaeologists, and ethnographers alike have characterized the Green River Basin as a frontier area, a cultural melting pot, or a transport route between the Great Basin, Great Plains, and Intermontane Plateau regions since early times—a place in which many different sorts of lifeways or adaptations have existed. This suggests that the archaeological record there might be confusing, being the accretion of materials from cultures of several types. Alternatively, however, the Green River Basin may be an area in which only a few relatively similar components from adaptations of different sorts existed.

THE ARCHAEOLOGY OF THE GREEN RIVER BASIN AND SURROUNDING AREAS

The history of archaeological investigation in the Green River Basin of Wyoming and surrounding areas is extensive, beginning in the 1930s and demonstrating a surprising amount of attention to such a remote and unpopulated area. In addition, much of the archaeological work in the area was initiated for cultural resource management—largely surface surveys required before large reservoirs and mineral exploration and exploitation projects were undertaken. Such surveys can provide high-quality baseline information to guide contemporary surface-directed investigations of the archaeological record.

Some of the earliest survey work in southwestern Wyoming was that of Renaud (1936, 1938, 1940). As his work was contemporary with much important Old World archaeological exploration, it is not surprising that Renaud, during summer trips to Black's Fork River near Lyman, Wyoming, classified some artifacts he found there as Lower Palaeolithic, assigning to them a "first interglacial" age (Renaud 1936:12). During his investigations along Highway 30-S, on "four long trips . . . undertaken in very wild and broken country," Renaud discovered more than forty sites containing large numbers of what he classified as Chellean coups-de-poing, handaxes, cleavers, Clactonian flakes, discoids, and Mousterian flakes, blades, and points. Following a trip to Europe to inspect similar artifacts in collections, he postulated that these were the remains of three distinct cultures. Renaud's Typical Culture, represented by the largest number of sites and highest density of artifacts, occurred on gravel-covered terraces and contained artifacts so highly patinated by the wind that "it was hard to distinguish these implements for collection purposes. This fact, of course, suggests great antiquity" (Renaud 1936:3).

The Typical Culture or Black's Fork Culture is represented by assemblages dominated by what Renaud interpreted to be handaxes or choppers—probably actually bifacial blanks or preforms for points or other bifacial tools. A Peripheral Black's Fork Culture, found farther from the highway and thus "marginal" (Renaud 1940:46), is similar to the Black's Fork Culture but contains fewer bifaces. The Sand Dune Culture, discovered where its name suggests, had an extremely high proportion of flakes (88.88 percent)—"no other culture approaches this excessive ratio" (Renaud 1940:56). Renaud felt that the Sand Dune Culture was more recent than the others. From Renaud's artifact photographs, it appears to me that most of the tools represent an extremely low investment of energy (broken cobble choppers and cores, and utilized flakes or irregular pieces of stone); there is a large number of unifacial tools, and bifaces are almost invariably preforms of some sort, that is, they are intermediate manufacturing products.

Early in the twentieth century, southwestern Wyoming achieved considerable archaeological notice due to the discovery of the Finley or Yuma Site (Renaud 1932) in a sand dune in the Killpecker (also spelled Kilpecker) dune field, about four miles southeast of Eden. The name "Yuma" was given to unfluted Palaeoindian points first found there by Renaud, and subsequently by Moss and others (Moss 1951). Moss felt that his geological studies indicated that in the past the Bridger Basin was more like the Plains than the Great Basin, with a grassland cover, shorter summers, and longer winters. He observed that when there is deep snow, moose, deer, and elk move out of the mountains into the foothills, where they could have been hunted by the Palaeoindians; an extinct species of bison, however, predominates the faunal assemblage at the Finley Site. On the basis of his geological work Moss placed the Finley Site at 7000–9000 B.P.; subsequent radiocarbon dating has yielded dates between about 8000 and 9000 B.P.

In the late 1950s and early 1960s the arid intermontane West experienced a great increase in archaeological attention, primarily due to government funding. In 1956 an early salvage survey was conducted at the Big Sandy Reservoir in the northeastern part of the Green River Basin by E. Mott Davis (1956), who found surface materials he interpreted as having been left by "migratory hunter-gatherer peoples who made very brief stops" on their way between the Plains and the Great Basin, as "climatic fluctuations . . . seem to have made the Bridger Basin an outlier of the Great Basin at one time and of the northwest Plains at another" (Davis 1956:86). This is perhaps the first statement of a basic tenet of southwestern Wyoming archaeology that persists to the present day—that the area is intermediate to or transitional between the Plains and Great Basin culture areas.

The 1960s saw more salvage-oriented survey archaeology in the Green River Basin. During a two-week field trip in 1961 Kent Day and David Dibble (Day 1961), working for the University of Utah, found twenty-two sites in an area soon to be flooded by the Fontenelle Reservoir at the center of the Seedskadee survey area. They felt that the basin had been sparsely inhabited in the past: "In no sense can the area be termed one of heavy site concentration" (Dibble and Day 1962:12). Most of their sites were found on or close to stabilized or active sand dunes, and in deflated areas they often found artifacts on interdunal hardpan surfaces. Lithic concentrations were found on the windward and thus eroded sides of dunes. Most sites had hearths lined or filled with cobbles (perhaps defining what they called sites?), and most artifacts they found were quartzite cobbles that were either fire-modified or had minimal cultural fracturing. Dibble and Day (1962:29) felt that this evidence "reflects the type of shifting, hunting and gathering economy practiced by the ethnographically known Wind River Shoshone." They thought that these people by preference camped on dunes at the edges of low terraces bordering the immediate Green River floodplain, and not in the floodplain itself. Only one of their sites appeared to have buried deposits (Dibble and Day 1962:40).

The next year Day and Dibble (1963) completed another survey in the soon-to-be Flaming Gorge Reservoir, about 100km south of the Fontenelle Reservoir in the Green River Basin. During several field sessions they found 121 clusters of artifacts. Again the largest number was found in sand dunes, both stabilized and active, and also in dune areas on alluvial fans. The clusters contained cobble-lined hearths, carbon-stained areas, points, blades, and bifacially chipped artifacts. Dune sites ranged in size from 13.5 to 225m square; "the limitation of living space was evidently governed only by the extent of soft sand" (Day and Dibble 1963:6). Day and Dibble felt that these were seasonally or temporarily occupied camps, similar to those at the Fontenelle Reservoir.

Twenty-four sites at Flaming Gorge were found in juniper-covered spurs on knolls, at some elevation and away from the river. These, according to the researchers, were multioccupation sites. They also found a number of circular stone alignments in open parkland, and ten rock shelters with petroglyphs. For the most part, they decided, people were in the area for "seasonal or transient exploitation of the riverine environment. This is also true of the area located within the Green River Basin some distance from the river" (Day and Dibble 1963:37). Past groups used vegetal resources, as shown by grinding stones and also by deer, antelope, bison, and fish and waterfowl from the river. The Duncan and Hannah points found at some sites, and a tipi ring at 9,000 ft. elevation, suggested relationships with the northwest Plains, and Day and Dibble felt that small triangular basal- or side-notched points were diagnostic of Great Basin associations.

At about the same time Floyd Sharrock, also at the University of Utah, was working out his own archaeological interpretations in southwestern Wyoming (Sharrock 1966). He postulated that the area "acted as a great synapse joining the central and northwestern United States" but with the Bridger Basin belonging "in most respects . . . with the desert zone, rather than the Plains steppe or semi-desert" (1966:2–3). The people who lived in the Bridger Basin exploited resources in a number of different habitats in the course of a yearly round. These resources included deer, moose, elk, beavers, ducks, rabbits, squirrels, badgers, mice, and a few grouse in the mountains and foothills around the basin (8,000–14,000 ft. elevation), plus antelope, bison, sage hens, badgers, coyotes, bobcats, rare reptiles, birds, rabbits, and insects, primarily in sand dune areas in the basin itself. Some sites occur on isolated plateaus (the remnants of pediment surfaces with resistant gravel caps), where antelope, sage hens, rabbits, doves, and other birds are found. Along the river there are many plants and trees, and there would have been fish as well.

Sharrock (1966:20) excavated the Pine Spring Site, in the southern part of the Green River Basin, and found three occupational levels, all of which he interpreted as "associated with the single activity of manufacturing finished artifacts (points, scrapers, etc.) from nodules and blocks of chert from the local outcrop." He found intermediate manufacturing stages from "roughouts" through projectile points, scrapers, knives, blades, and drills. Also present were firepits, bone fragments, grinding slabs and metates, and some pottery.

Sharrock refuted Renaud's theory of the Lower Palaeolithic origin of southwestern Wyoming culture; he also chastised Day and Dibble for at least implicitly going along with Renaud's scheme. Sharrock probably identified correctly the artifacts he found at the Pine Spring Site and those of the Black's Fork Culture as various stages of bifacial preforms. His extremely complex reconstruction of reduction stages, however (five stages, with sizes beginning at twelve inches in length, reduced to one to two inches), may well indicate the production of multiple sorts of bifaces, not solely tiny points. Sharrock wrote that the spatial extent of the "Black's Fork Typical Culture" corresponds exactly with the Lyman Surface, a terrace with cobbles and dunes between Granger and Lyman, and that many of Renaud's artifacts were really naturally fractured stones. Sharrock (1966:151) felt that Bridger Basin people, far from being influenced by Palaeolithic Europeans, were "provincial," making artifacts of wide-ranging styles but with a "local flavor." He noted that the Green River Basin presents no barrier to travel between the northwest Plains and the Great Basin, and that his archaeological observations indicated more affiliation with the Plains Culture than had been previously thought. The boundary between the Great Basin and the Plains fluctuated through time, he remarked, although "Plains influences perhaps extended farther into the Great Basin than Great Basin influences into the Plains" (Sharrock 1966:172).

In 1968 Waldo Wedel reported on the excavation of Mummy Cave, several hundred kilometers to the north of the Green River Basin. It was apparently occupied continuously since about 9000 B.P. and contained bone fragments representing thirty mammal and five bird species, including sheep and deer but almost no bison. According to Wedel, this cave was occupied by "people coming into the locality from widely different directions, but all of whom tended to adjust their lifeways to a mountain adapted subsistence economy" (Wedel 1968:184).

In 1972 Earl Swanson, Jr., published a work on his investigations of the Birch Creek Site in southern Idaho that is relevant to understanding the archaeology of southwestern Wyoming. He began investigating the archaeological record of Birch Creek because he believed the northern Shoshone "belonged to the mountains" (Swanson 1972:3), and that Birch Creek, which flows from the high mountains into an arid basin, would provide examples of all of the altitudinal variations within which people of past systems in the intermontane area would have lived. Swanson, in response to Steward and other authors who characterized the northern Shoshone as marginal, directed his research toward proving that they were marginal only if one was oriented toward Great Basin adaptations. The Shoshone were actually part of the Rocky Mountain ecological system, he argued, and they adapted to it when they lived there. "It may be that men simply borrowed altogether cultures as they found them while the people who left borrowed other cultures to replace what they lost like a new suit of clothes for an old discarded one" (Swanson 1972:11). This seems like a radically non-normative stance until one reads the next sentence: "What such people did in the interval without culture is unknown." Surely this was a private joke, which we may now enjoy with him, imagining a group naked of culture.

Swanson detailed a northern Shoshone lifestyle in an area environmentally similar to that of the Seedskadee, characterizing it as the "Bitterroot Pattern" of hunting and gathering, with the density of archaeological materials increasing in areas with maximum plant and animal diversity. He cited a correspondence between human and mammalian density in space and time, basing this on "a simple measure of the relationship between man and his natural setting . . . obtained by a rate of accumulation in which the number of classifiable artifacts is divided into the number of years in each phase" (Swanson 1972:188). Swanson was quite clearly postulating a generalist strategy in which the northern Shoshone made use of a broad range of resources.

Also in the early 1970s George Frison investigated and reported on the Wardell buffalo trap, five miles northeast of Big Piney, Wyoming, in the Green River Basin. This site, Frison (1973:3) felt, was located in a Plains environment, and it contained not only buffalo remains but also those of elk, moose, antelopes, jackrabbits, sage grouse, coyotes, badgers, and wolves. The area was, according to Frison (1973:3), "important in past population movements between the Plains, Great Basin, and the Colorado Plateau." Individuals or small groups stayed in the area hunting bison all year, with communal hunts in the fall. The Wardell site contained large numbers of points, bifaces, and flakes.

Frison's investigations of Wardell and other sites led to the publication of *Prehistoric Hunters of the High Plains* (Frison 1978), in which he included the Green River Basin as a peripheral Plains area. As archaeological sites on the Plains are small and hard to find, Frison (1978:13) admits, we have probably based our ideas about the past there on "a small fraction of the total evidence"—mostly large, animal-focussed sites. Frison divided Plains prehistory into Palaeoindian, Altithermal or Early Plains, Middle Plains Archaic, Late Plains Archaic, and Late Prehistoric Periods. The Palaeoindians were big-game hunters, the Clovis people depending largely upon mammoths, which were tracked by small mobile groups or individual hunters. The Folsom occupation was much more successful, based on hunting and gathering over large, environmentally diverse areas. Folsom technology involved a complex series of biface reduction stages, the transport of stone materials from distant quarries, highly prepared cores, composite tools, and many flake tools, some produced by biface reduction. Folsom prey species included bison, mountain sheep, deer, marmot, cottontail, and many other large and small animals.

When the dry Altithermal began, much of the game on which the Palaeoindians depended disappeared, and Early Plains period peoples began hunting small groups of bison with side-notched darts or by trapping them. The Middle Plains Archaic is marked by the dramatic appearance of the McKean Complex, and the movement of people onto the open plains and intermontane basins. The McKean Complex saw increased emphasis on plant food, shown by large numbers of roasting pits and much groundstone, and involved "the careful calculated scheduling of economic activity to coincide with food sources in a wide range of ecological areas from season to season" (Frison 1978:49). Stone circles also appeared during the Middle Plains Archaic, but such sites are noted for their lack of other cultural materials.

About 1000 B.C. the Late Plains Archaic (or Late Middle Prehistoric) began to replace the McKean Complex; these peoples' technology, presumably geared toward more specialized hunting, included corner-notched projectile points, multicomponent darts with foreshafts, and atlatls.

The Late Prehistoric Period, from about A.D. 500 until European contact, saw the introduction of the bow and arrow and pottery, although Frison (1978:66) felt that pottery is "intrusive" or "peripheral," and its introduction could have resulted from the blending of Athapaskan and Plains Woodland influences.

Jennings also discussed the prehistory of southwestern Wyoming, but he classed the area as peripheral to the Great Basin rather than the Plains (Jennings 1964, 1974). The prehistory of the Great Basin is, for Jennings, the expression of an extremely long-lived, uniform Desert Culture that developed in response to the diverse but constant pressures of the Great Basin environment. The development of Desert Culture roots is seen in the Desert Archaic, which lasted from about 7000 until 2000 B.C.; Desert Archaic people lived by preference in caves, gathered plants and seeds seasonally, made baskets, nets, and mats, used atlatls and darts, and had a wide variety of material items, most of them based on vegetable products. The Desert Culture or its traits were found throughout the Basin, as well as on the Plateau to the west and in some parts of the Southwest. In the central Great Basin itself, the Desert Culture lasted until European contact, while subsistence specialization in other areas superseded this generalist adaptation. Three basic, sequential traditions dominated the Desert Culture: the Basic Seed Gatherer Tradition (Jennings 1956, 1957; Meighan 1959) with a primary dependence on plant foods; the Big Game Hunters, who from 10,000 to 15,000 B.P. pursued large game (Jennings suggested giant sloths as likely prey, an idea he alone among Great Basin archaeologists espouses); and Specialized Lake Dwellers, who exploited aquatic resources. The later, partially agricultural Fremont tradition was simply an overlay on the earlier Seed Gatherer Tradition.

In 1975 David Madsen and Brian Berry initiated a largely chronological debate, involving northwestern Great Basin prehistory, which has relevance for southwestern Wyoming. They redefined the cultural stages in this area on the basis of radiocarbon dates, largely from Utah rock shelters, with the Early Archaic dating from about 10,000 to 5500 B.P. and the Late Archaic from 5500 to 2500 B.P., followed by a hiatus during which the Great Basin was abandoned, until 1500 B.P. This hiatus was followed by a Fremont "influx" (Madsen and Berry 1975: 404), which was superseded by a wave of Numic populations about 1000 B.P. The Early Archaic inhabitants of the northeastern Great Basin, contended Madsen and Berry, were semisedentary and inhabited relatively large villages on lake shores, exploiting aquatic resources. The later Archaic people pursued an "upland" (Madsen and Berry 1975: 403) subsistence strategy based on gathering and hunting at higher altitudes. Following the abandonment of the Great Basin during an exceptionally dry millennium, the agricultural Fremont people from the northern Anasazi periphery moved into the area, only to be quickly outcompeted by Numic hunter-gatherers (Shoshone, Paiute, Gosiute, Ute, and others). This latter occurrence, these authors feel, shows the great dependence of the Fremont people themselves on hunting and gathering; nonagricultural Fremont sites outnumber agricultural Fremont sites in the northeastern Great Basin by four to one (Madsen 1975).

Melvin Aikens (1976) challenged Madsen and Berry's cultural hiatus idea, also using stratigraphic evidence, and Madsen (1978) replied with six more cave sequences in which no dates between 2500 and 1500 B.P. could be found.

In the late 1970s and early 1980s archaeological fieldwork in the Green River Basin and surrounding areas increased in response to mineral exploration and development; interpretive emphasis shifted from the culture-area or trait list to palaeoenvironmental and adaptational reconstruction. Most of the cultural resource reports produced during this period are not strictly published and available.

An overview written for the Frontier Pipeline, just south of the Seedskadee area (Treat et al. 1982) is typical of such reports. It lists both Plains and Great Basin chronologies, finding that "Great Basin cultural influences are posited for southwest and south-Central Wyoming, the duration and intensity of which are unknown" (Treat et al. 1982:42). According to Treat, sites are distributed according to the location of resources, and "topographic diversity, in association with permanent or semi-permanent surface water and dune fields, *resulted in higher site densities*" (Treat et al. 1982:43, emphasis mine). Large sites thought by Treat to be long-term base camps have the most diverse as well as the densest artifact assemblages, which include tool repair and maintenance debris; smaller "limited function" (Treat et al. 1982:44) sites have fewer tool types and less manufacturing debris. The overview concludes that the project area is really "part of two culture areas . . . a mixture of Northwestern Plains and Great Basin cultural traits" (Treat et al. 1982:46), citing Kainer's (1980) conclusion that the area is "a frontier between two major culture areas . . . and reflects an ebb and flow of peoples and/or ideas . . . the intensity and duration of which are not well understood."

Excavations carried out at two sites in the Green River Basin in the early 1980s (Armitage et al. 1982; Mackey et al. 1982; Schock et al. 1982) were directed toward understanding the palaeoenvironmental, rather than cultural, basis of adaptations there. The Deadman Wash Site was a "camp site" (Armitage et al. 1982:1) in dunes, which, the authors imply, are attractive places to erect shelters. Ten stratigraphic components there date from between 8500 B.P. and A.D. 1500; large herbivores were hunted in early periods, while decreased carrying capacity during the Altithermal (7000 to 3000 B.P.) brought about the hunting of smaller game and an increase in the ratio of browsers to grazers among the prey. This middle to late Archaic period also saw a more equable balance between hunting and gathering than before. Using the number of radiocarbon dates available for the Green River Basin as a population indicator, the authors postulated that a low Altithermal population density slowly increased near the end of the dry period, and that Deadman Wash strata during this period, which contain the most debris, represent large group populations. Altithermal lifeways, the authors felt, were most like Great Basin adaptations, while Palaeoindian period adaptations were more reminiscent of the Plains. Essentially the same interpretation was given to the Cow Hollow Creek Site, a multicomponent mid-Archaic through Late Prehistoric lithic manufacturing and game processing location. The Cow Hollow Creek site, 100m square, is "atypical" (Schock et al. 1982:119) in that there are few diagnostic tools and a high proportion of flakes in assemblages there. The number of bone fragments increases over time, suggesting to the authors increased population and group size.

The research design for another cultural resources surface survey, for the South Haystack Coal Mine in Uintah County, Wyoming (Creasman et al. 1981), was directed at defining a plausible seasonal round for people in this area. It was postulated that mountains were used in the summer, foothills year-round but probably not in midwinter, and basins during the winter and not often in summer. The Haystack research employed the age composition of faunal remains, pollen analysis, and the presence and types of grinding equipment in assemblages to verify the seasons during which different areas were used.

Among the more recent publications to appear on Green River Basin archaeology are two papers in a volume on Plains archaeology (Osborne and Hassler 1986). In his article, Creasman (1986) uses geomorphological indications from published and unpublished sites to define erosional episodes that he dates about 7500–7000 and 4700–4500 B.P. Creasman took these episodes to represent extreme drought periods during the Altithermal; unlike other authors, however (see particularly Mackey et al. 1982), he felt that archaeological evidence shows that interior basins in Wyoming were heavily populated during the Altithermal. There was, however, a sharp decline in the frequency of dates during erosional episodes, a phenomenon that could be due to depositional processes as well as past population dynamics. During the Altithermal in general, the diversity of plant and animal resources increased and hunting focussed on small and medium game, unlike the big-game hunting strategies of pre- and post-Altithermal times.

In the same volume, Michael Metcalf (1986) takes issue with characterization of the Wyoming Basin as a frontier or a fringe area of other regions or culture areas; he feels that southwestern Wyoming shared "broad cultural traditions whose identifying traits occur over wide regions" (Metcalf 1986:1), but that there were important *in situ* cultural developments as well. Analyzing 199 radiocarbon dates ranging from 11,830 B.P. at the Pine Spring Site to 230 B.P. at the Eden-Farson site, he notes a great peak in the number of dates during the Late Prehistoric period, from about 1600 B.P. to 800 B.P. He finds no evidence in the Wyoming Basin for a very early Archaic culture, such as the Great Basin Desert Culture, but acknowledges that from 7300

B.P. to historic times many of the inhabitants of the basin were probably pursuing Archaic lifestyles. The increase in available dates during the Late Prehistoric is a panregional phenomenon, and this indicates to Metcalf that there had been high population levels across the prairie-plains ecotone from Iowa to Utah. He also contends that while there is no evidence of agriculture from the Wyoming Basin, Fremont people may have carried out many of their nonagricultural activities there.

THE ARCHAEOLOGY OF SOUTHWESTERN WYOMING AND RELATED AREAS: WHAT CAN IT TEACH US?

Several things can be said immediately about the archaeological literature relevant to southwestern Wyoming. First, although there are some differences in specific interpretations and the dating or names of different archaeological cultures through time, with later archaeology having a distinctly environmental emphasis, most authors tell essentially the same story. This is particularly evident in the nearly universal statements that the culture or adaptations of the past people of southwestern Wyoming represent in some way a blending, combination, or at least alternation of influences or people from at least two purer centers, the Great Plains and Great Basin.

How can the interpretations of archaeologists working in or worrying about this area be used in a positive way to help guide a distributional approach to its archaeology? Specifically, what can be said about past systems, their components, and how they might appear in the archaeological record in the Seedskadee area? What sort of alternative systems or adaptations are suggested by the archaeological interpretations?

Before answering these questions it is necessary to ask another sort of question, why archaeologists interpreting the archaeology of this area think and say what they do. This question has to do with paradigms, with the intellectual baggage that archaeologists bring to the archaeological record, the "received knowledge and beliefs that we use in viewing the world" (Binford 1985:2). Although it is often said that a systemic viewpoint and processual orientation are what separate the New Archaeology from the old, it may be that the most important distinction is the realization that everything we "know" about the past is interpretation, and that in order to evaluate it we need to know why we interpret things in one way rather than another.

ARCHAEOLOGICAL PARADIGMS AND SOUTHWESTERN WYOMING ARCHAEOLOGY

American archaeology developed alongside American ethnology, from which it received many of its directions as well as biases. When ethnologists and archaeologists, at almost the same time, began to attempt to understand the archaeological record of the New World, they took their cues and inspiration from observation of Native Americans. Ethnographic interpretations are as paradigm-dependent as archaeological ones. Binford and Sabloff (1982) have traced the beginnings of a dominant North American anthropological paradigm to early studies of the material aspects of culture as culture traits, initiated and expounded by Wissler (1917) and Kroeber (1939), and followed by major Great Basin and Plains ethnologists studying American Indians. The North American ethnological paradigm was based on a view of Native American cultures as relatively continuous over large, environmentally similar areas and long, climatically constant time spans, and on the observation that many contact- and historic-period aboriginal groups moved from place to place, almost immediately assimilating the "culture" (that is, the material traits) of groups already in the area.

This paradigm was translated for their own use by archaeologists, notably Krieger (1944), after whom Binford and Sabloff (1982:140) named the Kriegerian paradigm. Under this paradigm, one generates types of artifacts or patterns from the archaeological record and studies the continuity or discontinuity of their distribution through space and time. Culture types are collections of properties coherent in space, and this emphasis encourages the collection of formally similar data from many sites and inattention to undiagnostic (or noncoherent) traits. Properties unique to sites are not studied, and frequency variations between nondiagnostic artifacts are unimportant and are therefore ignored. The emphasis is on selective sampling for both the recognition of culture types and the reconstruction of past lifeways. Diagnostic items are compared using seriation methods, so that one arrives at an archaeological scenario of a series of cultural growths as new culture traits are added to the culture type, followed by collapse or abandonment in an area when "cohesion" is no longer seen between diagnostic elements. In some cases culture types are defined on the basis of single type-artifact appearance and disappearance. The artificial continuity of culture types over space encourages a truistic sort of "environmental determinism" to explain discontinuities in the occurrence of diagnostic elements in space and time, and recourse to explanations based on the blending of culture types when distributions of some but not all diagnostic elements seem to overlap.

One of the outstanding features of the archaeological literature interpreting the southwestern Wyoming archaeological record is that almost all authors postulate different kinds of blending of traits or cultures in one way or another. Renaud's cautious and early approach to the record (1936) posits blending on a very local scale: his typical Black's Fork Culture changes, within a few miles, to the peripheral Sand Dune Culture. Although Renaud's work was criticized almost to the point of ridicule by later authors (for instance, Spaulding 1948), his was the first *in situ* development scenario for this area and, strictly speaking, the only such scenario ventured for nearly fifty years.

More popular among archaeologists interested in this area has been the supposition of large-scale regional blending of traits and cultures based on the notion that this was a frontier, periphery, or boundary area between two or more cultural core areas. Davis (1956:86) felt that the Bridger Basin was an "outlier" of the Great Basin at some times and the Great Plains at others; Jennings (1964, 1974) saw the area as peripheral to the Great Basin, exhibiting an overlay of local traits on the Desert Culture tradition; and Frison (1978) thought the area to be peripheral to the Plains, but that the Archaic culture there was more closely related to a Basin adaptation. Treat et al. (1982) reiterated this position, illustrating that ideas of cultural blending on the Basin/Plains periphery have not been forgotten: the area is a "frontier," and saw an "ebb and flow of people and/or ideas" (Treat et al. 1982:46) over long periods.

A slightly different mechanism, involving the migration of peoples with different cultural repertoires in and out of the southwestern Wyoming area on a seasonal, short-term, oscillating basis, is proposed by other authors. Day and Dibble (1963) see different diagnostic artifact complexes in surface assemblages in the Fontenelle and Flaming Gorge Reservoir areas as indicating an alternation between peoples from the Great Basin and Plains. Wedel (1968) sees people from these areas and the Plateau to the west adjusting to an appropriate mountain subsistence economy through time. Swanson's (1972) fast, successive waves of Great Basin and Plains groups adopt appropriate adaptations like a "new suit of clothes." The idea of flexible, quickly alternating cultures may be a more realistic view of events in this area than other, longer-term schemes.

Other authors have interpreted the southwestern Wyoming area as representing a cultural blend or amalgam because it was a route of heavy travel throughout prehistory and historic contact times, a "great synapse" (Sharrock 1966:2) joining central and western North America, used by "provincial" people making artifacts of region-wide style but with a sometimes "local flavor" (Sharrock 1966:151). Frison (1973) sees this area as important in large-scale population movements between the Great Basin, Plains, and Colorado Plateau.

Another approach to the archaeology of southwestern Wyoming explains the blending or *in situ* change in cultures by reconstructing the chronology of population dynamics, movements ostensibly caused by long-term environmental change in southwestern Wyoming as well as the core Plains, Basin, and other areas. Madsen's (1975) and Madsen and Berry's (1975) hiatuses and influxes of different peoples (Madsen and Berry 1975:404), in which one culture disappeared or replaced another, are based on the frequency of radiocarbon dates available to the archaeologist. They see people during the Archaic period also shifting from closed-basin lakes to mountains, again relying on radiocarbon date frequencies. These population movements were apparently driven by long-term fluctuations in rainfall. In the 1980s other archaeologists suggested slow culture change in this area due to environmental variation over periods of thousands of years, with concomitant shifts in subsistence practices. They also used frequencies of radiocarbon dates to build cultural and population chronologies (Armitage et al. 1982; Mackey et al. 1982; Schock et al. 1982). Creasman (1986), again using radiocarbon dates as a population indicator, says that population declines and increases during and after the Altithermal period were due to game availability. Metcalf (1986), while arguing that the Wyoming Basin was not a peripheral or frontier area, also used radiocarbon dates to postulate a population decline and shift to basin utilization during the Altithermal period. In all of these reconstructions a peak in the frequency of radiocarbon dates is seen as representing the florescence of a culture or type of adaptation, and different cultures are separated from one another by periods of low frequencies of radiocarbon dates.

GREEN RIVER BASIN AND OTHER ARCHAEOLOGY: A CRITIQUE

It is easy to criticize such interpretations of the archaeological record with the advantage of hindsight, as all of us are prisoners of our paradigms. I shall do so now, although I will also make positive use of these interpretations of southwestern Wyoming archaeology. To begin a critique of interpretations involving blending or peripherality, I must ask, simply, "blending of or peripheral to what?" The answer, expressed in terms of the archaeological record—our only physical, contemporary data source—can only be "types of artifacts, or combinations of types of artifacts." The definition of different cultures based on differences in the appearance of diagnostic artifacts, is a classically Kriegerian procedure. Krieger and others based their ideas about the meaning of archaeological materials far more on the ideas and interpretations of ethnologists studying the extant cultures of the Plains and intermontane West than on any sort of analysis of archaeological materials. As they did so, they perverted ethnological ideas by translating directly from the types of instantaneous behavior and ideas that the ethnologists were studying to types of diagnostic artifacts in the physical archaeological record. One of the major thrusts of early ethnology in this area was that most cultures in the American West, especially those with "Great Basin adaptations," were extremely flexible over short periods, and certainly not inflexible over long time periods, as almost all archaeological schemes suppose. Short-term adaptive scenarios, such as those of Wedel (1968) and Swanson (1972), while perhaps outdated, may be more realistic sources of models than some later and more environmentally directed explanations.

This is so largely because environmentally based reconstructions of culture change over long time periods are dependent upon chronological assumptions that have not been carefully examined as to their validity. There are two components of long-term, chronologically documented culture change. One is the stability of cultures or adaptations over short periods, and the other is evolutionarily directed change over longer periods. Our ability to see cultural stability is seriously called into doubt by the low resolution of radiocarbon dating, which seems to be the basis for all recent cultural chronologies in southwestern Wyoming. With published variation figures for radiocarbon dates ranging from about fifty to more than five hundred years in the southwestern Wyoming area (Metcalf 1986), it is obvious than any discrimination of short-term (seasonal or even generational) alternation of culture types or adaptational types in this area is impossible, and must be relegated to the level of a serious sampling problem. In any case, the surface and subsurface archaeological record is probably usually the overlay of many separate behavioral events, and assigning datable deposits to diagnostic artifacts represents an exercise in futility.

Illustrating long-term, evolutionary, cultural, or adaptational changes by recourse to the frequency of available radiocarbon dates is even more tenuous, and it should be noted that most authors (see especially Creasman [1986], Madsen and Berry [1975], and Metcalf [1986]) acknowledge this problem, but rather summarily dismiss it. The archaeological record and our recovery of it are not simply the result of the frequency, duration, and intensity of past behavior. There are many qualitative differences between the dynamics of ongoing systems in the past and the archaeological record, things such as discard rates (including the discard of organic or burned materials that can be radiocarbon dated), and even more importantly the tempo between the discard of culturally modified materials and their natural deposition. These things vary between environmental settings, making it difficult to assign datable materials to the occurrence of diagnostic artifacts or sites that may be supposed to be system components.

Postdepositional processes can further affect the number of radiocarbon-datable deposits, suggesting that lack of such materials during extremely dry Altithermal times might also be the result of high erosion rates rather than low population densities (Creasman 1986). Further, rapidly alternating wet and dry conditions, such as could be expected in the arid West during drought periods, would also have a great effect on radiocarbon-datable deposits (Wandsnider, personal communication, 1986). Postulating abrupt cultural changes separated by thousands of years of adaptational continuity (for instance the persistence of the McKean Complex as a continuous cultural and adaptational phenomenon [Frison 1978]) is either a simplification of what must actually have happened or a totally misleading, sampling-biased fabrication.

In any case, even if the frequency of radiocarbon dates is accepted as a perfect indicator of population in an area, this sort of chronological approach must be seen for what it is: another culture-type argument, consisting simply of seriation using histograms of C14 dates instead of diagnostic artifacts.

Is this what we really want to know about what past people did in the Green River Basin, or anywhere? Thinking about this question leads to the conclusion that the reliance on a Kriegerian type-concept paradigm is not simply something that needs to be kept in the back of one's mind as one peruses the archaeological literature pertaining to the Green River Basin, or anywhere else. It is, rather, an insidious problem, one that may block our efforts at understanding the past in realistic ways. Human systems are composed of differentiated types of activities and sites. If we use a type concept, based on differential diagnostic artifact occurrences, to tell the difference between such adaptations we virtually insure that we will separate the integral components of these systems into different categories—into different culture types. If our paradigm includes the belief that cultures change, or evolve into other cultures, the different aspects of single systems will be classed into different time periods, based on the morphological characteristics of artifacts occurring together. Even if radiocarbon dates are available for some components of systems, undated components will be regarded as being of different types. Due to the differential preservation and visibility of radiocarbon-datable deposits, we see and date far too few occurrences for them to be used as any basis for grouping together the parts of contemporaneous systems (Frison 1978).

As an aside, but an important one for the present argument, I would like to reiterate what I mean by "a system." It is difficult to talk about systems, for the term may well be a primitive term in archaeology, similar to the ether of early particle/wave physics. By a system I do not mean a culturally distinct group or any sort of cohesive group of people connected in a genetic or even temporal sense. A system is a kind of adaptation, the parts of which are internally differentiated but form an integrated whole. This means that the characteristics of one component of a system depend on the other components. Systems components can be people (individuals or groups), things (artifacts or resources, for instance), places, or behavior. The archaeological record is composed of things and places as well, although the relationship between it and past systems is not a simple one. Dividing the places and things that were used by a single system into different "cultures" can only complicate this picture.

The analysis of the operation of systems is the goal of the archaeologist, but most archaeological interpretations focus on differentiating culture types to the detriment of understanding systems.

ARCHAEOLOGICAL IDEAS ABOUT ADAPTIVE SYSTEMS IN THE GREEN RIVER BASIN

One of the most positive aspects of most American archaeology is its focus on humans as part of the environment, and especially on subsistence practices. Although I am quite critical of some aspects of

Green River Basin and other archaeology, the archaeological literature summarized here can yield general ideas about the sorts of general adaptations that might be the cause of the archaeological record in southwestern Wyoming.

Although I explore the contribution of ethnographic accounts and ethnological interpretations in the next chapter, archaeologists may be seeing the results of unique adaptational systems not documented or imagined by anthropologists, and archaeological input is necessary as well.

Here I treat archaeological interpretations of the southwestern Wyoming archaeological record at face value. Instead of criticizing their inadequacies I shall explore these interpretations for what they may reveal about the different sorts of systems and systems components that might have been responsible for the archaeological record in the Seedskadee area.

Three major areas of interpretative focus may be important for understanding past systems: subsistence patterns or practices, settlement and mobility patterns, and technology. Of course these parts of systems are necessarily related, and taken together they may suggest general systems patterns.

Subsistence interpretations have been approached by archaeologists in two ways: on a very broad scale, with subsistence differences influenced by cultural stages or long-term climatic factors; and on a shorter-scale, intuitive level, dealing with what might be thought of as strategies to describe the exploitation of different species. The broad chronological approach in the literature relevant to southwestern Wyoming and related areas is for the most part based on the classic Plains-derived sequence of Palaeoindian–Archaic–Late Prehistoric (Jennings 1964, 1974; Frison 1978; Sharrock 1966; Armitage et al. 1982). Palaeoindian subsistence relied heavily on hunting large herbivores, while later Archaic subsistence shifted to dependence on a balanced or diverse range of resources: increased use of plant foods and at the same time a wider range of animals, mostly medium to small. In the Late Prehistoric period there was a shift back to larger animals, but plants remained relatively important.

This abbreviated chronological summary of subsistence is of course not limited to southwestern Wyoming, but forms the backbone of most archaeological summaries in adjacent areas as well, and in fact across our continent. In the vicinity of southwestern Wyoming, however, it is tempered by the proximity of the Great Basin, which is seen by some authors (Meighan 1959; Jennings 1964, 1974) as having its own, far more uniform chronological sequence. This sequence consisted of variations in the basic Desert Culture, including possible giant sloth hunting, which very early becomes the Desert Archaic, focusing on seed gathering, hunting and trapping of small animals, and in some areas the exploitation of aquatic resources. Metcalf (1986) says that there is no actual evidence of an Early Archaic focus on aquatic resources in the Bridger Basin, and that some mountain and foothill people throughout the area were Archaic, in the sense of having a very generalized and flexible subsistence base, until the historic period.

Other subsistence interpretations focus on more specific strategies, reasoning from animal behavior or from environmental reconstructions and inference. Frison (1978) sees the differences between archaeological materials and their distribution in Clovis as contrasted with Folsom as resulting from a marked difference in strategies for hunting mammoths and bison. Clovis hunters stalked individual animals or small groups, and as a result would have been mobile residentially; Folsom people hunted large groups of bison primarily in the fall, and would have lived in larger and more sedentary groups. At Wardell, a recent or Protohistoric bison trap site, Frison (1973) sees a strategy of communal bison hunts or drives in the fall, with year-round hunting by smaller groups of hunters.

Metcalf (1986) interprets the hunting of herds of predominantly male bison as a winter activity in the Wyoming Basin from Palaeoindian to Late Prehistoric times, although Day and Dibble (1963) assert that bison do not winter in the Green River Basin, according to ethnohistoric accounts. Instead, since Palaeoindian times the archaeological record there indicates to them "the type of shifting, hunting and gathering economy practiced by the ethnographically known Wind River Shoshone" (Dibble and Day 1962:29). Wedel (1968), also professing to be interpreting a Shoshonelike adaptation at Mummy Cave in northwestern Wyoming, describes a "mountain adapted subsistence economy" (Wedel 1968:184), and provides evidence for the utilization of birds, at least thirty species of mammals, many sheep, few deer, and almost no bison for nearly nine thousand years. Swanson (1972:2) reiterates that the northern Shoshone "belonged to the mountains." During the winter, according to Moss (1951), moose, elk, and deer were driven from the mountains by deep snows and moved into basin areas, including the Green River Basin, where they were heavily hunted.

Several authors comment on the Fremont people, who had the only agricultural strategy that has been suggested in the near proximity of southwestern Wyoming. Madsen and Berry (1975) see the Fremont people, even in their core area, as more dependent on hunting and gathering than on agriculture, with a ratio of four to one between the numbers of sites devoted to each activity. Metcalf (1986), even though he says there is no actual evidence of agriculture in all of the Wyoming Basin, feels that Fremont people must have visited this area often for nonagricultural purposes. In a somewhat far-flung comparison, Swanson (1972) likens the Fremont people, with their overlay of borrowed agriculture, to the Cochise-Mogollon, and compares the Birch Creek Cave site to Bat Cave in New Mexico.

More recently, a number of authors have supported their subsistence interpretations with environmental data. Mackey et al. (1972), on the basis of excavations at the Dead Man Wash Site in the Green River Basin, cite drier conditions during the Altithermal period as responsible for a decreased carrying capacity, which resulted in a subsistence shift toward smaller animals and more plant collecting. Creasman (1986) characterizes the Altithermal shift as one toward increasing diversity of plant and animal resources and strategies used to collect them, in contrast with pre- and post-Altithermal subsistence foci.

Other aspects of archaeological interpretations relevant to past Green River Basin area systems or their components are directed toward settlement and mobility patterning. Population dynamics, the differentiation of site types or functions, and speculation about why certain sorts of sites are located where they are figure prominently in these interpretations. Some population dynamics are expressed in terms of long-distance movement through the area, as people travelled from the Plains to the Great Basin or perhaps the Colorado Plateau (Frison 1973; Sharrock 1966), that is, "migratory hunting and gathering people who made very brief stops" (Davis 1956) on their way between different core areas. Wedel (1968:184), in contrast, interprets the Mummy Cave location as being a sort of focus of "people coming into the locality from widely different directions."

Reconstructions of seasonal rounds between settlements, or of the use of specific areas in relation to others, are somewhat more interesting in terms of defining past systems. Creasman et al. (1981) feel that while the general Rocky Mountain seasonal round entails the use of mountains in the summer, foothills in fall and spring, and basins in the winter, basins can actually be used year-round. Spring would have been the period of fewest available resources and highest mobility for monitoring and collecting the earliest available foods. Day and Dibble's survey of the Flaming Gorge Reservoir resulted in the discovery of sites in sand dune areas low in the Green River Basin, which they feel were temporarily or seasonally occupied camps, as well as sites along higher, juniper-covered knolls and spurs, which were occupied for shorter periods for the exploitation of foothill resources and were probably "oft-visited" (Day and Dibble 1963:7). The people responsible for the archaeological record in their immediate study area were there mostly for "seasonal or transient exploitation of the riverine environment. This is also true of the area located within the Green River Basin some distance from the river" (Day and Dibble 1963:37).

The location and populations of settlements have been explained by appeal to major palaeoclimatic trends. Madsen and Berry (1975) thus see the Early Archaic peoples in the northern Great Basin settled near aquatic resources in wetter times, and as semisedentary, with fairly large populations. As drier conditions prevailed in the later Archaic period, people moved to smaller sites in upland areas and moved to other locations more often. Similarly, Treat et al. (1982) speculate that both the open Plains and the lower basins of the Great Basin were abandoned during the Altithermal period in favor of foothills and upland resources. Creasman (1986), on the basis of radiocarbon dates from the Wyoming Basin, sees instead a heavy use of interior basins during the Altithermal, presumably at the expense of the Plains. Mackey et al. (1982) propose a decrease in total population, population density, and local group sizes during the dry Altithermal, combined with a more specialized seasonal migration pattern involving increased plant procurement sites.

Site types and character of reuse are suggested by some archaeological investigations, including excavations of the Deadman Wash Site (Mackey et al. 1982), a camp site where a wide range of domestic activities is represented, including lithic manufacture, cooking, hearths, and structures. At the Pine Spring Site Sharrock (1966) found three successive levels of reoccupation, each containing food debris and hearth remains, but interpreted its primary function to be lithic procurement and manufacture.

Several authors have speculated on the reasons that archaeological materials are located where they are. These begin with rather simplistic formulations reminiscent of predictive modeling. For instance, Armitage et al. (1982) feel that sand dunes are attractive because structures can be erected easily in soft ground. More complex, environmental and locational models usually cite diversity of topography and resources (Treat et al. 1982), or maximum plant and especially mammal diversity (Swanson 1972) as determinants of high densities of archaeological material or sites.

A final class of archaeological interpretations that might be useful in reconstructing the range and nature of past systems and their components in southwestern Wyoming deals with technology. These interpretations begin with descriptions of the range of materials found in different sites and suggest a contrast between assemblages containing large numbers of points, bifaces, knives or scrapers, and unifacial implements (for instance Frison [1973] at the Wardell Site and Davis [1956] in surface collections at the Big Sandy Reservoir), and those such as described by Schock et al. (1982) at the Cow Hollow Creek Site, which contained only four projectile points, eleven bifaces, and twelve other retouched artifacts, but many thousands of flakes.

A distinction between the reliance on hunting as opposed to plant gathering is often made by examining the ratio of flaked lithics to groundstone implements (Mackey et al. 1982; Treat et al. 1982; Creasman et al. 1981).

SYSTEMS AND THEIR COMPONENTS AS SUGGESTED BY ARCHAEOLOGICAL INTERPRETATIONS

As can be seen, the information about past Green River Basin systems and their components that can be gained through a review of the archaeological literature is of variable character and utility. It is often difficult to translate between what authors have said and its meaning in systems terms. This is not to fault archaeologists interpreting southwestern Wyoming archaeology, for most archaeology suffers from a lack of middle-range linking arguments to span the gap between the archaeological record and the interpretations given to it. In addition, it is impossible to list completely or even summarize usefully the totality of the archaeological record excavated at a site or discovered on a survey in articles or even large volumes. In order to make one's own interpretations from the facts of the archaeological record as recovered by other archaeologists, then, one would essentially have to reanalyze their collections.

Nonetheless, there are some qualitative and for the most part general conclusions that can be drawn from previous archaeological interpretations. They may help to suggest what sorts of systems, systems components, and strategies could be responsible for the archaeological record in the Green River Basin. I shall review these in outline form.

Subsistence and Strategy

Broad-Based Chronological or Climatic Interpretations
1. Dichotomy between big-game hunting in Palaeoindian and Late Prehistoric/Historic times and a general plant-and animal-gathering strategy in Archaic times (Mackey et al. 1982).
2. Three-phase classic temporal distinction:
    a. Palaeoindian: focus on large extinct herbivores; Clovis elephant hunting of individual animals with high residential mobility is one possible strategy, while later Folsom and other Palaeoindian strategies more dependent on hunters pursuing herds primarily of bison in large groups with lower residential and higher logistic mobility (Frison 1973).
    b. Archaic people, smaller residentially mobile groups, generalist strategy with relative balance between medium and small animals, and collection of a wide range of plants.
    c. Late Prehistoric strategy not quite as focussed on hunting large game as Palaeoindian, but less general than Archaic. Seasonal communal drives or hunting of bison and other herd animals, coupled with year-round hunting of single animals by individual hunters and some plant collecting (Frison 1973).
3. The alternative possibility that in Great Basin, some or all groups preserved an Archaic adaptation throughout archaeological time (Jennings 1964, 1974; Creasman 1986).

More Specific Subsistence/Strategy Interpretations
4. Bison herd hunting in fall (Frison 1973) and/or in winter in basins (Metcalf 1986).
5. "Mountain economy" based on large number of small mammal species, fowl, sheep, few deer, no bison (Swanson 1972) is basis of core Shoshone adaptive system.
6. Moose, elk, and deer hunting in winter in basins.
7. Existence of components of agricultural or horticultural

Fremont system in Green River Basin, although these components have not primarily agricultural but rather hunting-
gathering focus (Madsen and Berry 1975, Madsen 1975).

Settlement and Mobility Interpretations

General Settlement, Mobility Statements

1. Sites in Green River Basin the result of groups of people
   traveling quickly through the area on their way to and from
   other areas of economic importance, very brief stops only.

2. Sites created by people using the Green River Basin as a
   "peripheral" area for short-term resource extraction.

3. Seasonal round: mountains in the summer, foothills in the fall
   and spring, basins in the winter. Spring is time with fewest
   resources, highest residential mobility (Creasman et al. 1981).

4. Residential sites seasonally in low-lying, basin sand dune
   areas; higher juniper-covered knolls (foothills?) sites for
   shorter-term repetitive reuse for resource gathering (Day and
   Dibble 1963).

5. Seasonal exploitation of riverine environment, presumably
   locale of residential sites from which logistic mobility is
   initiated (Day and Dibble 1963).

Climate-Based Settlement/Mobility Interpretations

6. Great Basin Archaic pattern: Early Archaic, larger, more
   residentially sedentary near aquatic resources; Later Archaic
   (drier portion of Altithermal) upland focus, smaller groups,
   more residentially mobile (Madsen and Berry 1975).

7. Basins abandoned during dry portions of Altithermal (Treat
   et al. 1982).

8. Basins heavily occupied during Altithermal (Creasman 1986,
   specifically for Green River Basin).

9. During Altithermal, decrease in the total population and the
   population density of the area, also decrease in local group
   sizes (Mackey et al. 1982).

Site Type Differentiation Interpretations

10. Camp sites have hearths, evidence of cooking, structures,
    lithic manufacturing debris (Mackey et al. 1982).

11. Lithic procurement and manufacturing sites have evidence of cooking, hearths, lithic debris.

12. Sand dune sites preferred because structures can be erected more easily there (Armitage et al. 1982—these are, then, presumably residential sites, an interpretation agreeing with Day and Dibble 1963).

13. More sites in areas of higher topographic and resource diversity; more sites close to water.

Technological Interpretations

1. Broad distinction between two polar types of assemblages: one with large number of points, bifaces, unifaces, cores, also with flakes; other type of assemblage is dominated by utilized or unutilized flakes, with very few formal tools.

2. Distinction between hunting assemblages with flaked tools and plant gathering-related assemblages with groundstone.

5

GREAT BASIN ADAPTIVE SYSTEMS
INTERPRETED BY ETHNOGRAPHERS

Some ethnoarchaeologists have implied that the closer an archaeolog-ical manifestation and a living group are in space, time, and genetics the more relevant to one another they are (Gould 1968, 1978, 1980, for instance). This argument is clearly part of a strategy directed toward reconstructing the invisible part of past events at a specific place. It is more realistic to gauge the comparability of archaeologically represented and living groups on a systemic level—that is, to assess whether the operation and components of their respective systems are similar. Systems operating in a manner similar to those of the past inhabi-tants of southwestern Wyoming might, then, be found in many places around the world—or they might not be found anywhere within eth-nographic time.

I will not use the ethnographic record and its interpretations as the basis of any analogical translation from observations of living groups to the archaeological record. Here, I review what anthro-pologists have said about aboriginal inhabitants of the Great Basin and Plains for the same reasons I explored the archaeological litera-ture in Chapter 4: to arrive at ideas about alternative systems and strategies that might be represented in the distributional archaeological record there.

GREAT BASIN AND PLAINS ETHNOLOGY AND ITS RELEVANCE TO ARCHAEOLOGY

Observations and interpretation of the aboriginal peoples in the Great Basin and Plains begin in the later eighteenth century, with Father Escalante. Lewis and Clark journeyed through these regions on their 1804–06 expedition, soon followed by a wave of fur traders and a number of U.S. government expeditions between 1840 and 1880. The observations of most of these preprofessional (Baumhoff 1958) ethnologists for the most part are limited to names of "tribes" (a political category Europeans may have imposed upon aboriginal peoples) and are often grossly exaggerated (Hultkrantz 1970). Nonetheless, such accounts led professional anthropologists to focus on the arid West, particularly the northern Great Basin, beginning about 1900, with the work of Kroeber, Lowie, and Sapir. Steward's work with the Numic and other peoples of the area beginning in 1927 is often cited, although there are many other sources.

Steward's paradigm, through which he interpreted his observations and those of other anthropologists, was inherited from Wissler and Kroeber and formed the basis of most subsequent anthropological work in this area. Its central concepts are that culture is continuous or noncoherent rather than bounded, that material and ideological traits are transmitted by diffusion through space and time, and that people moving from one place to another freely adopt traits appropriate to that environment. Steward sees the Great Basin as culturally stable for thousands of years, with few external influences. "The elements that link it with neighboring areas occur predominantly along its margins, rapidly disappearing—inhibited no doubt by the slender local resources—toward its center" (Steward 1940a:450). There is very little import, he argues, to the boundaries of Shoshone groups shown on anyone's maps: "The concept of tribes among Shoshoneans is an anthropologist's fiction" (Steward 1940:147). Steward uses the term "Shoshonean" for almost all northern Great Basin groups, declaring them essentially similar to other Uto-Aztecan peoples of the province, including the Northern Paiute or Mono-Bannock, and the Ute-Chemehuevi or Ute and Southern Paiute (Steward 1940a).

Steward's paradigm is also the Kriegerian paradigm, which dominates American archaeology to this day. There are differences, however, between the ideas of early anthropologists, typified by Steward's approach to the Great Basin, and the archaeological Kriegerian paradigm. While anthropology's culture-area, diffusionist stance was undoubtedly what inspired early archaeologists, the translation of anthropological approaches into an understanding of the archaeological record involves a qualitative change. Steward and other anthropologists saw continuities, lack of cohesion, and diffusion in material items, but also in the events in which these material items participated, in human groups, and in the expressed ideas of those people: "Recent intermontane culture was not an unalterably integrated whole in any locality but consisted of elements of varying ages and origins that were stabilized and integrated by different factors and in different degrees of completeness" (Steward 1940a:447).

The cornerstone of Steward's interpretation of Great Basin aboriginal life is flexibility. Families, the self-sufficient economic units of the Great Basin peoples, adjusted the balance between hunting and gathering, travelled, organized labor, and changed their routes and "itinerary" in response to the availability of any and all foodstuffs: "Seasonal variation in rainfall and consequent crop growth frequently required that they alter their routine" (Steward 1938:232). Single-family units were a response to meager resources, low population density, and an annual cycle of nomadism; when resources were more abundant, there was increased interaction between families but still no "supra-family, or band, institutions." Great Basin inhabitants depended on plants for as much or more than eighty percent of their subsistence, but also hunted, trapped animals, or used anything else in a pattern of "multiple subsistence" (Steward 1940a:115–17).

It is surprising that this scenario was translated by archaeologists into the Kriegerian type concept, central to which is the interpretation of the archaeological record as the result of extremely cohesive (if sometimes discontinuous spatially), inflexible culture types with constant and distinct adaptations persisting over thousands of years. Virtually the only similarity between Steward's Great Basin aboriginal interpretations and those of type-concept archaeologists is that culture types are regional in scale. In attempting to understand translations between human systems dynamics and the archaeological record it is important to consider that anthropologists and archaeologists are looking at qualitatively different things, on a very different scale both temporally and spatially. This is so obvious that to assert it almost sounds absurd. Yet this is exactly what archaeologists have failed to do.

If our goal is to use the ethnographic record and its interpretations to understand systemic adaptations that may have caused the archaeological record, there are many questions that remain to be asked. Is what can be seen ethnographically a good example of the systems and their components that led to the formation of the archaeological record there? Are these the same people who caused the archaeological record (or does it matter)? What about modernization? In the Great Basin/ Plains area, what about introduction of the horse and its consequences? Is epidemic disease at European contact responsible for disjunctions between the archaeological and ethnographic record? The answers to these questions are difficult, for ultimately they are all "yes and no." The ethnographic record does not contain all possible adaptations or systems, but it certainly contains some. Herein lies one of the great potential contributions of archaeology to anthropology: its ability to represent systems that cannot be observed in operation today. Archaeological evidence may help inform us about adaptations that did not work and were not "selected for" into the ethnographic present.

In the Great Basin the question of whether observed aboriginal groups were representative of all past groups has been addressed by a number of authors. Some early anthropologists working in the area applied themselves to the origins of the linguistic groups there, seeing a relatively recent Athapaskan migration from the north down the axis of the Rocky Mountains by people bringing with them only a "simple hunting culture" (Huscher and Huscher 1942:82) lacking stone mauls or axes and grinding implements. Citing stratigraphic evidence from Lovelock Cave, Shimkin (1940:19) holds that "none of the early cultures so far discovered [archaeologically] can be matched at all closely by the existing ones of the Basin. Lovelock Cave shows modern northern Paiute remains as subsequent to, overlying, a culture with Basketmaker affiliations." He postulates that Shoshone–Comanche people were in southwestern Wyoming and southeastern Idaho by A.D. 1500– 1700, with northern Paiute to the west and Ute to the south. On the other hand, Earl Swanson, Jr., from excavations in southern Idaho, contends that the northern Shoshone's "Bitterroot Pattern" of hunting and gathering, and its technology, shows "evidence of cultural continuity in the Great Basin for 7,000–8,000 years" (Swanson 1972:11).

The question of just who the people of the Plains–Great Basin interface area are becomes even more confusing when more specific groups are examined. The literature is rife with taxonomies of groups, starting with broad subgroups of Uto-Aztecan (Numic) stock such as Shoshone, Bannock (also called Shoshone Bannock or Snake), Bohogue (or Bannock), and Northern and Southern Paiute (or Gosiute and

Chemehuevi). Finding uniform usage or depiction of group boundaries from account to account, however, is difficult. One of the most revealing "tribal identity" studies was carried out by Omer Stewart in advocacy of Bannock land claims (Stewart 1970). Reviewing a large body of published and unpublished accounts, records, and letters, he found that virtually no two accounts of boundaries or identity were similar. His short article contains thirteen maps derived from accounts of explorers, government agents, and anthropologists, which show vastly different Bannock and other "tribal" boundaries. On maps since 1841, he shows Shoshone, Waushakee Shoshone, Shoshone–Comanche, Wind River Shoshone, and Bannock as having "territory" in the Green River Basin.

Some of the differences in identity seen by early anthropologists in this area may stem from the confusing presence of horses, which were used by some groups but not by others. Stewart found that "the Bannock and the horse-using Shoshoni formed an upper class among the Shoshoni of Idaho, Utah, and Wyoming. . . . Their poor relatives, horseless foot-Shoshoni and Northern Paiute, remained in their traditional areas and subsisted by hunting and collecting seeds, roots, and insects. These poor were called the 'Digger Shoshoni' and 'Digger Paiute'" (Stewart 1970:225). Steward saw the horse as introducing some modern differences in some groups (for instance, he felt that bands in the area are posthorse [Steward 1970]), but also said that many groups never acquired horses and "continued to live very much like the people of the West" (Steward 1940a:496). He also observed that mounted Indians often moved without their families, as only a few male family members had horses. Shimkin (1947), studying the Wind River Shoshone, famous for their mounted warriors, calculated that mounted Shoshone could subsist for only about half the year on bison meat hunted from horseback, and that for the rest of the year mounted mobility was relatively unimportant. Hultkrantz's Tukudika, who inhabited mountainous areas between southwestern Wyoming and Yellowstone, were comprised "partly of an old layer of Shoshones ('walkers'), who retained the old way of living from the time before horses . . . and partly of pauperized Plains Shoshones, who had lost their horses" (Hultkrantz 1974:202; 1970). These authors viewed the horse as another flexible trait, an overlay upon an earlier adaptation or adaptations.

It is quite obvious that ethnologists' interpretations are colored as much by their paradigms as are those of archaeologists. At this point, shifting gears to employ relatively uncritically the interpretations of ethnologists, I shall review from an ethnographic viewpoint the categories of systems components examined earlier in connection with the archaeology of the area. These categories are subsistence and strategy, settlement and mobility, and technology. The components of systems are of course interrelated, and observations often cross boundaries between them. I view this as an alternative method for deriving ideas about past systems to be tested against the physical archaeological record, not as a direct translation between the ethnographic and archaeological records.

ETHNOGRAPHIC PERSPECTIVES ON SUBSISTENCE STRATEGIES

According to most anthropologists who have studied the region, the basic flexibility and lack of coherent structure among Great Basin and some nearby Plains groups was due primarily to the nature of the food quest, particularly the scarcity and low density of food in the entire area. Consequently, groups pursued a generalist subsistence strategy in which available foods were sought and consumed opportunistically. The great diversity of foodstuffs that may have been used at different times and places by the aboriginal inhabitants of the area is immediately apparent from the many food-related names given to local groups there. Thus, among the Gosiute there are the Hukunkuka (*stipa* eaters), the Kamuduka (rabbit eaters, Steward 1938), and among the more easterly Shoshone the Hukandika or eaters of unidentified seeds, the Tukudika or mountain-sheep eaters, the Padahiadika or elk eaters of the Teton Mountains, and the Yahandika (groundhog eaters) and Siptika (squirrel eaters) south of Pocatello. Hultkrantz (1974) delineated three general groups within the "eastern" Shoshone on his own ideas about their central subsistence food: the mounted buffalo eaters, sheep eaters, and dove eaters. His focus of study was the Tukudika (meat eaters, he says—called mountain-sheep eaters by others); he also identified other unmounted Shoshone in southern Idaho and northern Utah as Hukandika or dust eaters (including Kamodika, eaters of the black-tailed rabbit, and marmot and squirrel eaters, all of whom acquired horses very late), Pengwidika or fish eaters on the Bear and Logan Rivers in Utah, and the Haviodika or dove eaters of the Green River Basin in southwest Wyoming.

Haviodika, according to Hultkrantz, is a derogatory nickname given these people by mounted Shoshone. This remark points to the need for caution regarding the truth of food-related group names, for labels such as this are often given to groups by surrounding people rather than from within. Nonetheless, the profusion of northern Shoshone food-based group names underlines the importance of dependence on a wide range of subsistence items.

Food Species, Proportions, and Strategies

The observations of other anthropologists concern specific subsistence resources and occasionally strategies used in their procurement. In the Plains–Great Basin area, while subsistence strategies can generally be divided between gathering and hunting, there is a transitional area of small animal and insect collecting and trapping.

Steward (1970) volunteers that across the Great Basin, most groups depend upon plants for more than eighty percent of their subsistence. Relevant groups listed in Murdock's (1967) *Ethnographic Atlas* summary tables, however, show a somewhat less plant-oriented picture (Table 5.1).

Although the meaning and method of measurement of data in Table 5.1 are quite likely to be variable, it can be seen that none of Murdock's groups is more than fifty-five percent dependent on wild plants and small fauna. This may result from the inclusion of fishing as a separate category (or as a category at all—many authors may underplay the role of aquatic resources).

General accounts or lists of specific subsistence resources used in the northern Great Basin/Plains area emphasize a wide range of resources and at times shed light on what is probably an equally wide range of strategies employed in their procurement. Steward (1940a) classes the immediate area of my Seedskadee study as part of the Upper Sonoran Zone's Artemesia Belt, containing a xerophytic flora with few grasses, although he feels that the dominance of the sagebrush, rabbitbrush, and shadscale that now cover the area is probably due to grazing, and that the area would have been richer in grasses prehistorically.

The Gosiute Indians, according to Malouf (1974), earned the name "Diggers" because of their dependence on early spring greens, roots, and various grass seeds. Berries were also important along rivers. A number of groups of Southern Paiute gathered seeds "for weeks or months along streams and in sandhills" (Lyman 1930:120), and also gathered and dried berries there. One of the most important staple

Table 5.1. Dependence on various classes of subsistence resources as a proportion of total resources. [The numbers in columns 1–5 represent, respectively, percentage dependence on (1) wild plants and small fauna; (2) hunting, trapping, and fowling; (3) fishing; (4) animal husbandry; and (5) agriculture. Values represented are: 1 = 0–5%; 2 = 6–15%; 3 = 16–35%; 4 = 36–45%; 5 - 46–55%; and 6 = 56–65%].

Group	Relative Resource Utilization				
Southern Ute	3	6	1	0	0
Flathead	3	4	3	0	0
Wadadokado (Paiute)	5	3	2	0	0
Kidutokado (Paiute)	4	4	2	0	0
Kuyuidokado (Paiute)	5	2	3	0	0
White Knife	5	4	1	0	0
Bohogue (Bannock)	3	5	2	0	0
Gosiute	5	4	1	0	0
Uintah	3	4	3	0	0
Bannock	3	5	2	0	0
Wind River Shoshone	3	5	2	0	0
Hukundika (Shoshone)	5	3	2	0	0

seeds was sand bunchgrass or Indian ricegrass (Euler and Fowler 1966), which in the Great Basin ripens serially at increasing altitudes, providing a constant food source through the summer months. In northern Nevada bunchgrass was reaped and bound into sheaves for storage (Shimkin and Reid 1970), while at the same time sunflower seeds and cactus fruit were eaten. Northern Paiute groups also place summer-long reliance on both grass seeds and roots, the latter found both in marshy areas (*camas*) and in high, dry country (*epos*) (Kelly 1934). In areas with aquatic plants these were apparently heavily used as well (e.g., by the Toitekade, the tule eaters, in the Carson River Basin in Nevada [Shimkin and Reid 1970]). In many parts of the Great Basin, unlike the area of my Seedskadee study, pinyon nuts were an important wild plant staple.

Hunting recorded by anthropologists also encompasses a wide range of species, and at least two basic strategies. Communal hunting of herd animals is prominent in archaeological interpretations because of the spectacular nature of the remains it creates. Mounted bison hunting of course figures in most ethnographic accounts of the region, taking place on the open plains to the east of the study area. Communal drives, surrounds, or hunts also focussed on antelope (Steward 1940a; Reagan 1934), rabbit, and possibly waterfowl (Kelly 1934). Deer and antelope were also hunted by individual hunters or small groups in seasons not conducive to communal hunts, and mountain sheep were hunted in the mountains.

Most animal food species reported, however, are smaller, and were hunted individually rather than communally. Nonpursuit hunting methods are often cited, including traps, deadfalls, nets, rodent skewers, smoking, and flooding (Steward 1940). Animals hunted or trapped by the Gosiute included badgers, porcupines, mountain lions, wildcats, ground squirrels, prairie dogs, gophers, woodchucks, rats, muskrats, mice, chipmunks, weasels, lizards, snakes, and hares, although they "avoided skunks" (Malouf 1974). Shimkin and Reid (1970) report that one Toitekade hunter travelled more than thirty miles to net or trap woodrats (*Neotoma lipida*), which were smoked, dried, and returned to camp in oblong hampers made of grass.

Insects and their larvae are the smallest nonplant foods reported from the Seedskadee and relevant surrounding places (Steward 1938, 1940; Shimkin and Reid 1970). Even among the Wind River Shoshone, depicted by some as preferring bison and other horse-hunted game (Shimkin 1947), "a few persons (in the Green River country particularly) ate lampreys, ants, locusts, crickets, and owls" (Shimkin 1947:256). The Gosiute reported by Reagan (1934) collected large red ants and their eggs in baskets, and boiled these into a soup; fly larvae and dried grasshoppers were also soup ingredients. Malouf (1974) reports Gosiute use of Mormon crickets (*Anabrus simplex*), cicadas, grasshoppers, and ants and their eggs; crickets, particularly, were driven into crescent-shaped trenches about one foot wide and deep and up to forty feet long, roasted, and ground on metates for immediate consumption or storage (Malouf 1974:53).

Subsistence and the Annual Round

Reports of resource procurement and use within a seasonal or annual framework help bridge the gap between simple species lists, strategies, and settlement or mobility. A few examples of reports of annual rounds relevant to the Seedskadee area illustrate considerable agreement throughout the region. Steward's model, the most generally stated, has northern Basin peoples wintering in what is now the upper portion of the Artemesia Belt (including much of the Seedskadee project area) or along rivers; further to the south, where pinyon nuts were important, small groups wintered in the mountains near their nut stores. In the spring, when stored foods were meager, greens were sought in the lowest parts of basins, along rivers and lakeshores, where the snow first disappeared. In early summer seeds begin to ripen in arid valleys, and groups would travel as much as thirty or forty miles, often carrying water, to find them. In later summer roots and berries matured; if no roots could be found, stored seeds were consumed throughout the summer. The fall saw pinyon harvesting to the south and the congregation of game, which could be driven or hunted communally, to the north.

Manners's (1974) scenario for the annual round of Shoshone and Southern Paiute is similar. In early spring, greens were gathered along streams and rivers or in low sand hills. In early summer the focus shifted to seed gathering, an activity in which time efficiency is important due to the short time between the ripening and falling of many seeds. By contrast, in late summer root collecting was done at relative leisure. Early fall was occupied with pine nut storage or the transport and storage of grass seeds. Fall was a "time of plenty," when hunting trips were organized, and winter was spent in sheltered places "with friends" (Manners 1974:20), eating stored foods. Some men Manners met in a Grand Canyon winter camp also "hunted rabbits and sat around," (Manners 1974:132) while the women worked all day processing mescal. Some small game and fresh and dried fish supplemented other winter stores.

Whiting (1950), with the Northern Paiute, records a slightly different pattern. In May the first spring shoots appear and groups leave winter camps to find them; some roots occurring in good places where large numbers of families may camp are also gathered and stored at this time. Shortly afterward the men go north to fish for salmon, as do the women when the root harvest is over. Then families break off by themselves to hunt deer, sage hen, and birds, and to collect seeds and roots as they ripen. The first seeds to ripen are those of the sunflower. At mid-July families would come together to collect crickets, which were dried, roasted, and stored for the winter; the rest of the summer was spent in dispersed family units. In early September another harvest of seeds was stored, including grasses, saltbush, and chenopods. These species occurred in relatively limited areas, and during the harvest the largest groups of families were in association. In early November the families gathered their cached foods and transported them to winter camps where three to ten households stayed.

Again the picture is one of flexibility and generality. Winter camps seem relatively sedentary, but can be in mountains, foothills, or basins. Spring activities seem to center in valleys and basins. Seed and root gathering take place in early to late summer, again in basins, along rivers, in sand dunes, and probably at increasing altitude as the summer progresses. Seed gathering can involve either single family groups or larger aggregations. Small game (rodents, cf. Shimkin and Reid 1970), seeds and roots, and apparently fish in some cases are dried and cached or stored, a consideration that figures in the discussion of settlement and mobility below.

Nonfood Resources

Few of the authors whose works are reviewed here cite nonfood resources as determining the annual round or other important aspects of typical Plains–Great Basin mobility. It may be that these authors are unaware of other resource considerations or most nonfood procurement may be embedded in mobility for subsistence purposes. Steward mentions reliable water supply as being necessary for Shoshone winter camps, usually located at springs near the bases of mesas rather than on rivers, which were "too far from basic resources" (Steward 1940b:120). Dry camps were tolerable at other times of the year, although water had to be carried, a distinct possibility if waterholes were no less than thirty to forty miles apart. Kelly (1964) also observes that the presence of wood was an important factor for camps established in winter, but not at other times.

SETTLEMENT AND MOBILITY OBSERVATIONS AND INTERPRETATIONS

Ethnographic observations pertinent to settlement and mobility and interpretations of these data are among the most useful ethnological data for arriving at ideas about past adaptations and systems in the Seedskadee area. Anthropologists studying Shoshone, Ute, Gosiute, and Paiute groups in and around the Green River Basin of southwestern Wyoming, often supplementing their own observations with ethnohistoric data, have produced an amazing body of literature on settlement and mobility. As these authors did not follow set research, observation, and reporting formats, this information is, like other archaeological and anthropological data, of varying quality and completeness, and is somewhat difficult to integrate. Some authors write in general terms about what is typical of the "Shoshone," including a wide range of groups under this rubric (Steward is probably the worst in this regard). Others are obviously talking about unnamed groups and unobserved incidents. Thorough probing of ethnographic sources could doubtless pinpoint many of these observations.

Reconstructing ethnographic episodes would be a good strategy if one were seeking to compare (for instance) resource availability, environmental conditions, and appropriate strategies within ongoing systems, but applying this sort of specific reconstruction to the archaeological record would be difficult. It is all too easy, immediately after hearing about behavioral episodes, to imagine that the patterning in an archaeological site one has excavated is equivalent or directly comparable with that recorded in a known, living situation (see, for example, Todd et al. 1985).

Here, I shall use ethnographic observations and interpretations to arrive at ideas about alternative settlement and mobility characteristics such as occupation types, locations, and duration of use; the sizes of occupations; the reuse of places; routes and travel; and range sizes.

Occupation Types, Locations, and Duration of Use

Among the groups studied here, the most commonly delineated type of occupation, and the most discussed, is the winter camp. The locations, sizes, duration of occupation, reuse, and other aspects of winter camps seem variable, however, and some of the reasons for this can be defined. Steward's (1938) generalization is that the mountains were too cold for northern Shoshone groups to winter there (he includes Shoshone, Paiute, Gosiute, and Ute); instead they had winter camps in valleys or the upper portion of the Artemesia Belt in basins or along rivers. Winter camps were the most permanent association of families, some of whom remained there constantly during those months when plant foods were not available. In the summer the Shoshone dispersed into single-family groups, and Steward does not discuss what types of camps they occupied then. In contrast to this general pattern, the Owens Valley Paiute, who were dependent upon stored pinyon nuts as winter food, spent the early winter in small groups in the mountains and then moved to valley villages, presumably transporting stores there (Steward 1933).

Another general reconstruction of Great Basin Shoshone occupation types (Powell 1980) proposes relatively permanent winter villages where stored foods were eaten, along with dispersed hunting/gathering and occasional communal jackrabbit and antelope drives between March and October. Communal drives lasted only a few days or weeks. On this basis Powell postulates two types of settlements along with other specialized occupations.

In a more specific example of the Northern Paiute (Surprise Valley), Kelly (1934) describes places where seeds and roots were gathered and stored during the summer. Presumably at the largest or last of these the group took up residence at the beginning of winter, remained until the stored food was exhausted, and then moved on to the next storage location. In some years a group stayed at one place all winter, and in other years the group occupied two or more places during that season. The translation of one Paiute name for such a wintering ground, "where the river comes from the mountain into the open country" (Kelly 1934:77), suggests their location at canyon mouths. Gathering and caching activities took place in both lower and higher country, however, and winter caches might be located in those settings as well. Yet another type of occupation is implied by Kelly (1934) when she speaks of communal rabbit drives and waterfowl hunting in fall.

Another account of northern Paiute settlement (Whiting 1950) also suggests winter camps in foothills or near lakes in basins, with the locations and sizes of camps changing from year to year. During part of the rest of the year families were dispersed as units, but there were also congregations of families at places and times conducive to finding spring shoots (May), gathering and storing crickets (mid-July), and gathering and storing large quantities of their most important staple, the grass seed *wada* (*Suaeda depressa* var. *erecta wats.*), at which time the largest groups congregated.

Roth (1981), studying the Southern Paiute (Chemehuevi), distinguishes between the River and Mountain Chemehuevi on the basis of where they located their winter camps or home bases. At other times of the year Chemehuevi occupied hunting and gathering places on a "family basis," (Manners 1974:54), although during collective hunts many more people lived together for short periods.

Along the western edge of the Great Salt Desert the Gosiute had winter camps containing conical pole huts at the edge of the mountains; during the rest of the year they were more dispersed, using only circular sage windbreaks (Malouf 1974). An indirect indication of either the size or duration of winter camps is afforded by Malouf's (1974:96) reference to George Simpson's disgust engendered by the "immense piles of *faeces* voided by these Indians" around their habitations. While Gosiute communal antelope hunts were less frequent than those of some Basin groups elsewhere, larger numbers of people came together then.

Jefferson et al. (1972) found that the northern Ute wintered along the Green River, and that in the spring each family went its separate way until the next winter. Winter was the only time families were in close association (Reid 1972).

Murphy and Murphy (1960) show major Shoshone-Bannock winter camp areas at Fort Bridger in the Green River Basin, near Logan, Utah, and on the Bear River in eastern Idaho. These winter camps were relatively large, far apart, and occupied by mounted groups that hunted buffalo on the Plains in spring through fall.

Shimkin (1947) separates Wind River Shoshone settlement and mobility into foci, routes, and hinterlands. Foci are places where larger groups gather for considerable length of time, two to three months. Foci are phenomena not of winter (when these mounted groups break up due to fodder requirements), but rather of summer. Shimkin describes foci on the Black's Fork River in the vicinity of Fort Bridger, and near the headwaters of creeks flowing from the Uintah Mountains. At other times of the year smaller groups occupied the hinterlands.

To the north, unmounted Tukudika (sheep eater) Shoshone groups wintered in mountain creek valleys, although some occupied winter camps in the Green River Valley as well (Dominick 1936). Severe winters forced them to elevations well below 7,000 ft. Even winter Tukudeka groups were small. Hultkrantz (1970) feels that overwintering groups at Fort Bridger and in the Black's Fork River area in general were composed partly of buffalo hunters from Utah and Idaho on their way through to the Plains, partly of buffalo hunters from Wyoming who stayed for the winter, and partly of "fairly stationary groups of rabbit eaters" (Hultkrantz 1974:199). The Haviodika, or dove eaters, stayed for the greater part of the year along the tributaries of the Green River. After acquiring horses, the Green River Shoshone or Kucundika (buffalo eaters) wintered in the basin, and also pursued typical Shoshone hunting and gathering there during the spring and summer; in the fall, however, they travelled east to the Plains to hunt buffalo (Hultkrantz 1974). In contrast, the mountain-adapted Shoshone in east central Idaho wintered in forest areas (Swanson et al. 1969).

Occupation Size

All Paiute and Gosiute "local community" sizes listed by Murdock (1967) are given as fewer than 50 persons; presumably, these are winter camp sizes. Shoshone and Bannock local community sizes are listed as 50 to 99 persons, except for Wind River Shoshone (100 to 199 persons), and Hukundika, which are simply listed as "small extended families."

According to Steward (1940a:487), among the western (non-Plains) Shoshone, including northern Paiute and Gosiute, semipermanent groups numbered no more than 40 to 50 people, at maximum in winter camp. In a few lush settings, for instance the Owens Valley, groups of 200 or more could be found. During most of the year for most Shoshone groups, family bands averaging 6 persons were the basic economic and camp unit, although additions might bring this number to as much as 10 (Steward 1938:240). The mounted Shoshone and Fort Hall Bannock, wintering at Fort Hall, broke up into "groups of perhaps six related families" (Steward 1938:203) and travelled to southwestern Wyoming to gather and hunt various foods, and to hunt buffalo in late summer.

Two more specific examples that shed light not only on site size but also on the structure of settlement in winter camps are discussed by Steward (1940b). Steward observed northern Paiute in the Deep Springs Valley, which is 10 by 20 miles in size, as having 4 to 5 places of habitation. Fish Lake Valley, about 50 miles long but narrow, contained 8 contemporaneous occupations. Each local aggregate or family cluster contained 1 to 5 "camps" or nuclear families, averaging 2 families (Steward 1940b:132). Clusters ranged from 4 to 29 persons, averaging 12.4, while individual nuclear families ranged from 2 to 12, with an average of 6.2.

Steward contrasts this with Kelly's data on Kaibab Paiute, whose minimum economic unit was also a local cluster of camps or nuclear families that travelled together hunting and seed gathering. Kaibab Paiute winter residences consisted of 1 to 7 camps or nuclear families. "These camp sites or headquarters" were located at water and firewood sources. The average camp consisted of 7.5 persons, slightly larger than his Deep Springs Valley and Fish Lake Valley groups. The total Kaibab camp cluster ranged from 4 to 39 persons, averaging 12. "The winter sites, of camp clusters, were somewhat grouped in ten major areas where water sources were concentrated. . . . the sites in some of these were fairly close while other were scattered within 10 to 30 miles" (Steward 1940b:134).

Winter camps described by Whiting (1950) among the northern Paiute ranged from 3 to 10 households, with group sizes and the locations at which families wintered changing from year to year. These winter camps were not the largest congregations of people; this instead took place at times in the spring and fall, when certain roots and grass seeds matured in relatively restricted areas for short periods of time. A northern Paiute group, the Wadatkuht in the Honey Lake area of Surprise Valley (Riddell 1960), occupied winter camps as small as a single family, while another winter village had 6 houses and 34 people.

In other seasons, Southern Paiute associations, according to Euler and Fowler (1966:49), consisted of small extended family groups or even single individuals. This contemporary observation is supported by a note of Father de Smet's, from the early 1840s, that southern Paiute "are seldom seen more than two, three, or four together" (Manners 1974:87).

The Reuse of Places

Although the southern Kaibab Paiute tended to reoccupy the same general locales during the winter, sheltered places where they congregated "with friends," during the summer they returned to other sorts of "home bases" according to Manners (1974:20, 22), where reliable water supplies could be found at springs at the feet of plateaus. Manners also seems to suggest that not only home bases but also other sorts of locations were reoccupied by Kaibab groups, although not necessarily annually: "While the pattern of ripening [seeds] involved erratic movements from year to year, the general territory within which the gathering might be done was limited by a group's familiarity with suitable camping places and water" (Manners 1974:77).

The Chemehuevi had winter home bases (Roth 1981) to which they habitually returned, both in the mountains and near rivers, but they were away from these bases for most of the year. Chemehuevi reported on by Laird (1976:24) wintered at certain places for a number of consecutive years; in one area all available "little valleys" were occupied by "clusters of families."

Kelly's (1934) description of northern Paiute storage or caching during the growing season, and subsequent reuse of these foods at serial locations during the winter, leaves little doubt that plant processing or at least storage places were reoccupied within the span of a year. She does not say if they were reoccupied from year to year, however.

Riddell's Wadatkuht (Surprise Valley Paiute) separated during their seasonal hunting and gathering rounds, but returned to a permanent winter village year after year (Riddell 1960:22).

Some Ute groups apparently also maintained permanent winter camps in sheltered spots where food was stored, to which they returned annually (Reid 1972). Ute structures or "bivouacs" consisted of rough shelters of bark, juniper, or sage with a central hearth; each of the 10 to 40 families in a group traveling together had its own bivouac. One particularly exciting passage in John Wesley Powell's notes confirms (in winter?) the reuse of places by Ute groups, and also informs us about its consequences in the archaeological record.

> It is very rare that a site for a camp is occupied a second time and though they all go again year after year to camp near the same spring or small stream they invariably seek a new site for their bivouacs each time. When they leave a camp their bivouacs are not destroyed and so on coming to a customary camping place of the Utes, it gives the appearance of having been occupied by a very large tribe, and persons are easily led to suppose that thousands have been encamped there when in fact perhaps a small tribe of a dozen families have been the only persons who have occupied the ground for many years (Fowler and Fowler 1971:53).

Powell's use of the term "site" in this passage seems to imply the immediate rather than general location of activities, and may parallel Steward's (1940a) recounting of Kelly's "camps." Both of these accounts cast an interesting light on contrasts and parallels between the ethnological and archaeological use (and appropriateness) of the intuitive and unqualified concept of the site.

Travel and Routes

Early observations of Northern Ute groups by Powell are also revealing in terms of route reuse, supporting the idea of fixed seasonal rounds and the revisiting of places. The people observed by Powell were "nomadic," traveling a "grand circuit" for several months of they year; Southern Utes accomplished this round on foot while the Northern Utes had horses. Dragging lodge poles year after year over the same routes left distinct "lodgepole trails" (Fowler and Fowler 1971:39). Horse transport is, of course, not the only method by which lodge poles might be dragged; the use of dogs or people for carrying burdens including lodge poles, tents, food, and water is documented for

Plains groups in general (Wedel 1963) and among the Tukudika and other horseless Shoshone groups (Dominick 1936; Hultkrantz 1961, 1974). Wedel (1963) estimates that a dog can carry a load of slightly less than 50 lb. and as much as 25 lb. of water 5 to 6 miles per day. At European contact, trains of hundreds of dogs were observed on the Plains to the immediate west of the Rocky Mountains.

Little additional specific information about travel and routes is available in the literature surveyed. Most maps show general and "logical" travel routes, many through the Green River Basin from the Salt Lake area and central Idaho in the west to the Wind River Mountains and Plains and basins to the east (Murphy and Murphy 1960). Hultkrantz (1970, 1974) feels that some of the groups observed through ethnographic time in the Green River Basin were traveling through, and that others were relatively constant occupants of the Basin, either gathering and hunting there all year, or leaving only for short periods to hunt buffalo on the Plains.

Shimkin's (1947) separation of Shoshone settlement and mobility into foci, routes, and hinterlands, which he felt to be appropriate to describe these portions of the Wind River group's system, classified routes as relatively high-mobility use of areas, with subsistence activities taking place along the way. Hinterlands are similar to routes, but presumably involve the less mobile activities of smaller groups than those along routes.

Range Sizes

The term "range" is meant to reflect the idea of the distances travelled by people, as well as the differential use to which they put areas of varying distances. The bits of information on range sizes that reach us through the ethnographic and ethnological literature are as fragmentary as those for other systems component categories. Several are intriguing, however.

Steward saw mobility among Great Basin groups occurring almost entirely in the spring, summer, and fall but particularly in the early summer. "Sometimes, if information reached them that certain [seed-bearing] species were abundant in another [mountain] range, the entire family crossed one or more valleys, traveling 30 to 40 miles to procure the harvest" (Steward 1938:18). The Owens Valley Paiute in the spring and summer moved as much as 20 miles or more in all directions from their winter camp (Steward 1933, 1940a). Both of Steward's "range" descriptions here sound as though they pertain to residential mobility in which consumers and producers move together.

Gosiute families reported by Malouf (1974) congregated from several adjacent valleys to join communal hunts about every 10 years. Malouf estimates that their yearly rounds extended over an area 100 miles on a side (1974:93).

Shimkin's (1947) taxonomy of Wind River Shoshone mobility, which he divides into foci, routes, and hinterlands, is the most explicit statement about ranges of different sorts and sizes in the ethnographic literature, although the exact sizes of these ranges are not specified. Shimkin also notes that the Wind River Shoshone knew about areas considerably greater than their territory and visited them occasionally.

OBSERVATIONS AND INTERPRETATIONS PERTAINING TO TECHNOLOGY

Technology, as the term will be used here, refers to all stages of the manufacture and use of implements or any other culturally modified physical materials. It would be an archaeologist's dream come true to discover detailed accounts of the organization of tool manufacture and use among living groups—that is, technology within a systems context—but of course organization is no more obvious or visible to anthropologists than to archaeologists. References to technology in the ethnographic literature, for this reason, are largely limited to mentions of the appearance and use of individual tools or lists of tools as cultural traits.

Steward (1940b) provides a good example of tools as cultural traits: ollas for water carrying, baskets, and seed knives of stone, bone, and wood are typical of Great Basin native cultures. Other "traits" of the seed-gathering complex are poison arrows, rodent skewers, and blinds. In an earlier, more focussed study of the Owens Valley Paiute, Steward (1933) noted large, bifacial, ovoid or slightly pointed stone knives used with and without hafts for skinning and cutting.

Other studies of Northern Paiute groups mention bone awls, digging sticks, large flakes or stone blades used as knives for cutting meat and fish among the Kupadokado (ground-squirrel eaters) of Humboldt Sink (Heizer 1970), and stone knives and scrapers made primarily of obsidian by the Surprise Valley Paiute (Kelly 1934). These people used two sizes of stone knives, the smaller for skinning and the larger for butchering, and carried them with their firedrills. Some smaller knives were hafted and other were not, including "large blades which appear to be giant spearpoints" (Kelly 1934:141). Stone scrapers were used to work hides; these may have been manufactured, but along with the arrow points she saw being used (by the Surprise Valley Paiute) may have been "found archaeologically" (Kelly 1934:141)—reused from archaeological deposits.

Observing Northern Paiute, Whiting (1950) saw stone knives and scrapers used to flesh deer hides. The knives were of flaked obsidian or a white stone, and had 3- to 8-in. blades and wooden handles. A knifelike saw of flaked flint was used to cut down trees. Riddell (1960) reports stone skinning knives referred to by Northern Paiute as "people skinners," 3 1/2 to 4 in. long and about 1 1/2 in. wide, which were ovoid and bifacially flaked over their entire surface. One end of these knives was rounded and the other pointed. A flint drill or punch was used for working skins, and flint or obsidian was also used for making skin scrapers "shaped like an oyster shell" (Riddell 1960:50). "Flint Mountain," a hill near Gerlack, Nevada, was the source of the stone, and these tools were also scavenged from two well-known archaeological sites in the area.

Dominick (1936), observing the Tukudika (sheep eaters) in the Green River Basin and the mountains to the north, reported that most modified stone materials he found on their archaeological deposits were in the form of flakes from cores.

To the south, the Southern Paiute used hafted stone knives as well as knives of bone for butchering and seed plant cutting (Steward 1940b). Steward also reported corner- and side-notched points in use in the Owens Valley, and ground stone slabs, metates, and vessels. Unhafted flakes were also used as temporary knives and scrapers for shaving wood. Euler (1964) describes flat metates, large oval manos, large stemmed points, and small triangular points in the southern archaeological record attributable to the Paiute.

Kaibab tools (Kelly 1964) included digging sticks sharpened with a stone knife, as well as stone drills and metates obtained from prehistoric deposits. Drucker (1937) noted chipped stone skin scrapers and knives in use by the Chemehuevi.

SYSTEMS AND THEIR COMPONENTS AS SUGGESTED BY ETHNOGRAPHIC RECORDS

To conclude this review I shall summarize the general characteristics and components of these systems suggested by ethnographic records. Anthropologists have generally interpreted observations of material culture and social interactions in this area as indicating a flexible situation in which tribal or group boundaries or names are unimportant or ambiguous markers of adaptation types. For this reason I shall consider all of the different sorts of adaptations suggested for nearby Great Basin and Plains groups as possibilities for the Green River Basin.

Subsistence and Subsistence Strategies

General
1. Generalist strategy with reliance on a wide variety of plant and animal foods
2. Dependence on shoots and seeds, ripening beginning in spring at lowest elevations of basins, and progressively at higher elevations
3. Storage of grass seeds, insects, and possibly small game and fish; during collection of these resources, subsisting on other nonstored resources from immediate area
4. Communal hunting of herd animals, including bison, antelope, rabbit in basins, low foothills
5. Individual hunters pursue animals (including single or small groups of those hunted communally) throughout entire area
6. Trapping of smaller animals; often involves considerable logistic mobility

Annual Round
7. At winter camps, reliance on stored foods and opportunistic hunting or gathering
8. Spring foraging in lower parts of basins, along rivers and lakes, and in sand dune areas; storage of grass seeds and insects
9. Later summer, roots and berries gathered in addition to grass seeds

10. Fall pinyon harvesting where possible, also communal hunts or animal drives. Stored grass seeds still important

11. Most nonfood resource procurement embedded in subsistence mobility?

12. Winter camps on tributaries of major rivers, streams, or in areas with reliable springs due to water and wood availability. Water and wood availability probably not critical considerations in short-term, family camps at other times of the year.

Settlement and Mobility

Types and Duration of Occupation
1. Winter camps ubiquitous, but variable in location, size, duration of occupation, and reuse frequency. Located in valleys or upper portions of Artemisia Belt, at canyon mouths, in foothills, basins, or near lakes and rivers or their tributaries. Expect annual reoccupation in most suggested cases.

2. Some winter camps where food was stored during spring, summer and fall; when stored food gone, move to next camp with stored food. These are obviously reoccupied within the annual round.

3. Winter camps usually the largest regular association of families during the year, although this may be reversed for mounted groups due to winter fodder requirements

4. Communal hunt or drive camps between March and October; maximum of a few days to a few weeks occupation. Large, short-term congregations could also be expected in areas of exceptional concentration of briefly available resources (grass, roots, insects). Both of these types of occupations might be expected to be reoccupied, but probably not annually— communal drive occupations only every ten or more years?

Settlement Sizes
5. Maximum winter village or camp size probably 50 persons or fewer, sometimes single families; higher for some mounted groups

6. During most of year, camp size 6 to 10 persons (family unit) for foragers

7. "Winter camps" not necessarily congregated units, may be spread out in family groups or "clusters" of 4 to 39 persons each (average about 12), scattered within as much as a 30 mile radius. Such "winter camps" would not appear to be single units in the archaeological record.

8. Nonwinter communal drive or hunt camps might be considerably larger than winter camps, but very short-term; same for aggregations in exceptional food areas.

The Reuse of Places

10. Reuse of appropriate locales with reliable water and wood annually during the winter months

11. Reuse of other locations not as regular, may be either more or less often than annually

12. Serial reuse of places where foods stored or cached during winter—reoccupation more often than annual, for different functions

13. Reuse of places might not involve direct superimposition of houses, features, activity areas but rather reuse of general area

Travel and Routes

14. Reuse of routes implies reuse of places or areas

15. Possible high-speed travel routes through Green River Basin to and from other areas

Range Sizes

16. Some family seed gathering mobility involves episodic travel of 30 to 40 miles

17. Normal residential mobility around winter camp areas (Owens Valley) as much as 20 mile radius

18. Estimated annual Gosiute rounds (Malouf 1974) 100 square miles, or 5 to 6 miles radius

19. In addition to foraging and logistic radii, larger area of infrequent mobility of which groups had some knowledge

Technology

1. "Material traits" of foraging seed gathering people not simple, many planned elements: baskets, ollas, bows and arrows, large bifacial knives

2. Nonlocal materials from some distance used by some foragers

3. Possible major dependence on previously used places and recycling of discarded materials, tools for raw material; reuse of previously discarded tools. Reuse and recycling may involve the use of materials cached by the later users themselves, or may span much greater time periods between initial discard and later reuse. Viewed in this way, discarded nonlocal lithic resources may be extremely important sources of raw materials.

4. At least some mention of flakes from cores used as tools

5. Skin working with knives and scrapers "shaped like an oyster shell" (Riddell 1960)

6. Discarded materials on known Tukedika (sheep eater or foot Shoshone) occupations observed to be primarily cores and flakes

7. Both corner- and side-notched points used contemporaneously in Great Basin

8. Stone drills, knives used for woodworking.

6

ALTERNATIVE SYSTEMS, THEIR COMPONENTS, AND THEIR EXPRESSION IN THE ARCHAEOLOGICAL RECORD

-- -- -- -- -- -- -- -- -- -- -- -- --

Archaeologists and ethnologists have provided two bodies of interpretation of aboriginal lifeways in the Great Basin, respectively. In some cases their interpretations are complementary, although there is also a great deal of variation. Beginning with these differences and similarities, I intend to suggest alternatives for landscape usage and the places within it.

To determine which systems or components may actually be responsible for the archaeological record, it will be useful to develop some archaeological expectations, stated in terms of assemblage contents. The term "assemblage," here denotes any collection of artifacts and other archaeological materials found together and analyzed at any scale. The scales of analysis I apply to assemblages recorded in Wyoming's Green River Basin range from 5 through 500m for the same assemblages. At no time during these analyses do I assume that any scale of assemblage—any cluster of archaeological materials found together—participated in a single uninterrupted behavioral episode. In other words, assemblages are not taken to be sites.

Instead, I seek archaeological expectations that can be evaluated using measures sensitive to the spatial scale of clustering and repetition of the patterning of various classes of artifacts. These expectations are based in turn on middle-range linking arguments concerning mobility and site-type differentiation, mobility and technological organization, scheduling and time constraints, the occupational history of use and reuse of places, and lithic production "trajectories."

Developing expectations about assemblage content variability among different systems components might at first seem tantamount to reconstructing systems and their parts, or to testing suspected systems to see if they were really in operation in the Green River Basin in the past. Indeed, this approach has been taken by some authors (Bettinger 1977; Thomas 1971, 1983). But my goal is to provide a basis for determining measurable variables in distributional survey and to assign meaning to distributional generalizations.

COMPARING ARCHAEOLOGICAL AND ETHNOGRAPHIC INTERPRETATIONS

Although archaeologists and ethnographers may have a common basis for their interpretations of past systems in southwestern Wyoming and surrounding areas, the overall pictures presented by these two groups are quite different. The archaeologists' scenario is one of well-differentiated subsistence types or phases occurring across wide regions (the Great Basin, the Plains, or both) for long periods (thousands of years). The number of phases varies with the author—two or perhaps only one for Desert Tradition adherents (following Jennings 1964); three (Palaeoindian, Archaic, and Late Prehistoric) for most authors; and the occasional suggestion of a fourth, the agricultural Fremont, although Fremont manifestations in southwestern Wyoming presumably were represented only by nonagricultural components.

The ethnographers present a more uniform but internally differentiated picture. Early authors such as Steward and Kroeber stressed the sameness of adaptations across the Great Basin, characterizing them as evolutionarily simple and spanning at least 10,000 years. Their tendency to "emphasize the typical and overlook the variability of modal behavior" (Thomas 1983:26), has been tempered more recently by the recognition of a "startling array of temporal, spatial, long-term, and short-term variability" among adaptations of this region. Expressing this in another way, Fowler (1982:121) sees "considerable variability in *actualized* patterns in the region, while at the same time . . . similarities in the *generalized* pattern." This is not simply the effect of time scales of observation; for instance, from an inspection of some ethnographic accounts, Kelly (1964) finds evidence of several simultaneous, "actualized" settlement patterns in small areas.

Archaeological and ethnographic accounts differ in more specific terms, too. One dominant archaeological theme is that the Green River Basin largely contains the record of transient camps, or people for whom this high arid steppe was peripheral to a central base of operations elsewhere. Implicit in such reconstructions is the assumption that these people exploited enormous areas. There is also some suggestion from archaeologists examining lithic material sources that very large logistic ranges were exploited, with radii of perhaps hundreds of miles (Goodyear 1979; Frison 1973). While ethnographic accounts of unmounted family groups document extreme cases of movement up to 40 miles for seed gathering in bad years, they generally report annual radii no more than 20 miles, and in some cases as little as 5 miles. If people with this kind of range used the Green River Basin (which measures about 80 miles on a side), it is difficult to label such usage peripheral. The ethnographic record does, however, also mention visits to the Green River Basin by transient groups.

Archaeologists focusing on the Green River Basin area have interpreted the record as indicating that basins were used in the winter as the locations of residential camps, foothills were exploited in the spring and fall, and mountains in the summer. Winter residences in basins were extensive, especially in dune areas, which, due to ease of construction, are supposedly ideal for longer-term camps. In dry Altithermal times the Green River Basin and other basins were even more densely occupied by Late Archaic peoples than during later periods. Spring to fall camps were smaller and, at least implicitly, reoccupied only rarely, except for large communal game drive locations. Multiple-occupation sites such as Pine Spring (Sharrock 1966) or Deadman Wash (Mackey et al. 1982) are usually seen to have been occupied only at a few times separated by long intervals (sometimes only once per cultural phase).

In contrast, ethnographers report the locations of winter residential camps to have been quite variable (on rivers, in foothills and canyons, and in the upper portions of the Artemesia Belt). They also report a wide range of different types and frequency of reuse. Accordingly, the winter camp locale is reused year after year by most groups. Some locations where plant foods were gathered and stored in the spring through fall may also be occupied in the winter while stores are consumed, or visited during the winter by groups retrieving stores through journeys of as much as one day each direction (Fowler 1982), indicating an overnight or longer stay. Both of these strategies for using stored foods virtually ensure that camps used in one season for one function will be used in the next in different ways. Such serial reuse of places must take place at frequencies higher than once a year. Frequent mention of the reuse of travel routes in the ethnographic record suggests that many other locations must have been reused at least annually. The ethnographic record is a story of the frequent and constant reuse of places at a far higher temporal resolution than will ever be measurable archaeologically.

While the winter camp is the largest longer-term gathering of families, even larger groups congregate for purposes of communal animal hunts or drives (usually coupled with social events such as Thomas's [1983] *fandangos*), and also at places where abundant vegetal resources are clustered. Both of these latter types of camps or congregations are short-term occupations (probably no more than a week or two), have specialized purposes, and might be located without concern for any resources but those that are concentrated on. Congregations at the locations of clustered plant resources might occur annually or every few years; there is some evidence that communal drive sites were used again only at much greater intervals, and perhaps not actually reoccupied at all.

Ethnographic settlement sizes typically range from fifty people or fewer at winter encampments (although camps may not have been nucleated, sometimes consisting of distinct households separated by considerable distances) to residential foraging groups of 6 to 10 individuals.

Archaeological and ethnographic interpretations of technology also differ. Archaeologically, two general kinds of artifact assemblages, in various blends, comprise the record: a hunting tool kit dominated by projectile points, bifaces, unifaces, cores, and flakes; and a gathering or domestic (women's) tool kit with utilized and unutilized flakes, few if any formal tools, and ground stone. Ethnographic accounts show the tool kits of seed gatherers to be quite complex, including many planned elements and using nonlocal materials. A possible major dependence on lithic materials scavenged from old archaeological sites appears in the ethnographic literature, another strategy that would result in places being reused for functions different from their initial uses. The existence of scavenging somewhat alters ideas about the almost exclusive dependence on quarry sites for lithic materials, a concept that serves as the implicit basis for most archaeological discussion of lithic sources, territory, and the sizes of foraging or travel radii.

TYPES OF SYSTEMS AND COMPONENTS

Given the wide range of possibilities suggested by archaeologists and ethnographers for what the aboriginal inhabitants might have been doing in the Green River Basin and surrounding areas, what kinds of systems and their components might be represented? In other words, how might the use of the landscape and places within it have been differentiated?

Considering this question in a study area in Monitor Valley in central Nevada, Thomas inspected the subsistence and mobility strategies of the Reese River Valley Shoshone, the Kawich Mountain Shoshone, and the Owens Valley Paiute. These groups, he felt, demonstrated such a wide range of variation in settlement pattern, mobility, procurement and resources, and political organization that they could serve as examples of extremes within the Great Basin. On the basis of this examination he proposed different sorts of "sites and nonsites" that would have served as settlement nodes.

Residential bases are properties of all groups' settlement systems—Steward called them headquarters—where a full range of domestic activities takes place, including food preparation, consumption, and storage; and tool fabrication, maintenance, and use. The residential base is the focus of hunter-gatherer life, and "its importance is reflected in the archaeological record." The "assemblage level consequences" of the residential base are hearths, fire-cracked rock, a wide variety of faunal and floral remains, fabrication tools, tool manufacturing debris, and discarded broken or worn personal gear. Residential bases are where one intends to carry out lithic manufacturing tasks, so they exhibit a wide range of lithic reduction, including "both ends of the manufacturing sequence" (Thomas 1983:73–78).

Field camps are temporary centers of operation where a special-purpose group eats, sleeps, and maintains itself while away from the residential base. Thomas sees these as primarily places where groups stay during communal activities; they should contain specialized equipment and be biased toward either plants or animals but not both. Other camps may be occupied by logistically organized hunting parties (field camps and observation stations, in Binford's [1980] terms) and contain a small artifact inventory of curated personal gear, debris from limited artifact maintenance, and only specific stages of lithic reduction.

Caches must be common but relatively invisible in the archaeological record, although material buried in pits that are deflated by erosion should form tight clusters. Tool caches should occur near the place where it was intended to use the tools.

Locations should be common to both foragers and collectors, according to Thomas, and are the places where daily extractive activities are carried out. Their archaeological visibility should vary radically, most must be of low visibility, and artifact losses at locations should be extractive tools and debitage.

Thomas then considers the variability in annual positioning strategies exhibited by the three Shoshone groups examined. The Owens Valley groups had foraging radii of about 8km and logistic radii of 24km; in the Reese River groups' logistic radii were 60 to 80km; and the Kawich Mountain Shoshone had a slightly larger, 8 to 10km foraging radius, but no real logistic range, as they were always residentially mobile. Using these figures and the mobility patterns they imply, Thomas deduces five basic regional mobility strategies that may have operated in the Monitor Valley.

1. *A strategy of high residential mobility,* in which foragers could have exploited all of Monitor Valley; one would expect low-density residential bases and locations to result from this strategy, with a few caches concentrated in areas of high bulk resources.

2. *A strategy of seasonal fusion and fission* "monitored from within the camp/foraging radii" (Thomas 1983:139), consisting of the exploitation by "mixed-mode forager-collectors" who occupy established residential bases in several optimal areas and pursue both local foraging and wider-ranging logistic strategies throughout the rest of the valley. This strategy should produce a series of high-visibility base camps surrounded by locations, field camps, and extensive seasonal caching systems.

3. *A strategy of seasonal fusion and fission* "monitored from within the logistic radius" (Thomas 1983:140), essentially the same strategy as just described, but with residential bases located outside the valley and only logistical visits to Monitor Valley. Archaeologically, this strategy should produce field camps, high-visibility intercept locations, and an absence of residential camps.

4. *A strategy of minimal residential mobility* monitored from within the camp or foraging radii, meaning that collectors could have operated from nearly permanent residential bases within the valley and pursued both foraging and logistic strategies there. This would appear archaeologically as a few very high visibility residential bases, with signs of high investment in facilities surrounded by locations and field camps.

5. *A strategy of minimal residential mobility* monitored from within the logistic radius, consisting essentially of strategy 4, with the difference that the permanent residential base is located outside the valley. Archaeologically, this should appear as highly visible intercept locations, field camps, and caches, with an absence of residential sites.

Thomas's mobility strategies and the settlement systems they represent are valuable, since they acknowledge variable use of landscape and locations. His conclusions on what to look for to confirm the existence of these strategies, however, may be evaluated less positively. Thomas seems to view the operation of systems and their translation into the archaeological record as episodic, with a system positioned in one set of places creating a corresponding set of frozen archaeological consequences. The nonsite concept seems largely forgotten. Thomas identifies different phases of his postulated systems components by the presence or absence of different sorts of sites, which can be recognized archaeologically by the functions of the artifacts and features they contain.

If, as I have suggested and as Thomas himself suggested in earlier writings, the archaeological record can be expected to be a composite overlay of episodes of behavior resulting from many uses of places, it may be very difficult to distinguish overlaid field camps from residences simply through a functional interpretation of all items found at a place. As we cannot expect the episodic or annual expression of systems (as types of adaptations) to overlap perfectly, but instead to be repositioned across the landscape, we should see not whole systems in any area but rather the result of greater or lesser overlap of their components— that is, the spatial scale of their recurrence. Previously, I likened this to looking at systems through a small window. We cannot hope to distinguish between residential bases within a valley or study area and "their" corresponding field camps, locations, and caches.

For these reasons I have modified Thomas's expectations somewhat.

I would expect to find components of Thomas's strategies 1, 2, and 4 in the Green River Basin and similar Great Basin settings in general. Renumbered and rephrased, these are:

1. A strategy of high residential mobility in which foragers exploited the area, using serially occupied residential camps from which foraging trips of a day or less were undertaken.

2. A strategy of seasonal fusion and fission, in which large multifamily residential camps were occupied during one portion of the year. Foraging as well as logistic forays were undertaken from these camps. At other times the camps broke up into small, residentially mobile foraging groups.

3. A strategy of minimal residential mobility coupled with high logistic mobility, represented by large permanent residential bases with high investment in facilities and highly specific, repeatedly used logistic field camps and staging locations.

I add another possibility suggested by the archaeologists and ethnographers:

4. A strategy (or more realistically a component thereof) consisting of temporary camps of highly mobile and logistically organized special-purpose groups passing through the area, with neither residential bases nor procurement activities related to the area at all.

ASSEMBLAGE CONTENT AND SYSTEMIC ORGANIZATION

In the remainder of this chapter I shall develop some general expectations about variability in assemblage content among the different sorts of systems and their components suggested above. I intend this to illustrate the rationale behind the collection of distributional data in the Seedskadee survey.

Perhaps the most popular approach to developing expectations about assemblage content is to posit the functions of certain artifacts, usually "diagnostic" tools. These assumptions are usually based on such criteria as edge angles (Wilmsen 1970; Gould 1968; Gould et al. 1971; White 1967; White and Thomas 1972), edge shapes and sizes (Knudson 1973), or other assumed functions—ground stone for grinding, scrapers for scraping, knives for cutting (such as Thomas 1973, 1983). There are a number of problems with such direct translation from behavior to the archaeological record. Tools that are manufactured and used expediently probably exhibit variable design characteristics; tools that are the focus of greater design specificity and thus more "formal" or "diagnostic" are carried from place to place and may perform many functions, or be modified to meet situational needs. The locations of these formal, curated tools in the archaeological record informs us about their discard, which is only the endpoint of their history of use. In other words, two different tools might be used for the same type of task, or two similar implements for different tasks, depending on their roles within an overall system rather than simply their shapes or other formal characteristics.

Even intensive examination techniques, such as the identification of animal protein or microwear (Keeley 1974, 1980) on tool edges and surfaces, can really be counted on only to inform us of the tool's most recent use, not its use history or rationale for making it. Even more importantly, however, direct functional interpretation of the contents of assemblages makes it impossible to compare assemblages of different types in terms of general, crosscutting variables. An assemblage with cutting tools is a cutting (male, butchering) assemblage; one with scraping tools is a scraping (perhaps female, hide-working) assemblage. One with both is a mixture of the two. That different tools can be expected to occur in different mixtures in tool kits resulting from successive components of organizational systems was demonstrated twenty years ago by Binford and Binford (1966) in an article that also underscored the difficulty of dissecting and interpreting multivariate patterning.

My approach to developing expectations about assemblage content is, instead, to focus on assemblage content variables that crosscut assemblage and artifact types. I develop these expectations with reference to recent middle-range theories, for it is my feeling that we are presently undergoing a middle-range theory revolution, in which different avenues of inquiry are converging on generally applicable interpretive methods for archaeology.

Mobility, Settlement, and General Technological Strategies

The key to understanding variability in tool manufacture, use, and discard, according to Kelly (1985), is to understand a tool's role—that is, the placement of activities in which a tool is used, in relation to the mobility strategy and distribution of raw materials across a particular region. Binford has suggested that there are qualitatively different types of tool roles, such as personal gear, site furniture, and situational gear. Personal gear and site furniture are both "anticipatory" (Binford 1979:261), being manufactured and maintained with planned or unforeseen uses distant in time, space, or both, while situational gear is responsive to immediate needs. Personal gear belongs to a person, while site furniture essentially belongs to a place, to be used there by those who visit it. Anticipatory personal gear is designed to have relatively long use life, and rarely wears out in the context of its use; personal gear is manufactured and maintained in residential camps. The only components of personal gear that one might expect to find in places where they are used are parts of broken items, for instance point tips.

Personal gear, manufactured at leisure and with some activity in mind, should exhibit relatively large design and labor inputs, and should often look formal or diagnostic (that is, such gear can often be classified by shape). The form and material of situational gear, on the other hand, should vary according to the specific demand in each instance in which it is produced.

The distinction between local and nonlocal materials is often used in attempting to discriminate between curated, personal gear and situational implements (Francis 1980; Gould 1980; Gould and Saggers 1985). Actually, in a truistic way, all lithic raw materials are local. When people need raw material they look around where they are; if materials can be found on the ground, they may be used situationally, and if not, personal gear can serve as the source of material for situational tools. If a material must be transported, considerable effort should be expended in economizing its use, and little material should be discarded. If raw, unmodified material is abundant, replacement rates of situational implements may be very high. The recycling or resharpening of personal gear into situational tools, or both, should be a property of field or special-purpose locations.

At residential occupations lithic manufacture should vary with the scale and nature of the group's mobility from that camp and the more general patterns of mobility before and after that occupation. Kelly (1985) distinguished four general flaking techniques commonly employed in lithic manufacture and reduction.

Bipolar flaking produces sharp flake tools quickly and expediently from small nodules or tool fragments; bipolar flakes usually cannot be retouched extensively.

Microblade techniques can be used on small nodules as well, but preparation of the core and platform wastes some material. Microblade techniques result in flakes with high edge-to-mass ratios, which are of uniform size and are easily interchangeable as hafted elements. Microblades are thus made when tools are designed for long-term use and particular roles.

Percussion flaking requires fairly large nodules, and is used when the only requirements are that a tool be sharp and easy to handle. Percussion flaking produces low edge-to-weight ratios, and is used for expedient tools.

Biface techniques require high time and energy investments, and are used to shape a tool into a specific form. Biface edges are durable, can be resharpened, and bifaces can also serve as cores for the manufacture of situational tools.

The techniques used for manufacturing in any situation, then, should vary with the physical properties of available lithic material and with anticipated use of the tools produced:

1. At residential locations, where manufacture of anticipatory tools occurs, available materials should be regulated by the scale of a group's systemic mobility. Collecting groups can be expected to embed their resource procurement within relatively long-distance travel undertaken for other purposes (Binford 1979; Binford and Stone 1985). Embedded lithic procurement renders economic value distinctions between stone from local and distant sources meaningless. At residential sites occupied by collectors, both expedient tool manufacture and the fabrication of personal gear may thus involve either local or nonlocal materials. The nature of raw materials used at nonresidential collecting camps and locations should depend not only on material availability, but also on time constraints.

2. Foraging groups with high residential and low logistic mobility have smaller short-term land use radii and greater problems with the transport of things from residential bases than do collectors. For this reason, the nature of a foraging group's lithic technology should be heavily influenced by lithic materials that can be found in an immediate area. It is tempting to think of these as being "local" or "untransported," but abundant references in the ethnographic literature point to the seeking of previously-used

places—archaeological sites, in essence—as sources of raw materials. In general, if raw materials are abundant, one would expect foragers to rely heavily on percussion flaking, resulting in high ratios of waste to utilized flakes. Scavenging of worn or broken and discarded (and thus small) tools for raw materials for other tools may be indicated by an increased use of bipolar flaking techniques.

The distinction between foraging and collecting used throughout these discussions is, of course, heuristic. Most subsistence strategies should be seasonally variable, and as stone collecting is often embedded in logistic mobility, which should vary in scale or even occurrence seasonally, "lithic source variability as indicated in primary debris should be correlated with the geographic position of the residential site" (Binford 1979:270) and the scale of nonresidential mobility.

The final phase of a technological strategy, discard, should also vary with mobility and settlement differentiation. Manufacturing debris, often referred to as debitage, is of course discarded—usually just dropped—where it is created; this fortunate fact helps define the use of places on the basis of "trajectories" of staged lithic manufacture. Some more general patterns of discard and abandonment can also be postulated:

1. Residential occupations should be the locus of the discard of worn-out items of durable personal gear because they are refurbished there, and replacements (in good condition) are taken out on subsequent forays for special purposes.

2. Special-purpose locations should have the highest incidence of recycling and reuse of personal items, reflected in high incidences of utilized flakes from bifacial cores, or bifacial thinning flakes. Discarded material should also reflect an inverse relationship between the reuse of personal gear and the abundance of situationally produced gear from untransported raw materials.

Time Budgeting and Technology

Torrance has suggested an interesting avenue of middle-range inquiry that may help link mobility and settlement with the archaeological record through a consideration of the time constraints met by different technological strategies. Reasoning that rates of energy capture are important whether the available energy is scarce or not (a stance that flies in the face of most optimal foraging models), Torrance sees technology varying with both the severity and the character of time stress. Slotting embedded activities, such as lithic procurement, into more important subsistence tactics is one way of using time efficiently (Torrance 1983:12). Another is staged manufacture of lithic and other implements, in which materials or items at various stages of completion are carried and worked on during down time, for instance while waiting for game at hunting stands. Such staging may allow the input of large blocks of time that would not be available at residential camps, with resultant increased complexity of tool kits. Tool kit complexity, and thus presumably efficiency for specific tasks, in turn speeds task completion. In collecting systems, this balance between time-stressed tasks and long periods of down time should be highly adaptive. Torrance suggests characterizing tool kit complexity by using measures of parts' per tool or components per tool kit, following Oswalt (1973, 1976), accordingly:

1. The diversity of tools within a functional class, measured by counting the tool types present, should be negatively related to the amount of time available to complete a job; a small amount of time should correlate with large tool kits. This is due to the increased efficiency of specialized tools, and the fact that many specialized tools are required to carry out a set of tasks comprising an activity.

2. Where many nonspecific tasks must be accomplished, on the other hand, general-purpose tool kits with relatively fewer elements and lower diversity should be expected. The number of tasks that must be undertaken is roughly correlated with the number of resource types comprising a group's diet. Specialist collecting strategies call for tools with limited but specific functions and few possible alternatives; it is beneficial in such situations to devise special-purpose tools, each of which is used for only a few tasks. Thus more kinds of tools are required. Investment in special-purpose tools by generalists is unnecessary.

Time stress occurs when more than one thing needs to be done at once. Torrance (1983) suggests that planning for specific activities and manufacturing and carrying specialized tool kits is one solution to this problem. Time budgets may also be stressed by spatial incongruities between places where time is and is not available. One answer to such problems is the caching of technological items. Schlanger (1981), in the course of an ethnographic survey of literature on more than than 80 hunter-gatherer groups, has found that caching commonly occurs when there are strong seasonal differences in the utility of tools and equipment. People in seasonal environments may maintain two or more sets of tools and equipment, leaving behind those inappropriate for the upcoming season for reuse during the following year's occupation of a seasonal camp.

The extent of tool caching depends on the overlap of activities from one place to another and the degree of redundancy in the tool inventory (specificity or generality in Torrance's terms), making caches "a potentially important case in discussions of the relationship between location of use and location of archaeological discovery" (Schlanger 1981:2). For instance, things are cached when conditions make their continued use uneconomical, or, they are cached where they are no longer needed. Where there is high redundancy in the location of seasonally utilized places, the first season's equipment may be cached at the second season's habitation. Where there is seasonality but uncertainty about whether a place will be reoccupied next year, tools and equipment may be cached at some intermediate location. Securely cached items at nonhabitations might, therefore, indicate some stability in recurrent resource location over a period of time.

Distinguishing cached technological material in the archaeological record can be difficult. Schlanger (1981) points out that if places with caches are actually reused for the purposes for which tools were left behind, these things might be used up over time, and caches should be relatively empty. The archaeological recovery of caches might therefore indicate some sort of "break in the system," where the intent to return was not realized. McAnany (1986), however, suggests a possible consequence of caching that might be measured with assemblage content data. Special-purpose tools are of course more likely to be cached than general-purpose gear; patterns of wear or edge damage on special-purpose tools should be more homogeneous than those on general-purpose tools. In addition, the longer or more often a tool is cached the longer its use life will be. High labor-input, formal, specific-use tools that still have useful lives found in an archaeological context may be indicative of tool caching strategies. Finding many identical artifacts together (many bifaces or preforms of the same type, for instance), a pattern often taken by archaeologists as diagnostic of caching, is probably indicative more of staged manufacture than it is of caching things for later use.

The Staging of Lithic Manufacture

Torrance (1983) suggested that the manufacture of specialized, labor-intensive lithic implements might be undertaken at a hunting camp or station during down time. Under relatively high logistic mobility and when tool manufacture is complex—things that should occur together—such down time could be expected to occur regularly but in small packages, resulting in the staged manufacture of both carried tools and those used and left at specific locations. Staged manufacture should take place in episodes, between which items might be stored in a residential context or carried to the next nonresidential location, with discontinuity in stages representing "transport junctures" (Binford 1979:268). In other words, the manufacture of personal and household gear within a highly differentiated collecting system could be embedded in other activities, just like lithic procurement. Staging of manufacture is a response to the intermittent work schedules typical of logistically organized groups.

The production of personal and household gear might take place in any context under such a technological strategy, at logistic camps as well as at residences. While tools in different stages of manufacture are carried between different places, the debris from their manufacture fortunately is not, providing the archaeologist with means of measuring the nature of staged manufacture. In very general terms, manufacturing debris at special-purpose sites intermediate between residential sites and procurement sites (hunting camps or stations) might include considerable debris from working on partially finished staged items, but should not contain those items themselves, exhibiting "disjunctive tool-to-debris relationships" (Binford 1979:270). As situational implements are manufactured from raw materials provided in at least some instances by personal gear, the finished tool is not the endpoint of this process. Tools are "continuously and reliably rejuvenated, or changed into other tools, or used as cores for the derivation of new tools" (Goodyear 1979).

Unravelling the complex process of staged lithic manufacturing promises to provide another middle-range tool by which assemblages can be compared in a general way, and several recent efforts have focused on its measurement and analysis. Lithic technology, according to

Pokotylo (1978), involves three basic classes of physical elements: fabricators used in tool manufacture and maintenance, debitage or discarded waste, and finished tools; only debitage is consistently left in the place where it is created, making it perhaps the most important class of lithic material for understanding the relationships between places and what was done at them. As flaking stones is a subtractive process (Deetz 1967:48), the debris from successive stages of manufacture (or "reduction," after Pokotylo 1978:161) bears evidence of prior working.

Just what are these stages, and how can they be measured? Muto (1971a, b) considered each flake removal during lithic reduction to be a stage in the technological process; other less extreme but variable approaches to discerning reduction stages have been offered by Collins (1975), Katz (1976), Knudson (1973), and Phagan (1976). In an effort to devise unambiguous and easily measured criteria for identifying manufacturing stages, Pokotylo (1978) examined and exhaustively measured a large collection of lithic materials collected in the Upper Hat Creek Valley of British Columbia. Reasoning that "the entire range of technological behavior is unlikely to occur at the same place," (Pokotylo 1978:163), his goal was to divide these materials according to their participation in five technological stages (after Collins 1975):

1. acquisition of raw materials
2. core preparation and initial reduction
3. primary trimming
4. secondary trimming
5. maintenance or modification, or both

Pokotylo first divided his assemblages into platform-bearing flakes, cores, tools, and shatter (debitage without platforms). He measured twenty-three attributes on platform-bearing flakes; he then subjected these measurements to a factor analysis to assess their redundancy in distinguishing between stages. They were reduced to five major factors:

1. flake size measures, contributing to 54.2 percent of the total variation;
2. ventral and dorsal flaking angles, contributing to 20.2 percent of the total variation;
3. dorsal surface scar count, contributing to 9.2 percent;
4. striking platform architecture (size, angle), contributing to 9.1 percent; and

5. ventral surface lipping/bulb of force, responsible for 7.4
   percent of the total variation.

These factors are best represented on platform-bearing flakes by measures of weight, ventral flaking angle, dorsal flake scar count, striking
platform width, and presence or absence of a bulb of force.

Pokotylo examined cores with reference to their weight, shape, presence or absence of cortex, number of flake removal surfaces, pattern
of flake removal, and several other characteristics; he distinguished block
shatter from flake shatter (flakes without platforms); and typified tools
on the basis of their edge angles. He then subjected flake, tool, core,
and shatter characteristics to a Ward's Error Sum cluster analysis of
the standardized City Block distance matrix to produce a dendrogram
of site similarity from which site clusters of types were derived. These
were compared to environmental characteristics of the study region.
Although the final results of this exercise are far from easily interpretable, Pokotylo's demonstration that both tools and manufacturing
debris must be examined to understand site utilization (Pokotylo
1978:321–22) has encouraged other archaeologists.

One of these is Martin Magne (1981, 1983), who saw the necessity
for controlled lithic reduction experiments rather than simply assuming that certain variables were the best indicators of otherwise unknown
reduction stages. Magne undertook lithic replication experiments with
a number of stone workers, numbering all of the flakes produced in
precise order of their production. He measured flakes to within 5mm
and removed from the experiment all debitage above an average size
of 30g that he thought could be further utilized (and he reasoned, would
have been in actuality). While most previous studies (for instance, Stahle
and Dunn 1982; Fish 1976b, 1979; Collins 1975) had examined only
complete flakes, that is those that are unbroken and have platforms,
Magne measured all platform-bearing flakes and portions thereof. Three
broad classes of flakes were separated: platform-remnant-bearing flakes,
biface reduction flakes with lipped platforms, and bipolar reduction
flakes exhibiting crushing at two platforms or evidence of a blow from
two directions.

Magne divides his reduction stages into only very general categories—
early, middle, and late—for analytical purposes. Early-stage reduction
includes core reduction (single platform and bipolar); middle-stage
reduction encompasses trimming stages, including all reduction events
of marginally retouched tools and the first half of reduction in unifacial

and bifacial tools; and the remaining half of uniface and biface production is late-stage reduction. Following Pokotylo (1978) and Katz (1976), Magne subjected measurements from his debitage to a factor analysis to assess redundancy. The six variables Magne (1983) measured, and their expected relevance to determining reduction stages, are listed in Table 6.1.

In Magne's analyses platform scar count was the best indicator of reduction stage, and weight was relatively unreliable. All of the variables measured were useful, however, in distinguishing stages. Generally, platform-remnant-bearing flakes with cortical or unfaceted platforms are early, those with two platform scars are middle-stage, and those with three or more are late-stage; biface reduction flakes have three or more scars on acute-angled platforms. Shatter and bipolar flakes with cortical or plain surfaces are early, those with two dorsal scars middle-stage, and those with three or more dorsal scars are late.

To gain a "regional perspective on lithic assemblage variability" (1983:195) in a study area in British Columbia, Magne examined variability in reduction stages represented by flakes in assemblages associated with house pits, cache pits, fire-cracked rock, and in isolated lithic assemblages without other associations. A number of previous discussions of lithic reduction have emphasized economic considerations in procurement and use, suggesting or demonstrating that sites near raw material sources should contain earlier reduction stages or assemblages with longer trajectories (Ahler 1975; Butler and Lopinot 1982; Chapman 1977; Jeffries 1982, 1983; Pokotylo 1982; Raab et al. 1979). In order to test this assumption Magne examined the proportions of late-stage chert and obsidian (nonlocal in his area) to basalt (local) and found no significant differences; in one area it appeared that the local basalt might in fact be conserved. This result reinforces those of several other experiments oriented toward detecting economization in raw material types through the examination of reduction sequences. Morrow (1982), examining Late Archaic assemblages in Illinois, found no stage differences in the use of local versus nonlocal lithic materials, and decided that these people's range must have included both sources. Johnson (1983) interpreted similar results in a Mississippi study as indicating that there may be differential economizing under different systems, or that what may look like economizing in some cases may really be attributable to variation in the scale and tempo of the use of different places (that is, different purposes of mobility).

Table 6.1. Six variables measured by Magne (1983) and their expected relevance to the determination of the reduction stage at which flakes were removed from cores during the manufacturing process.

Flake Characteristic	Expectation
Weight	Decreases through reduction process
Dorsal scar count	Increases through reduction process
Dorsal scar complexity (scar directions)	Increases through reduction
Platform scar count	Increases through reduction
Platform angle (dorsal)	Decreases through reduction
Dorsal cortex cover	Decreases sharply following initial core reduction

Magne (1983) also found striking differences in the material making up debitage of various stages as opposed to tools in sites. He interpreted sites with large amounts of early debitage and no tools as primary manufacturing sites, those with later debitage and few tools as maintenance locations, those with many tools and much late debitage as reoccupied tool maintenance locations, and those with many tools and little debitage as places where tools were used over long periods but little maintenance was carried out.

While some foundation for the utility of examining lithic reduction stages and the empirical measurement of these stages has been laid, there is still work to be done in interpreting their meaning. Recent research by Camilli (1985, 1988) and Larralde (1988) in this direction are promising. They examine reduction stages not to reconstruct those stages and thereby arrive at statements of functional analogue, but to determine whether reduction stages as indicated by debitage, and the comparison of debitage with tools in assemblages, are keys to the episodal history of the use of places.

The Occupational History of Places

"Occupational history" refers to the manner in which a place is reused. One way to approach the interpretation of occupational history is through a consideration of assemblage texture (Binford 1980). A coarse-grained assemblage is one that is composed of discarded materials from events taking place over a relatively long time, for instance an assemblage formed at a permanent residential camp over the course of a year or many years. As many activities take place over this time within a relatively limited area, the resolution between archaeological remains resulting from specific events and associated debris is low.

Fine-grained assemblages, on the other hand, result from the accumulation and sedimentary encapsulation of debris over very short periods, for instance in special-purpose camps or locations over a period of days or even hours. In fine-grained assemblages there is high resolution and correspondence between debris and events. Mobility is the primary cultural factor determining the texture of assemblages. Other things being equal, high mobility should result in finer-grained assemblages, and low mobility in those with coarser grain. Another factor that may or may not be equal is the degree to which events within the system and at different places are serially differentiated; this tends to increase with latitude and thus resource specialization.

Coarseness of grain reduces the interassemblage variability among residential sites of a system and increases the "complexity and scale of assemblage content referable to any given occupation, assuming, that is, responsiveness of assemblage content to event differentiations" (Binford 1980:18). Assemblages from long-term residential locations should look relatively similar but be internally complex; shorter-term occupation should be highly variable, constituting a "noisy category" (Binford 1980:18) or what might look like a number of different categories under analysis.

Another way of looking at this relationship is that differences in interassemblage variability between residential and special-purpose locations should be attributable to differences in mobility patterns, while differences within these groups should reflect the types of activities performed at places and the variable situations affecting the execution of these assemblages (Camilli 1983b). Coarse-grained residential camp assemblages should accrue a full range of tool manufacturing and maintenance debris, while finer-grained assemblages should not exhibit all stages of manufacture. Fine-grained assemblages from short-term occupations, even if they result from identical activities, may be quite different due to the recycling of personal tool kits of variable condition, or to special situations (Camilli 1983b:4).

In terms of debitage, two basic types of assemblages should be seen, if staging of manufacture is held equal.

1. One type should be fine-grained assemblages containing flakes generated from tools and cores carried in personal tool kits,

exhibiting trends in flake morphology that reflect specific technological strategies.

2. The second type should be coarse-grained assemblages generated at residences, with flake debris representing all aspects of stone tool manufacture and not necessarily a single production strategy. A wider variety of flake forms can be expected within coarse-grained assemblages, coupled with less variability between them compared to special-purpose locations.

The occupational history of places is not necessarily completely self-evident from the general nature of assemblage contents, however. To further examine the nature of the reuse of places, Camilli (1983a, 1989) breaks assemblages down in a taxonomy reflecting differences in occupational history rather than function or their role in a settlement system. **Single occupations** are places used only once. **Multiple occupations** are areas that have been reused, resulting in partially overlapping distributions of items generated during separate and unrelated occupations. **Reoccupation** entails the reuse of a specific place; while reoccupations are separate events, they are not necessarily unrelated, as they often result from the reuse of specific structures, processing features, and other facilities, as well as the possible reuse of lithic materials already there. Multiple occupations seem to characterize the residential locations of foraging groups studied by ethnographers (Yellen 1976:67; Fowler and Fowler 1971:53), while more logistically organized people tend toward more highly overlapped reoccupations (Binford 1978; Hitchcock 1982; Gould 1968).

Tool roles should differ with occupational history, and this difference should be reflected in assemblages resulting from different types of occupations. Site furniture is to be expected in (and may often be the cause of) reoccupations. Storage of site furniture, coupled with the low use rates and long lives of such items, should ensure that furniture frequencies are not directly related to the number of tool users or the frequency of use of a place. In other words, there should not necessarily be any direct relationship between amounts of site furniture and assemblage size. If duration of occupation is measured using such variables as amounts of discarded debitage or expedient implements, frequencies of site furniture should not vary in a regular fashion relative to such measures. These expectations provide a means for identifying site furniture in assemblages and indicate that furniture should be diagnostic of reoccupations.

I have used the caveat "other things being equal" above. Unfortunately, when discussing the relationship between artifact frequency and anything else, frequency itself may not be equal. The amount of culturally modified material found at a place depends not only on intensity or duration of use, of course, but on material economization, reuse, and tool curation. A more general measure of assemblage content is afforded by variety (a simple count of tool types compared to the total number of tools in an assemblage) or diversity (a variety measure corrected for equability or evenness of proportions of each artifact type).

In an obvious way, assemblage variety or diversity measures should be useful in determining which assemblages are more specialized than others; those with low variety or diversity could be the result of only a few specific activities (Larralde 1985). A recurrent theme in recent archaeological literature holds that assemblage variety or diversity is inevitably correlated with assemblage size. While this may be true in a purely statistical sense, this does not mean that one should find a positive ("Yellen model") correlation between variety or diversity and assemblage size in all archaeological situations. In a recent analysis of assemblages from west central New Mexico, Larralde (1985) noted a number of situations in which the relationship between diversity and assemblage size was negatively correlated. She sees these as unexpected and therefore scientifically interesting cases that might indicate intense single or less intense multiple episodes for one or a small number of functions.

Camilli (1983a, 1985, 1988), in fact, proposes three different models of assemblage diversity compared with size.

1. One is a direct or "growth in size:growth in diversity" model, such as that proposed by Yellen (1976) for !Kung Bushmen and Jones et al. (1983) for assemblages in general. This sort of relationship should hold when locations are reused for functionally different purposes. This might be the case at residential camps into which a variety of foraged resources are introduced, where the assemblage should thus increase in variety and size with longer occupation.

2. Another model is a "constant relationship" (Camilli 1983a) or "linear growth model" (Larralde 1988), in which a diversity threshold can be postulated beyond which assemblage size should increase but diversity should not. Such a relationship might be expected in assemblages at special-purpose locations

in logistically organized systems; at these places a number of different activities may be carried out, but they are likely to be related to a small number of subsistence strategies (such as hunting certain animals). In addition, both subsistence and manufacturing activities are planned and partitioned in such a system, with assemblages more directly reflecting tool production strategies rather than simply situational needs.

3. A third model is a "growth in size:decrease in diversity" model, in which the highest frequencies of items in assemblages correlate with the lowest diversities. This sort of relationship would result from processing of single or small numbers of products in a redundant way, possibly during a number of occupations, in conjunction with tool recycling; few formal tools and large amounts of debris therefore might be expected, with continued use of the place contributing to tool specificity rather than heterogeneity. Unfortunately, certain analytical problems may preclude the universal application of formulations that measure diversity across a wide range of spatial assemblage scales. In particular, very small assemblages (in terms of number of items) should be difficult to discriminate among.

An even more complete understanding of different types of occupations requires consideration of measures incorporating the physical areas assemblages occupy. As there are no bounded sites in many situations, it is obvious that the concept of assemblage area is from the outset analytical. The discussions of assemblage content and area-related variables reviewed in this chapter have been based on arbitrary measures of site or "scatter" (Camilli 1983b:1) size. Given the data collected in the course of almost all archaeological surveys, this is a practical direction. Using distributional archaeological data, however, a better way of thinking about assemblages produced by overlapping occupations can be based on scales of content patterning.

The raw frequency of materials compared to scatter size may be significant in inferring the existence of different types of occupations. Simply, multiple occupations, which do not completely or wholly overlap, should be larger than single occupations or reoccupations. In multiple occupations, scatter area and artifact frequency should be closely related. In scatters resulting from reoccupations, the relationship between site area and debris frequency should be dependent on the degree to which

additional space requirements accompanied different occupational episodes. With strictly superimposed distributions, the area may remain
the same while the amount of debris increases, although there is not
necessarily any relationship between site area and amount of debris
(Camilli 1989:10–11). If there are additional space requirements at
subsequent reoccupations, however, site area might increase with debris
frequency in a manner similar to that at multiple occupations.

Differences in artifact and debris density within multiple occupations and reoccupations should be conditioned by the degree of overlap of the distributions from occupational events or activity areas.
Distributions formed by continuous discard with little overlap may have
the same densities as single-occupation sites, while in superimposed
reoccupations (other things being equal) densities should be higher.

A more complex area-to-density measure devised by Camilli (1983a,
1989) for examination of occupational history is density per unit area,
or DPUA. DPUA expresses the relationship between the density of artifacts in an assemblage and its spatial extent. For instance, two clusters
of artifacts might have similar densities, but one could be twice the
size of the other. The larger "scatter" would have half the density per
unit area of the smaller one. Low measures of DPUA should be the
result of multiple instead of single occupations, because multiple occupations probably do not overlap wholly and thus should increase in
area without building up higher densities of occupational debris. Superimposed distributions from reoccupations should have higher DPUAs
than single occupations.

ASSEMBLAGE CONTENTS OF SYSTEMS COMPONENTS

The final section of this chapter lists types of systems components—
"sites" in a living sense—that could result from each of the four strategies postulated for the southwestern Wyoming study area. From this
we may develop some expectations about distinguishing differences in
assemblage content; these expectations may further be segregated in
terms of the middle-range arguments discussed previously.

The Four Strategies

Four systemic strategies have been suggested as probable or at least
possible in the Green River Basin.

1. High year-round residential mobility with serially occupied camps from which only foraging trips are made
   a. short-term residential bases, likely reoccupied annually
   b. foraging locations, probably not reused in any sense but continuously distributed throughout foraging radius
2. Seasonal fusion and fission, with large multifamily residential camps occupied during the winter, from which foraging and logistic forays are launched; during the rest of the year, single-family residential foraging groups
   a. large, multifamily residential bases, reoccupied annually
   b. foraging locations within their foraging radii, continuously distributed
   c. logistic locations associated with these seasonal residential bases, probably reoccupied annually or more often
   d. during the other part of the year, under family residential mobility, like 1a and 1b above
3. A system of large permanent residential bases and highly specific, redundantly used logistic field camps and locations
   a. large residential base camps, permanently occupied
   b. year-round foraging locations within foraging radius of these permanent camps; relatively continuous but low-density use
   c. year-round logistic camps, almost certainly reoccupied for redundant functions or a small group of functions
4. Temporary camps of highly mobile people "passing through" the area; as a component, temporary "logistic" staging-type travel locations with little procurement activities of any sort in the area

Types of "Sites"

The component types listed above under each possible systemic strategy type condense into seven different categories:

1. short-term residential foraging bases (1a, 2d);
2. foraging locations (1b, 2b, 2d, 3b);
3. semipermanent or seasonal multifamily residential bases (2a);
4. permanent multifamily residential bases (3a);
5. logistic locations used from semipermanent, seasonal residential bases (2c);

6. logistic locations used from permanent residential bases (3c); and
7. traveling camps (4a).

Assemblage Contents

Table 6.2 lists some expectations about assemblage content for each of the seven component types above. They are arranged according to the middle-range research areas discussed previously in this chapter. Not all of these sets of expectations—or, necessarily, any of them—are perfectly represented by any assemblage content measures. Just as systems can contain mixes of strategies, so can the assemblages they produce. Even single-episode occupations may contain portions of several strategies or purposes; multiple occupations, as discussed previously, are quite likely to for functionally different reasons. What is more, overlap of materials left by different components of one sort of system, or even components of more than one type of system, may occur in many places.

There are several general things that quickly become apparent from Table 6.2. First, it should be noted that different systems contain some components that cut across system boundaries. Foraging locations, for instance, should occur in almost all possible adaptations, with the possible exception of that partially represented by traveling camps. Short-term, residential foraging bases should be found year-round in one adaptation, and seasonally (spring and fall) in another. In contrast, the "logistic locations" class has been separated into two types: logistic locations associated with semipermanent seasonal bases, and logistic locations from permanent, year-round bases, as these may result in different sorts of assemblage contents.

Most schemes for separating functionally different assemblages concentrate on the formal nature of artifacts; in Table 6.2, the major difference between lithic technology in assemblages from different sorts of system components is the degree and manner of utilization of local and nonlocal raw materials, and the presence of site furniture. These variables are conditioned by the extent of systemic mobility and the degree to which places are revisited and reused for planned purposes.

Time utility and stress is seen in the archaeological record as complexity or its absence and as specificity or generality of tool kits. Caching is also an important measure of time stress, and may affect assemblage content in a somewhat counterintuitive way. The most complex assemblages may be those at semipermanent multifamily base camps, because the adaptive system of which these are a part also involves a completely different, contrasting sort of subsistence strategy and mobility during other parts of the year. Conducting a dual strategy within each annual cycle would require maintaining two separate tool kits, with far more complex manufacturing and caching activities than should be found in annual base camps.

The appearance of staged manufacture is probably one of the most straightforward sets of expectations to operationalize, with variability among locations being a far more important statistic than a simple list of stages found in an assemblage. The differentiation of manufacturing stages as seen in separate assemblages should be controlled, in general, by the degree of mobility involved in the logistic components of a system, the redundancy of travel routes, and variability in time stress, providing down time interspersed with the procurement of specific resources.

Table 6.2. Archaeological assemblage content expectations for seven Green River Basin occupation types.

Short-term foraging base [1a, 2d]	Foraging location [1b, 2b, 3b, 2d]	Semipermanent multifamily base [2a]	Permanent multifamily base [3a]	Logistic locations: from semipermanent seasonal bases [2c]	Logistic locations: from permanent year-round base camps [3c]	Travelling camps [4a]
			STAGED MANUFACTURE			
all stages of manufacturing, mostly local materials	early stages, mostly situational tools very late stages, economizing for tools from non local materials (manufactured from personal gear)	local material: all stages nonlocal material: possibly not early stages	all stages of lithic manufacture represented for all materials	middle and late manufacturing stages present	highly specific later manufacturing stages (high variety of stages)	mostly only late manufacturing stages, from nonlocal material only early stages from local material
			OCCUPATIONAL HISTORY			
high resolution	high variability among assemblages	moderate interassemblage variability	low resolution	high resolution	high resolution	high resolution
low internal variability	*Single Occupations*	internally complex (caching)	low interassemblage variability	high interassemblage variability	moderate interassemblage variability	low interassemblage variability
internally simple assemblages	low assemblage diversity	*Reoccupations*	internally complex	*Multiple Occupations*	may be internally complex	*Single or Multiple Occupations*
Multiple Occupations	small or continuous scatters	very high assemblage diversity	"*Reoccupations*"	moderate assemblage diversity	*Reoccupations*	low assemblage diversity
low assemblage diversity			moderate assemblage		low assemblage diversity?	

(continued)

Table 6.2. (continued)

Short-term foraging base [1a, 2d]	Foraging location [1b, 2b, 3b, 2d]	Semipermanent multifamily base [2a]	Permanent multi-family base [3a]	Logistic locations: from semipermanent seasonal bases [2c]	Logistic locations: from permanent year-round base camps [3c]	Travelling camps [4a]
growth in size: growth in diversity model		constant relationship between assemblage size and diversity (threshold model)	diversity [special case of animal drives: very low assemblage diversity]	direct size: diversity relationship model	constant (threshold) size: diversity model	constant (threshold) size: diversity model
			constant size: diversity—threshold low?	area and amount of debris positively correlated	area remains the same, amount of debris increases	area increases, amount of debris increases
			GENERAL TECHNOLOGY			
personal and situational tools: all stages	situational tools only—broken personal gear?	personal, situational tool manufacture: all stages and worn out or broken tools	personal, situational gear manufacture: all stages and worn out, broken tools	situational gear: from local material or personal gear	situational gear from local material and personal gear	situational gear from local material and recycled personal gear
raw materials relatively "local," economizing of nonlocal materials	no site furniture	raw materials: probably wide range, little "economizing," even during early stages of manufacture	raw material: probably wide range, little "economizing"	middle and late stages of manufacture using recycled nonlocal material	staged manufacture, nonlocal material, middle and late stages and recycling	not so much staged manufacture—only late stages, extremely "nonlocal" material from personal gear only
portable technology: bifaces, core carrying			much site furniture	highly specialized technology: blades, bifaces?	much site furniture	
bipolar techniques of manufacture		site furniture expected		some site furniture		no site furniture
little site furniture						

Table 6.2. (*continued*)

Short-term foraging base [1a, 2d]	Foraging location [1b, 2b, 3b, 2d]	Semipermanent multifamily base [2a]	Permanent multi-family base [3a]	Logistic locations: from semipermanent seasonal bases [2c]	Logistic locations: from permanent year-round base camps [3c]	Travelling camps [4a]
			TIME UTILITY AND STRESS			
relatively simple, general tool kits or high variability in complexity of tool kits among assemblages	high variability in tool kit complexity	time stress, highly complex tool kit	time stress evidenced by highly complex tool kit	staged manufacture	staged manufacture during down time	very high tool kit complexity, but probably not represented in discard
general purpose tools dominant	general purpose tools, expedient	special purpose tools in use	special purpose tools	caching but not necessarily specific to that location	high tool kit complexity	no tool caching
little or no tool caching	no tool caching	general purpose tools/other special purpose tools cached	no tool caching—but many stored raw materials, tools in different manufacturing stages		much tool caching, specific to that location	

7

DISTRIBUTIONAL FIELDWORK:

AN EXAMPLE FROM

SOUTHWESTERN WYOMING

-- -- -- -- -- -- -- -- -- -- -- -- --

This chapter outlines the details of a distributional archaeological survey designed to explore some of the propositions set forth in previous chapters and to provide data with which the analytical potential of survey results may be examined. An unfortunate fact of survey archaeology is that information gathered during the course of one survey can rarely be compared with data from another. This may be in part because each archaeological situation and survey area is unique. It probably has as much or more to do, however, with the fact that there is no uniformity in, nor are there often even attempts at controls on, the ways that archaeologists find and measure the archaeological record.

As the result of long discussions with colleagues at the University of New Mexico, I (and at least some of them) became convinced that in order to understand the surface archaeological record a survey methodology that completely ignores "sites" was necessary. The entirety of the archaeological record that can be discovered within relatively large, contiguous portions of the landscape needs to be located, its constituents (artifacts, not sites) must be mapped with relation to one another, and relevant characteristics of these materials must be recorded in a consistent manner. We had heard about and investigated previous surveys that sounded as though they fulfilled these requirements, and found that most of them focussed only on densities of items, made use of unspecified or unintensive discovery procedures, or were directed toward sampling small and often inconsistent portions of very large areas.

An opportunity to design a survey that met our own requirements arose in early 1983, when the Bureau of Reclamation contacted the National Park Service's Remote Sensing Division to request help with a Class I survey of about 185,000 acres around and below the Fontenelle Reservoir, and surrounding the Seedskadee National Wildlife Refuge on the Green River in southwestern Wyoming. The Bureau of Reclamation was interested in a "predictive model," based on existing site data and guided by remote sensing, that would aid in planning future surveys in this area. In order to check the results of the remote-sensing-aided predictive model, a "ground truth survey of a small sample of the project area" (Ebert 1982:1) was also proposed. The Seedskadee survey described here evolved from that "ground truth" survey. Support for this survey, which I acknowledge thankfully, was provided by the Bureau of Reclamation through the National Park Service. Although I designed the survey method, it was put into operation and directed in all phases by LuAnn Wandsnider and Signa Larralde, then employed by Chambers Consultants and Planners of Albuquerque.

THE STUDY AREA

The study area lies in the Green River Basin in southwestern Wyoming between 41°35′ and 42°12′ north latitude, and 109°25′ and 110°13′ west longitude (Fig. 7.1). The area, drained by the Green River and for the most part between 2,000 and 2,700m in elevation, is located between the upthrust belts of the Wind River and Gros Ventre Mountains and is bounded by a low divide from the Washakie and Great Divide Basins to the east (Knight 1950).

The mountain ranges in the region are composed of Precambrian sediments surrounded by more recent Cambrian to Cretaceous rocks. The strata of the Green River Basin itself are superimposed on Cretaceous rocks, and consist of poorly cemented Eocene lacustrine and fluvial beds made up predominantly of sandstones and shales. These sediments were dissected during the late Tertiary and Pleistocene, creating a landscape dominated by stepped terraces capped with gravels. Fluvial, aeolian, and gravitational processes have further altered the landscape in post-Pleistocene times, giving rise to a varied and diverse topography when considered on a small scale.

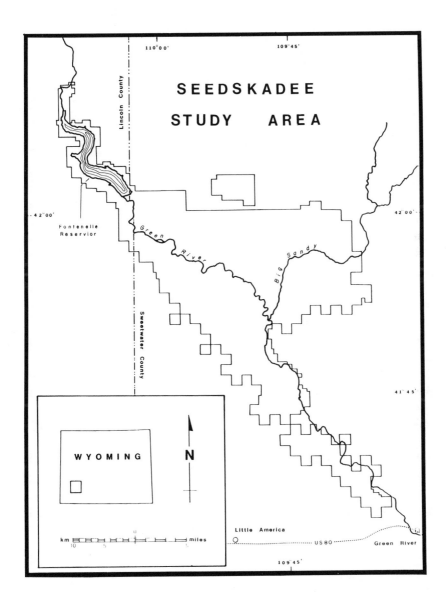

Figure 7.1.

The Green River Basin is semiarid today and probably has been for some time, receiving generally less than 400 to 500mm of rainfall annually. Even on high plateaus and slopes vegetation is quite sparse, usually covering not more than 20 percent of the ground surface. A more detailed account of the nature and diversity of the topography in the study area can be found in a discussion of geomorphic mapping later in this chapter.

Steward classified the Green River Basin, along with most of southwestern Wyoming, as "Upper Sonoran Zone: Artemesia Belt" (Steward 1938:17), characterizing it as an area of xerophytic flora and few or sparse grasses, dominated by northern desert shrubs including sagebrush, little sagebrush, little rabbitbrush, shadscale, and winterfat, none of which he felt were important aboriginal food sources. He observed that grasses are now found predominantly along stream margins, but may have been more prevalent in areas now covered by rabbitbrush and shadscale prior to grazing by cattle and sheep. This description is probably attributable at least in part to Steward's overall inclination to see the Great Basin as impoverished; grasses, especially thickspike wheatgrass (*Agropyron dasystachyum*), Indian ricegrass (*Oryzopsis hymenoides*), bluebunch wheatgrass (*Agropyron spicatum*), and Sandberg bluegrass (*Poa sandbergii*) grow along with big sagebrush (*Artemesia tridentata*), Gardner saltbrush (*Atriplex* spp.), and winterfat (*Eurotia ceratoides*) throughout the basin, joined by cottonwood (*Populus* spp.) in the riverine lowlands and juniper (*Juniperus* spp.) on ridges and hillsides (Treat et al. 1982:24). Long lists of edible plants and plants otherwise useful to the aboriginal population can be found in Treat et al. (1982), Zier and Peebles (1982), and Reynolds (1983). Some of the animal species that could have been exploited in the past are discussed in Chapter 4, and the above references also include extensive faunal species lists.

"SAMPLE" DESIGN

An unstratified random sampling design was employed to distribute 30 sample units 500 meters square within the Bureau of Reclamation's survey area. This was accomplished by superimposing a grid of 500-by-500m squares (61.77 acres), numbered by rows and columns, on a 1:2,000,000 scale map and choosing random row and column numbers for sample squares. Sampling was by replacement, giving each grid square an equal chance of being chosen, and units were surveyed in the order in which they were chosen. This sort of probabilistic sample allows the prediction of statistics descriptive of characteristics of the universe from which the sample units were drawn (Mueller 1974). The random sample covered slightly more than one percent of the study area, about 750ha or 1853.1 acres. Due to time and funding constraints only 25 of the units were surveyed (625ha).

Neither the choice of sample unit locations nor the sampling fraction is important in the research and conclusions discussed here. I shall not regard the data collected during the Seedskadee survey as any sort of statistical sample, but rather as a record of all cultural items located during intensive survey within relatively large contiguous portions of the landscape. The important sample property, then, was the size and shape of the sample units. A unit size of 500-by-500m was chosen because it was believed that squares this size would cover many times the dimensions of artifact patterning that should take place as a result of specific cultural events, or the occupation, multiple occupation, or reoccupation of single places. Larger contiguous areas might be even better choices for this sort of survey; 800-by-800m areas have been used in at least one recent distributional survey with promising results (Camilli et al. 1985).

Survey unit locations were transferred from the 1:2,000,000 scale map to 1:24,000 U.S. Geological Survey quadrangle maps and 1:80,000 black-and-white aerial photographs, to aid in their location in the field.

FIELD METHODS

The Seedskadee survey was conducted during July and August of 1983 with a crew of ten to eleven people who expended a total of 369 person-days of effort. Fieldwork was undertaken in three phases: artifact discovery, mapping, and attribute coding.

Artifact Discovery

The first step in artifact discovery is locating each sample unit in the field. One corner was located and staked, and then the sides and other corners located using a compass and 100m tape. Two opposite sides of each square were marked at 25m intervals with blue pinflags to serve as a guide for transect control. Two to four such units can be set up in this manner per day.

The discovery crew was composed of five people who, guided by the pinflags along opposite sides of the units, walked parallel 5m transects. Each discovery crew member flagged each artifact or feature found within the 5m-wide transect with an orange pinflag, and counted each flag put down with a tally counter. At the end of each 500m sweep these counts were noted, as well as time and general conditions of terrain, light, weather, and so on. The discovery crew was able to cover about one sample unit per day in this manner.

Mapping

Following discovery, one or both of the other two survey phases was carried out. The mapping phase consisted of measuring the three-dimensional point location of each flagged artifact, as well as mapping the sample unit corners and their relationship to the nearest survey benchmark. The mapping crew consisted of at least two members: an instrument person and a rod person, and sometimes a third who would write down instrument readings as they were called out, thus saving operator time. A Leitz-Sokkisha electronic distance measuring (EDM) theodolite was used to measure distance (to the nearest centimeter) and vertical and horizontal angles (to the nearest second), over distances as great as 1.7km, as the rod person held a range pole and corner prism above each flag. Instrument accuracy allows the "worst case" measurement of point locations—that is, across the 707.1m diagonal of a square—to within a 5cm cube. Most shots were much shorter and therefore more accurate than this figure. Flags were numbered consecutively as shots were taken, with numbers communicated by radio to the instrument person. In many cases only one instrument station was used, but topography required several on some survey units. In all, 6,045 artifact locations were mapped in this way.

Due to the high density of artifacts in some areas, a grid recording system was used to place artifact proveniences within 1-by-1m grid squares. Another 10,073 artifacts were mapped in 48 grids with variable numbers of 1-by-1m squares. Corners of the grids were also mapped in with the EDM and tied to the closest benchmark or benchmarks.

Attribute Recording

The attribute recording crew was composed of three experienced lithic analysts. When the recording crew preceded the mapping crew into a discovered unit they marked numbers on the orange pinflags. In addition, recording crew members carried red pinflags with which they marked additional artifacts they found. These were, of course, mostly found in areas where the recording crew spent the most time, that is in areas where large number of orange-flagged items were. Attributes coded for each artifact will be discussed and described at the conclusion of this chapter. Artifact attributes were recorded on Fortran coding forms and feature attributes on feature description forms.

The number of people working on the mapping and recording crews was flexible, allowing additional crew members to be used for mapping when artifact attribute recording was slow, and vice versa. As the work of the discovery crew was relatively fast, they joined the mapping and especially attribute recording crews from time to time when several units had been "discovered" and were awaiting mapping and recording.

EXPERIMENTAL CONTROLS

Prior to the initiation of field activities, it was decided to incorporate three experimental controls into the Seedskadee survey. Two of these were methodological, having to do with the accuracy and consistency of the discovery process and artifact attribute coding. The third was an experiment in mapping and measuring surface geomorphological processes that might affect the visibility and integrity of the surface archaeological record. These experiments will be the subject of more concentrated work in the near future by other authors, and I shall review them only briefly here, although the geomorphic characteristics of different sample units will figure in the discussion of spatial analysis in Chapter 7. Detailed accounts of the methodological experiments and their results can be found in Larralde (1984), Wandsnider and Larralde (1984), and Wandsnider (1984), while the geomorphological mapping experiment is discussed by Wandsnider and Ebert (1983).

Discovery Accuracy Experiment

In an attempt to assess the effectiveness and accuracy of the discovery procedure used in the Seedskadee survey, particularly the completeness of recovery given the relatively intense 5m survey interval, an artifact seeding experiment was conducted in one of the survey units. This experiment took place approximately midway during the survey, after discovery crew members had had a chance to become accustomed to the surface conditions in the study area and to a survey method that was new to many of them. The experiment was designed to assess how much of the archaeological record in any of the areas might have been missed by the survey crew, and additionally in what circumstances items remained undiscovered.

One of the survey units, Unit 24, was seeded with 202 modern, introduced artifacts or control items: 107 washers 1.5cm in diameter and 95 concrete nails 5cm long. Washers and nails were chosen because they have nonnatural shapes, just as many older, prehistoric or historic artifacts do, and these shapes aid in their recognition. Sixty of the washers were painted a light buff color similar to that of surface sediments in the survey unit and 47 were painted flat black; 58 of the nails were buff and 37 black. Unit 24 is a relatively unspectacular area containing small arroyos, an alluvial flat dominated by sheetwash processes and greasewood, and a gentle rise covered with grass and sagebrush on one side. Vegetation was sparse except atop the rise. Sediments are consolidated, so no footprints were left during the seeding operation to provide clues to the discovery crew.

The control items were distributed throughout the unit, without the knowledge of the discovery crew, in two basic ways: in clusters and individually. All of the isolated control items and the centers of the clusters were mapped with the EDM. Two days later the discovery crew was informed at breakfast that they were to flag washers and nails in addition to "real" artifacts in Unit 24.

A total of 133, or 66 percent, of the control items was discovered by the crew. This number included 70 percent of the washers seeded and 61 percent of the nails; in terms of color, 60 percent of the buff control items were found while 71 percent of the black items were. Far more interesting than these figures is the fact that while only 22 percent of the isolated control items were discovered, 80 percent of the clustered ones were. There is also a strong correlation between the percentage of items within each cluster that were found and the density of the clusters. While most of the seeded items were discovered by the discovery crew, the recording crew accounted for approximately 10 percent of the discoveries.

One obvious conclusion to be drawn from this experiment is that for some reason people find more items in clusters than when these are isolated. Although it is probably human nature to look harder in a place where other things already have been found, it might also be that archaeologists have convinced themselves that artifacts occur in bounded clusters that are intrinsically sites. In effect, we may manufacture such clusters, even in situations where the archaeological record is continuous. Additional experiments with truly random and even distributions of control items might help bear this conclusion out.

What solutions are there to this problem? The proportion of the archaeological record that is discovered might be increased in a number of ways. More intensive survey, or surveying each unit twice, might be possible. Paying crew members per artifact discovered rather than by the hour might even help! Factors that control discovery may be natural (lighting conditions, weather) or inherent in the crew (attitude, eyesight, recent partying), however, and will vary from situation to situation. A better solution might be to provide a means of controlling for discovery rates in all distributional surveys; this could entail the systematic seeding of every area surveyed.

Lithic Recording Precision Experiment

While the seeding experiment described above was designed to test the accuracy of discovery, another Seedskadee survey experiment was devised to test the precision or consistency of the recording of attributes of lithic materials. Most archaeological analysts accept the consistency of lithic attribute coding without question, but it has been demonstrated that even a single coder changes measurement criteria over time (Fish 1978). This is compounded, of course, when more than one coder is involved, and particularly when many coders are used over long periods, such as when artifacts are collected, brought back to the laboratory, and measured over the years by dozens of students. Categories used in artifact attribute measurements are analytical constructs, and never "true" or inherent, so there is virtually no way to ensure consistency other than through constant checks or other ways of discovering biases.

The great majority of the lithic artifacts measured and coded for attribute states in the Seedskadee survey were handled by three data recorders. All artifacts were coded in the field, with the recorders working closely together, over the short period of only ten weeks. All coders had considerable previous experience in lithic analysis, and upon entering the field in Wyoming they trained in pairs for several days. The Seedskadee lithic data is probably a best case example of coding precision. In order to determine just what this level of precision was, a lithic test assemblage was manufactured and two hundred items were chosen from it to be coded by each of the three recording crew members. Some cryptocrystalline rocks that had angular shapes but were not fractured by man were included. Coders were instructed to code these items using the forms and conventions of the Seedskadee survey, both of which had been tested in the laboratory for their workability prior to the survey.

The results, which are reported in detail by Larralde (1984), suggest that while coders are quite consistent in their measurements of continuous variables such as size, and only slightly less so in estimates of ordinal variables such as percentage of cortical cover or dorsal flake scars, they may agree far less on measurements of nominal scale variables, for instance the discrimination of angular debris, or number of striking platforms per flake. The precision of measurement of seven noncontinuous variables ranged from 9.3 to 34.7 percent disagreement among the three coders.

At first this might be taken to mean that the Seedskadee data are at least partially suspect, but it should be remembered that the data may be far more precise than many other lithic attribute coding efforts carried out using more coders, untested forms, ambiguous definitions, and over far longer periods. Like discovery proportions, coding precision does not render data either true or false, it is merely something else that needs to be controlled for. I suggest that this is something that all archaeologists need to concern themselves with in all projects.

Mapping of Surface Processes

In Chapter 1, I argue that natural, cultural, and methodological junctures lie between the systemic behavior of past people and our interpretation and understanding of this behavior through the archaeological record. The two experiments described above were directed toward illustrating and controlling for methodological biases that can alter this understanding; a third experiment carried out in conjunction with the Seedskadee survey was designed to help gauge the effects of natural, depositional and postdepositional processes on the archaeological record.

While the geomorphological processes responsible for the nature and dynamics of surface and immediately subsurface sediments, and thus the archaeological record, are increasingly recognized as important by archaeologists (for instance, Foley 1981a, b; Gifford 1981; Kornfeld

1982; Rick 1976; Wood and Johnson 1978), there is seldom any attempt to assess the effects of natural processes on the archaeological record in any specific place. This is probably because of the difficulty of mapping and classifying the nature and extent of these processes.

The geomorphological mapping experiment carried out during the Seedskadee survey had two objectives: to derive information that could be applied to the understanding of the natural component of patterning in the Seedskadee distributional data; and in a more general way to explore methods by which archaeologists can quickly and effectively come to some understanding of depositional and postdepositional processes. Geomorphological mapping in the Seedskadee survey and its implications for analysis of the archaeological record are being explored in depth by LuAnn Wandsnider (Wandsnider and Ebert 1983c) and will be described only briefly here.

The Seedskadee project area and surrounding areas, totaling approximately 559,000ha (1,380,000 acres) were examined using remote sensor data, primarily a 1:100,000 enlargement from a single Landsat multispectral scanner color composite scene, and 1:80,000 stereo black-and-white aerial photographs. Using these two complementary data sets, boundaries of areas in which different geomorphological surface processes are dominant were drawn on a 1:100,000 map (an enlargement of the base map used during the choice of sample unit locations). Fifteen geomorphological zones were identified, falling under six major headings (Fig. 7.2).

1. *Terraces* formed by fluvial processes, of varying degrees of activity, on relatively flat surfaces, within which channel and overbank deposition and sheetwash are dominant processes

2. *Playas and flats* consisting of flat areas of slow deposition of fine sediments alternating with aeolian erosion

3. *Dunes*, which in the study area consist not of continuous fields but are interspersed throughout badlands, flats, along watercourses, and at mesatop scarps where wind velocity changes cause sediments to be dropped

4. *Badlands* consisting of eroded shales with dense, reticulate drainages, interspersed with flats and dunes

5. *Mesatops* or dissected remnants of earlier surfaces, capped with resistant gravels

6. *Agricultural areas,* which are extensively levelled and

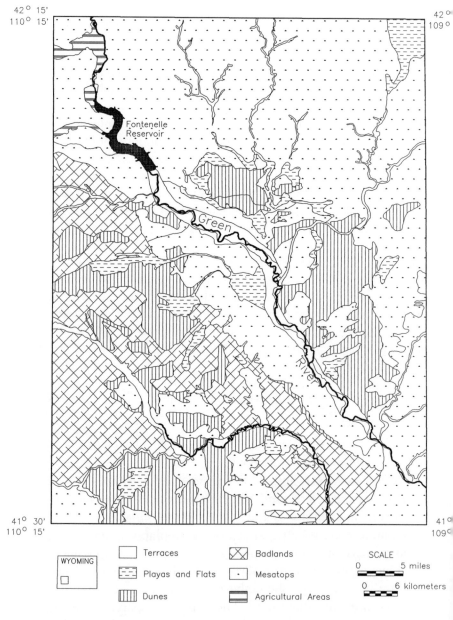

Figure 7.2. Geomorphological surface process areas in the Seedskadee study area, compiled through aerial photointerpretation and digital image analysis.

disturbed, and probably need no further archaeological consideration. In some parts of the country, archaeologists have used the fact of agricultural plowing to great advantage in discovering artifacts in areas of otherwise prohibitive ground cover. The Seedskadee agricultural areas, however, were designed to be irrigated by waters impounded by the Fontenelle Dam, and were formed by wholesale earth moving.

The dominant geomorphological processes in each of these zones were characterized, and this information has been presented in detail elsewhere (Wandsnider and Ebert 1983a, 1985). In the course of the Seedskadee survey it was found that this geomorphological classification had immediately apparent implications for understanding the general appearance of the archaeological record from place to place. In areas of sediment deposition, such as active terraces and slopes at mesa edges, few artifacts were discovered; the relatively inactive mesatops exhibited artifacts and features in many instances, but visibility there was low due to dense gravel cover. Dune and badland areas had, in many cases, spectacularly high artifact densities. In dunes, artifacts may be quickly and gently deposited after they are dropped, preserved with relative spatial integrity, and exposed with regularity, to the advantage of the archaeologist.

Of course the high densities of artifacts found in these areas obviously reflect the intensive use of these places. Other places, however, where postdepositional processes have resulted in the encapsulation of archaeological materials within sediments and where they thus cannot all be seen during surface discovery, may contain just as many artifacts as do badlands and dunes. They may or may not have been just as intensively occupied or used. Those authors who record high densities of artifacts in sand dunes and then infer that large, long-term camps were placed there because these are "good places to stay," need only camp in such a place to be disabused of their notion. (Although perhaps not. One survey report from Wyoming—which I shall not identify here to spare its writers public embarrassment—notes large numbers of artifacts in a sand dune field. The authors, apparently having once tried camping in dunes, wonder at length about why people would have placed their largest camps there—and especially why they would camp mostly on the windward side of the dunes!)

Other observations made on the basis of this mapping experiment were not so encouraging, however. In many units it appeared that the scale of geomorphological processes affecting the patterning of the archaeological record—for instance, the natural bounding of scatters imposed by dune edges—is probably very close to the scale of ethnographically documented debris scatters. The scale of mapping that was possible using Landsat images and small-scale aerial photographs, therefore, is probably too gross to provide any sort of control on the patterning of items even within the 500-by-500m units. Photointerpretation of newly available 1:12,000 scale aerial photographs of the Seedskadee survey units (Wandsnider n.d.) has shown that larger-scale aerial photos can be used to map differential surface processes within areas of this size, with discrimination of only a few meters in some cases.

GENERAL RESULTS OF THE SEEDSKADEE SURVEY

Although the analysis and interpretation of Seedskadee survey data will be dealt with on a more detailed level in the next chapter, a few very general results of this distributional survey were strikingly apparent even during fieldwork. The first of these is that when one looks for artifacts as if they might be anywhere they are everywhere. Only two of the survey units contained very few lithic artifacts, and there were cultural materials in all of the geomorphological zones inspected. On average, artifacts occurred at quite low densities, about 0.03 per square meter, a figure comparable to that estimated by Foley and discussed in Chapter 2.

Another immediate conclusion is that a distributional survey strategy such as that used here can result in very high information yields when compared to site-oriented survey. In a period of approximately seven 10-person weeks 17,000 artifacts were discovered, their locations very accurately mapped, and their formal attributes coded. To gain some perspective, the approximately 170,000 spatial and formal artifact attributes gathered were compared with the information produced each time a site is recorded. In Wyoming, as in several other Great Basin states, the state archaeologist requires site data to be recorded on the Intermountain Antiquities Computer System (IMACS) site form (University of Utah 1983). This form is long, complex, and arranged so that entries can be quickly computerized. The information that can be included and encoded on an IMACS form was counted, and it was calculated that the 170,000 Seedskadee attributes contained information equivalent to 3,300 IMACS forms. In other words, in order to derive as much information as provided through the coding of the 17,000 Seedskadee artifacts, a site survey would have to locate and complete IMACS forms for 528 sites per square kilometer there. Distributional archaeology costs more than site survey per unit area, but perhaps not per unit of archaeological information recovered.

An immediate, pragmatic observation is that a multicomponent crew organization such as that used in the Seedskadee survey allowed each group to work at its own rate, greatly increasing the flexibility and thus the speed and effectiveness of this sort of survey—at least per unit of information gained—over that of traditional survey, in which, when a site is found, everyone leaves his transects and converges to help guess at largely indefinable site dimensions and other characteristics (Plog, Plog, and Wait 1978).

MEASUREMENT AND CODING OF ARTIFACT ATTRIBUTES

Seedskadee lithic data were recorded on Fortran coding sheets using an attribute coding template for chipped and ground stone. A ceramics coding form was also taken into the field but was not used, as no ceramics were found. The chipped and ground stone coding categories, definitions, and format were derived from previous sources, primarily Camilli (1983a) and Camilli and Nelson (1983), with the object of yielding information regarding reduction stages, artifact breakage, and use or wear, as well as allowing the discrimination of artifact types, edge treatment, and recycling. The forms and definitions were tested in the laboratory, using lithic collections, for workability prior to field use by Eileen Camilli, Signa Larralde, and LuAnn Wandsnider. Information categories were designed for computer entry. The information categories coded and their identifiers are listed in Appendix A.

After the first few units had been surveyed and mapped, and the lithic attributes measured and coded, it became apparent that the large number of artifacts and the relatively comprehensive data recording undertaken for each artifact would require (1) a sampling approach within units; (2) reducing the number of units to be surveyed; (3) reducing the number of measurements taken on artifacts, or some combination thereof. As the object of distributional survey is to discover, map, and analyze all cultural materials (artifacts and their attributes) over contiguous areas, and not simply to guess at what is there, the sampling approach was rejected. In addition, data collected from several units was inspected statistically, and it was found that weight—which was being measured with small, sensitive spring scales by the recording crew, a time-consuming procedure—was closely correlated with a measure of artifact size. Weighing artifacts was thenceforth discontinued at substantial saving in time.

8

EXPLORING SCALES OF PATTERNING
IN THE ARCHAEOLOGICAL RECORD
WITH DISTRIBUTIONAL DATA

-- -- -- -- -- -- -- -- -- -- -- -- --

Obviously, almost any artifact-based analysis that has been suggested
and performed by archaeologists can be applied to data collected during intensive surface survey. Most surface survey data are not collected
at artifact-level resolution, but data of high resolution are often collected during excavations. In many excavations, artifacts are point-
plotted or segregated in small grid units. A short survey of some recent
analytical goals advanced by archaeologists using excavation data illustrates the range of analyses that have been suggested as appropriate
for application to high-resolution archaeological data.

INTUITIVE OR SEMIANALYTICAL APPROACHES TO
PATTERN ANALYSIS

Before examining truly quantitative approaches to spatial pattern analysis, it is worthwhile to touch upon the sort of semianalysis that is
common in archaeology today. Encouraged by increasingly sophisticated computer graphics packages, such semianalytical approaches are
literally quantitative, as they are based in part upon numbers of items
and their locations. In what is probably the most common approach,
the locations of items (artifacts or sites) are represented on a map of
the study area (survey area, site). In a variant that is rapidly gain-

ing popularity, densities are derived from the locations of all or different sorts of mapped archaeological items and represented as contours or surfaces.

That an experienced archaeologist can look at an array of points or a representation of densities, recognize clustering, the association of artifact types, and other spatial patterning in these data, and interpret the past is an appealing idea. We have all thought along these lines many times in our archaeological careers, but is not always easy or even possible to interpret spatial patterning in such an expert manner. Even if the patterning that can be recorded in the archaeological record actually represented frozen moments in the past (which it does not), this would be the case. This is because the recognition and the definition of spatial clustering, the association of artifacts with one another, associations between different types of artifacts, and patterning in derived measures such as density and diversity are wholly dependent upon the scales and resolutions at which patterns are observed.

The reason we cannot reliably recognize spatial clustering is that we are not able to comprehend patterns visually at a wide range of scales at one time. It is essentially a hardware problem. Just as individual streets and houses cannot be represented on a map of an entire state, we are physically restricted in our ability to represent and interpret nested scales of spatial patterning.

Figure 8.1 illustrates the locations of chert and quartzite artifacts (represented by crosses and triangles respectively) in survey unit 28, a 500-by-500m square surveyed during the course of the Seedskadee project. Figure 8.1a is an index map showing the subareas illustrated in the succeeding figures as the study unit and its artifact distributions are progressively "zoomed in on."

In Figure 8.1b the distribution of chert and quartzite items in the entire survey unit is shown, with the index map superimposed. One can discern five or perhaps six places where the symbols cluster strongly, in fact overprinting to form dark patches where patterning is indistinguishable. It is interesting to note that these major clusters appear to be on the order of one hundred meters in diameter, and to think about what this could mean in an area said to have been used only by small groups of hunter-gatherers.

In each progressively higher-resolution figure, patterning at smaller scales can be discerned, but of course the lower-resolution patterning visible in the preceding figure is obscured. In Figures 8.1c and d (250 and 100m square), it becomes apparent that there is subclustering within the major clusters, and that chert and quartzite may be clustered at different places. At 50 and 25m resolutions (Figs. 8.1e and f), the overall distribution of items seems almost uniform. This is approximately the sample unit size at which hunter-gather camps described by ethnographers should be distinctly discernible. In Figures 8.1g and h (10 and 5m square), virtually nothing that could be called clustering or even patterning is detectable. Ten meters is about the maximum window perceived by an archaeologist walking a survey transect on the ground. The Seedskadee survey crew walked and searched for artifacts in 5m transects. Virtually no patterning of even the simplest sort is measurable or interpretable at this small scale.

A somewhat different approach to interpreting distributions visually, illustrating the futility of trying to do so, is demonstrated in Figures 8.2a–f, a representation of a surface defined by densities of artifacts in Unit 28. The data used to create each surface in the figures are the same; the only difference is the exaggeration of the z-axis, which represents the density of artifacts per square meter. The maximum density of artifacts found within 5-by-5m subunits of Unit 28 is 0.9 per square meter, which at the scale at which the 500m square unit is represented would not be discernible at all given an unexaggerated z-scale.

In Figures 8.2a and b, in which the z-scale is exaggerated by factors of 25 and 50, the six clusters distinguishable in the largest-scale "zoom views" (Fig. 8.1) appear as small topographic highs. These might be interpreted as six sites, were one presented with these data at this resolution. The picture begins to change, however, as the z-scale exaggeration is increased in the succeeding figures. When the z-scale is exaggerated by a factor of 200 (Fig. 8.2c), it is clear that there is density patterning between the previously discrete highs, in some cases perhaps altering the perception that they are separate. Are some of the previously distinguished bumps really part of the same "site?" The clusters that seemed discrete in the early frames of Figure 8 appear to coalesce as the z-scale is exaggerated by a factor of 500 (Figure 8.2d). When the z-scale is exaggerated by factors of 1,000 and 3,000 the peaks are lost (another hardware problem!) but are quite obviously meaningless anyway. There is continuous density patterning throughout the entire 500m square survey unit at these resolutions.

In Figures 8.3a–c, densities of artifacts in Unit 28 are again represented, this time with isopleths or contour lines. Densities between 0 and 0.9 artifacts per square meter are shown at 5 items per m^2 contour intervals in Figure 8.3a, and several distinct density peaks are separated by areas of low density (between 0 and 0.05 artifacts per square meter). Figure 8.3b shows the same contour lines as does 8.3a, with the addition of dots representing the centers of 10m square grid cells that contain at least one artifact. It is clear that there are many such grid cells that are missed at a resolution of even 0.05 artifacts per square meter. In Figure 8.3c only the density interval between 0 and 0.05 artifacts per square meter is shown, contoured at an interval of 0.01 artifacts per square meter. There are quite clearly several types of density patterning in different portions of the survey unit that might be subject to interpretation. But what, exactly, does a density of 0.01 artifacts per square meter mean? We simply have no theoretical basis for interpreting derived measures such as the density of artifacts. What is more, our perception of such measures is completely controlled by the spatial scales and the resolution (contour interval, z-scale) at which they are viewed.

Because of our limited visual interpretation capability, it is necessary to seek another way to comprehend spatial patterning and its repetition across the archaeological landscape. Truly quantitative methods that make positive use of the fact that perceptions change as differing spatial scales are examined provide at least a partial answer.

Figures 8.1a–h, 8.2a–f and 8.3a–c follow, text resumes on page 186.

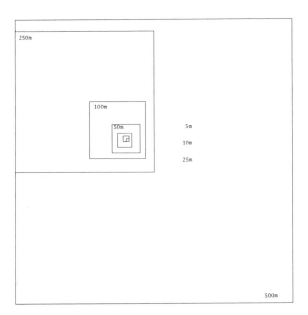

Figure 8.1a

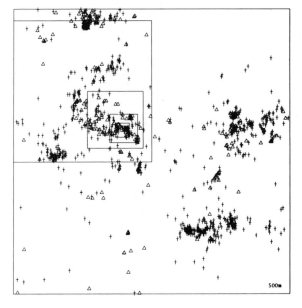

Figures 8.1b

Figure 8.1a–h. Chert (crosses) and quartzite (triangles) artifact distributions viewed through successively smaller "windows" within Seedskadee Unit 28, a 500m x 500m survey area. Window size and position are shown in 8.1a–b. When viewed at each map scale, even though the data remain constant, patterning among artifacts and materials varies.

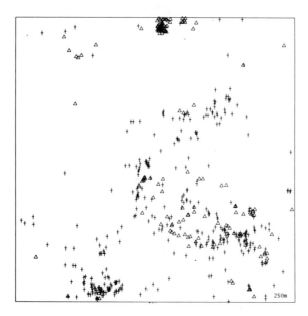

Figure 8.1c. A 250m x 250m portion of Unit 28 (see index map, Fig. 8.1a).

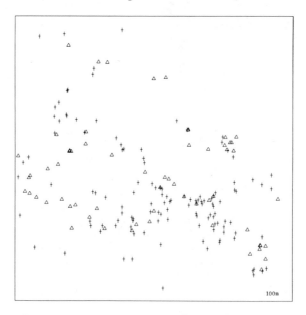

Figure 8.1d. A 100m x 100m portion of Unit 28.

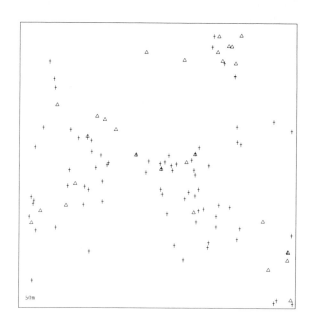

Figure 8.1e. A 50m x 50m portion of Unit 28.

Figure 8.1f. A 25m x 25m portion of Unit 28.

Figure 8.1g. A 10m x 10m portion of Unit 28.

Figure 8.1h. A 5m x 5m portion of Unit 28.

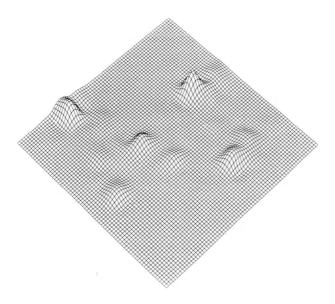

Figure 8.2a. Unit 28 Density: Z Scale 25x

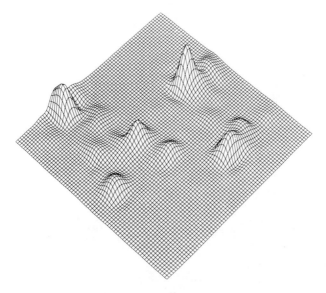

Figure 8.2b. Unit 28 Density: Z Scale 50x

Figure 8.2a–f. Pseudo three-dimensional representations of surface densities of all archaeological materials in Seedskadee Unit 28. The data represented in Figures 8.2a through 8.2f are the same but are represented with varying z-axis scale figures. As the z-axis scale factor increases, what at first seem to be separate concentrations of materials begin to look "related," then merge into a bewilderingly "continuous" density distribution.

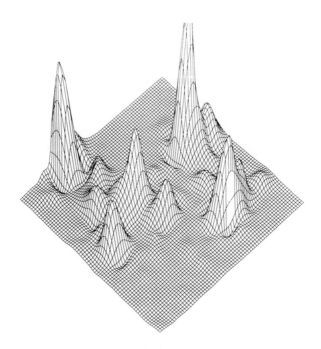

Figure 8.2c. Unit 28 Density: Z Scale 200x

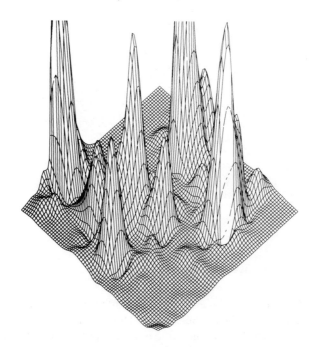

Figure 8.2d. Unit 28 Density: Z Scale 500x

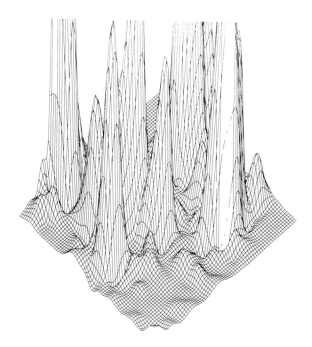

Figure 8.2e. Unite 28 Density: Z Scale 1000x

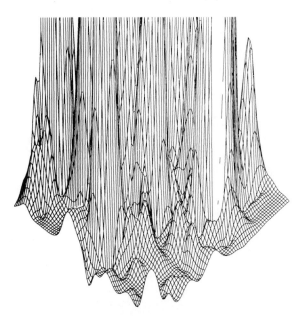

Figure 8.2f. Unit 28 Density: Z Scale 3000x

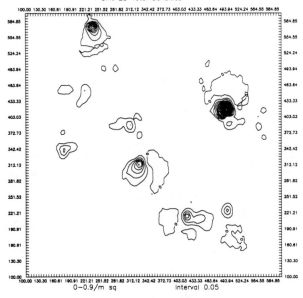

Figure 8.3a. Surface densities of all artifacts in Seedskadee Unit 28 represented by isopleths, or contours. This figure shows a range of 0.0 through 0.9 items per square meter, at an interval of 0.05 items/m². At this resolution relatively few "artifact clusters" are discernable.

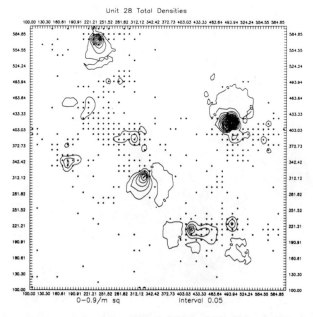

Figure 8.3b. Surface densities of all artifacts in Seedskadee Unit 28, same resolution as Figure 8.3a, with superposition of all 10m x 10m grid cells containing at least one artifact. Many areas actually containing artifacts were clearly "missed" by the isopleth map in Figure 8.3a.

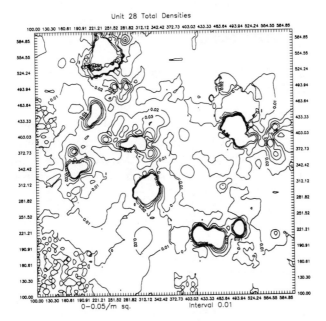

Figure 8.3c. When densities of 0.0 through 0.05 items/m² are mapped with a density countour of 0.01 items/², it becomes clear that there is a relatively continuous distribution, albeit low density, throughout Unit 28.

GOALS OF QUANTITATIVE SPATIAL AND ASSOCIATIONAL PATTERN ANALYSIS

In a recent and comprehensive survey of spatial analytic approaches to the archaeological record, Christopher Carr defines four primary goals of archaeological analysis. These goals are derived from those suggested by Whallon (1973), stated as four questions (Carr 1984:106-07):

1. Are the artifacts of each recognized functional type randomly scattered over space, aggregated into clusters, or systematically aligned?

2. If the artifacts of a given type are clustered, what are the spatial limits of clusters of that type?

3. Whether or not the artifacts of given types are clustered, randomly scattered, or systematically aligned, do artifacts of different types tend to be similarly arranged such that, for example, their frequencies vary together or they are associated spatially?

4. If the artifacts of several types both cluster and are arranged together, what are the spatial limits of multitype clusters?

"The first, second, and fourth operational questions reflect concern at the inferential level in defining activity areas. The third question is posed in response, at the inferential level, to defining tool kits" (Carr 1984:107).

Carr cautions that these goals are not likely to be fulfilled through a straightforward sequence of statistical operations of spatial and associational analysis, because most of the archaeological record is formed by processes that result in overlapping and polythetic depositional sets. **Depositional sets** are those things discarded during human activities, as distinct from **activity sets** (sets of artifacts used in episodic, ongoing human behavior) and **recovery sets** (the things archaeologists find in the archaeological record). In fact, there are reasons to expect all three sorts of sets, particularly depositional and recovery sets, to be **polythetic** and **overlapping** (Carr 1984).

Sets overlap when their members share some of the characteristics required for admittance into their respective sets; this is an "external" property of sets. The difference between monothetic and polythetic sets is an "internal" (Carr 1984:120) property of the sets; polythetic sets share a large number of characteristics, but no single state is essential to group membership. As I interpret them, Carr's reasons for believing that most sets of phenomena found in the archaeological record will be overlapping and polythetic are based on reasoning from an "if I were there" perspective. Such reasoning is of a reconstructive nature. Some of Carr's specific reasons for believing that most discovery sets are overlapping and polythetic are:

1. differential deposition (discard) of artifacts within their life histories (artifacts within an activity set enter the archaeological domain at different times and locations with respect to their manufacture);

2. size-sorting of artifacts (he implies this is mostly behavioral; large items are discarded conveniently, while smaller ones are discarded or lost anywhere, perhaps along the lines of primary and secondary discard);

3. curation and differential wear and breakage rates affect discard locales;

4. the multipurpose nature of tool types—one tool can be used for a number of functions;

5. the compound nature of tool types—a number of tool types can be used for a single function;

6. recycling of artifacts, by which one sort of tool is made into another tool type and used for different purposes than its first use;

7. "mining" of artifacts, which occurs when people come back to a location "over an extended period of time" (Carr 1984:123) and tools are used again by later occupants for different purposes;

8. incomplete recovery of artifacts by archaeologists;

9. classification of artifacts based on stylistic rather than actual functional criteria;

10. overly divisive artifact classifications formulated by archaeologists; and

11. misclassification of artifacts.

It is clear that in thinking about reasons for expecting overlapping and polythetic sets Carr crosses and recrosses the boundary between behavioral and archaeological domains. Nonetheless, these reasons are complementary to the systems-based behavioral reasons for expectations of overlapping and polythetic depositional sets that I have out-lined in earlier chapters.

The goal in analyzing the archaeological record, Carr goes on, is the discrimination of tool kits, sets of artifacts deposited together as the result of episodic discard, in the archaeological record. He implies that these sets of artifacts are not only depositionally related, but were used together during episodic activity, and are representative of those activities themselves. The four questions asked earlier outline four steps by which spatial and associational analyses are applied to allow these sets to be discriminated in the archaeological record. Each of Carr's four original questions can, of course, be asked empirically of any sort of spatial data. Certainly, they can be asked of the distributional archaeological record. But what are the implications, on theoretical and methodological levels, of asking these questions? The first two questions deal with gauging whether or not artifacts are clustered and at what scale, and are to a great extent methodological, sampling-level questions. Of course we expect the products of human activities, including discard, to be clustered at some scale or scales, and in fact this can be demonstrated in the archaeological record everywhere. In a sense, however, clustering is definitional: its existence and recognition depend upon the packages one samples in. If sites are those packages, then the only clustering measurable will be at scales the same size, or smaller, than sites.

Questions three and four carry even heavier theoretical baggage along with them. As I argued earlier, the surface archaeological record in almost all places is probably the result of many overlapping, associ-ated and unassociated episodes of discard collapsed by depositional and postdepositional processes into polythetic, contemporary sets. Whether artifact types are spatially correlated in clusters or in more uniform distributions, there is no assurance and in fact no way to tell whether these types were associated within behavioral episodes in the past.

If the archaeological record is the record of overlapping distribu-tions of discard episodes over long periods, and if episodic discard events take place at different time scales than do depositional events, then we may never really be able to sort them out and identify distinct discov-ery sets that can be translated into depositional and activity sets at any level of reconstruction. This dramatically directs what we are inter-ested in thinking about. It means that no matter whether frequencies of artifact types correlate or appear to be coarranged, or whether there are multitype clusters, we can probably never tell whether they were associated at instants in the past. This negates the validity and in fact the possibility of fulfilling Carr's (1984) and Whallon's (1973) last two goals, which are directed implicitly toward isolating things that are coassociated as tool kits. We know that people use tool kits, but indentifying them in the archaeological record, especially given the disjunctions between manufacture, use, discard, deposition, and discovery, is a tenuous proposition at best.

What are we left with? Metaphorically, the information available to the archaeologist through analysis of the archaeological record is a time exposure of the structure of human reuse of the landscape. One way this structure can be analyzed and measured is by examining the spatial scales of repetition of the patterning of artifacts and their characteristics, which may be very complex.

In order to pursue the recognition of such patterning, we must focus on Carr's questions 1 and 2. To interpret the complex patterning we should find, a deductive approach ultimately may be most rewarding intellectually, although it may also be far more difficult than inductive explanations.

THE APPROPRIATENESS OF DISTRIBUTIONAL DATA

Archaeological excavation data are often comparable to distributional data in resolution—that is, in the precision with which the locations and characteristics of artifacts are recorded. There are two major differences between excavation data and distributional survey data, however. One of these has to do with what archaeologists who are excavating think about the archaeological record they uncover. It is often assumed without question that the materials found in depositionally distinct strata are behaviorally related. There has been some recognition that postdepositional natural processes may disturb strata or their contents; when disturbance is detected, however, it is seen as distorting the ideal sealed situation. Excavation data are also either explicitly or implicitly seen as being horizontally bounded. Radiating test trenches are used to see where the deposits "lens out" or end, and a boundary is drawn to focus excavation on productive areas of the site. Actually, boundaries of excavation are probably just as often drawn on the basis of economic practicality. Excavation is slow and expensive, and one cannot excavate forever in all directions; excavated sites must be of a reasonable size.

The irregular, roughly circular shape of the boundary thus drawn causes problems acknowledged by Whallon (1973) in partitioning the site into squares and rectangles for dimensional analysis. A far greater problem facing dimensional analysts using site data, however, is that as one doubles the grid size again and again the maximum extent of excavation is quickly reached. The scales of spatial patterning that can be investigated using these data are extremely limited.

Distributional data differs in that it extends over large areas, in the case of the Seedskadee data 500m squares. As the Seedskadee locational data were recorded in some cases at millimeter resolution, and the lowest resolution used was 1m square grid units in areas of very high artifact density, a great range of scales of patterning can be explored. This spatial range covers areas that most archaeologists would be willing to acknowledge as being much larger than most "sites" (at least those of hunter-gatherers), down to areas smaller than one would expect for many single-actor activity areas—a range of more than five orders of magnitude.

Here I shall concentrate on spatial scales of landscape use, using a graphic and intuitive sort of analysis of variance. Of course, any other sort of analysis involving artifacts and their associations could be performed with this data base: correlations, cluster analyses based either on spatial or formal properties of things, factor analysis, and many others. Looking at spatial scales of patterning among different artifact types is something that can be done only with distributional survey data, particularly at relatively large scales.

A SIMPLE MATHEMATICAL METHOD FOR THE ANALYSIS OF SPATIAL SCALE

The analyses described here attempt to define and measure spatial scales in artifact distribution, artifact characteristics, and indices derived from such characteristics. Several mathematical methods can be used to measure scales or frequencies in spatial clustering, or the lack thereof. Among them are the Poisson method (Kershaw 1964), dimensional analysis of variance and covariance (Grieg-Smith 1952, 1983; Kershaw and Looney 1985; Whallon 1973), nearest neighbor analyses (Morisita 1959; Whallon 1974), Fourier and other power spectrum analyses (Gonzales and Wintz 1977), and segregation analysis used in concert with clustering algorithms of various sorts (Pielou 1961).

I shall not attempt to specify ideal mathematical methods for analyzing distributional archaeological data. Plant ecologists have worried about detecting and describing the distributions of their data—which are in many ways like those of archaeology—for more than twenty years. Presently, they use dozens of methods and at times heatedly discuss their applicability to different situations.

I prefer to use one of the simplest and most generally applicable of the plant ecologists' spatial analytical techniques: dimensional analysis of variance (after Whallon 1973), also called the variance-to-mean ratio (Grieg-Smith 1983:61) or, in Kershaw and Looney's (1985:129) terms, the analysis of a contiguous grid of quadrats. This method is based on changes in the variance about the mean of counts of items or mean values of properties or characteristics of those items as they are sampled with varying sizes of units in a sample grid placed over their distribution.

While the distribution of points in space is an empirical fact, it is also a fact that our comprehension of spatial distributions varies with differences in the scales at which we sample it. If distributions over a large area are sampled with many extremely small sample units or observations the result is a large number of units containing small numbers of items, regardless of how the items are actually distributed. This is the Poisson distribution, in which the variance between individual observations is approximately equal to the mean number of items per observation (Carr 1984:144). As the size of sample units approaches the scale of clusters or patterns in the actual distribution, the histogram of items per observation becomes increasingly bimodal, with some sample units containing large numbers of items and others no items or small numbers of them. In this case, the variance is high compared to the mean number of items per sample unit. As observation unit sizes are increased still further the mean number of items per unit becomes more equal, and therefore the variance becomes small again when compared to the mean.

Using this property of sample unit sizes, the scale of clustering of a set of items or their properties as distributed in space can be assessed by subjecting the same universe to measurement by overlaying the universe again and again with sample grids of varying sizes (Kershaw and Looney 1985:129). In order to compare the variance with the mean at different sampled grid sizes, the variance-to-mean ratio for data expressed as integral counts (Grieg-Smith 1983; Whallon 1973) or the ratio of

$$(\text{variance} - \text{mean})/(\text{mean})^2$$

for continuous data (Grieg-Smith 1983) is related to the sample unit block size by means of a graph (Kershaw and Looney 1985).

My adaptation of the ecologists' methods is illustrated in Figures 8.4 and 8.5. This example utilizes data from the Seedskadee Project survey Unit 28, which have already been presented.

Figures 8.4a–f show Unit 28, with the locations of chert artifacts marked by small triangles and those of quartzite artifacts by crosses. In successive frames of this figure the 500-by-500m survey unit is divided into samples cells 5, 10, 25, 50, 100, and 250m square.

For illustrative purposes, integer counts of chert debitage (unutilized flakes and angular debris) are used in the calculations. A histogram illustrating the count of chert debitage per cell (along the x-axis) and the number of cells containing that number of items (the y-axis) is also presented for each sample grid size. At small sample grid sizes in relation to the scale of clustering or patterning in the actual debitage distribution, most cells contain no items. Many other cells also contain very few items, and very few cells (in this example, only one) contain many items. This is a classic Poisson distribution (Carr 1984).

In each frame of Figure 8.4 the variance-to-mean ratio (VMR) is also calculated. The mean is calculated on the basis of all of the cells—in the case of the 5m grid, for instance, 10,000 cells, including those with no debitage. The variance is the square of the standard deviation of the means.

As the sample grid size increases, more grid squares contain larger amount of debitage and the tail of the Poisson distribution becomes longer while its peak (the number of cells with no debitage, or a very small number of these items) diminishes, as shown in Figures 8.4c and d. The VMR increases. At the grid size that best accommodates the dominant scale or scales of patterning in the distributional data—in this case, a grid size of 100m for chert artifacts—the histogram becomes almost level, with a widely spaced distribution along the x-axis (that is, the variance peaks). The VMR reaches its highest point. At a grid size of 250m the variance relative to the mean has decreased, indicating that the sample grids are now larger than the scale of patterning in the spatial data. (In the VMR analyses presented later in this chapter, scales up to 500m result from the use of the means and variances among 25 survey areas 500m square, distributed about the overall Seedskadee study area.)

In Figure 8.4g the VMRs resulting from sampling Unit 28's chert debitage (y-axis) are graphed against the grid cell size (x-axis). The VMR clearly peaks at 100m, indicating the dominant scale of patterning or clustering in the distribution of the chert debitage. By itself, this observation is perhaps somewhat trivial, but it becomes less so when the scales of patterning of different sorts of items are compared. Figure 8.5 presents VMR-to-grid cell size graphs calculated for chert and quartzite artifacts (all chert or quartzite items within the cell lumped together), debitage (unutilized flakes and angular debris), tools (biface 3s and utilized flakes or other utilized items), and cores and bifaces (cores and biface 1s and 2s). Varying scales along the y-axis (the VMR value) have been used to permit comparison. Some immediate differences between the scales of clustering in quartzite and chert items are apparent. All classes of chert items examined appear to peak at 100m, although chert cores and bifaces also exhibit a weaker peak at 10m, and the stronger peak extends from 50 through 100m. Quartzite debitage and tool VMRs do not peak, but continue to rise through 250m scales, indicating that perhaps the scale of their patterning is greater than 250m. Quartzite cores and bifaces exhibit a different VMR picture entirely, being uniformly high at low scales and dropping off slightly at 250m.

Behavioral interpretation of such specific patterning is difficult. Nonetheless, it is clear from this analysis that quartzite cores and bifaces (which are probably also cores) are more evenly distributed than are chert cores and bifaces. What is more, chert materials are uniformly clustered at a characteristic 100m scale, while quartzite materials are not. It is tempting to speculate that chert materials were more carefully collected and transported than quartzite—in other words, chert was more a part of the curated portion of the technology in this area than quartzite.

Visual inspection of such graphs allows the interpretation of the scale or scales at which the phenomena examined cluster, indicated by peaks on the graph. In addition, the height of peaks in variance-to-mean ratio as opposed to block size graphs indicate the intensity of clustering (Kershaw and Looney 1985:133).

Here I shall use variance-to-mean graphs in a relatively general and intuitive way. When using such graphs, plant ecologists (Grieg-Smith 1983; Kershaw and Looney 1985) and archaeologists (Whallon 1973) have attempted to assign confidence limits, levels between which the patterning they display may be the result of chance. I shall not do so here in view of the general level at which I am using the dimensional analysis method. While chi-square and t-tests give the appearance of objectivity, the researcher must always subjectively determine acceptable cutoff levels. It is my feeling that even extremely subtle patterning may convey important information about the distributions of archaeological materials over large areas. Certainly at the present state of our knowledge we cannot conclude that it does not. In any case, the ultimate test of the validity of perceived patterning must depend on whether such patterning corresponds with our ideas about what the archaeological record should look like and why, rather than on statistical criteria.

I have departed from the method illustrated by Whallon (1973) and by plant ecologists in at least one important respect. In their dimensional analyses of variance the grid squares are increased by doubling their areas in each successive step (1, 2, 4, 8, 16, 32, and so on). This is done by changing the shape of the cells from squares to rectangles to squares. If, however, the shapes of distributions remain constant, or if they are different for distributions of different things, then alternately changing the shape of the sample grid units may introduce interpretive difficulties. In Whallon's (1973) examples, this appears to be the case: the variance-to-mean values seem to oscillate, at least for small grid unit sizes. In my dimensional variance analyses, grid cell sizes have been decreased from units 500m square through 250, 100, 50, 25, 10, and 5m squares progressively. Some show variance-to-mean ratio oscillation and some do not. When using consistently square sample grid units in dimensional analysis, therefore, changes in the inflection of the graphed lines, in addition to simply their peaks, may have interpretive significance.

There may well be methods of looking at the spatial scales comprising the archaeological record that are more accurate, of higher resolution, and ultimately more easily computed and interpreted than the dimensional analysis of variance used here. In this book I have concentrated on the reasons we might want to look at spatial scales in the archaeological record; if these reasons are adequately demonstrated we should spend our analogue of the plant ecologists' twenty years deciding what the best methods for us to use are. With the mathematical expertise that exists within archaeology today it should not take us that long.

Figures 8.4a–g and 8.5a–h follow, text resumes on page 206.

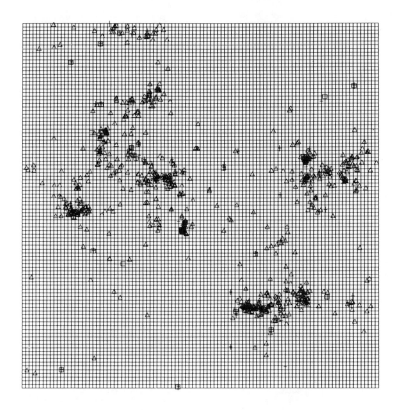

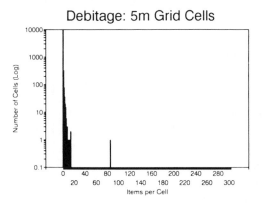

Debitage: 5m Grid Cells

Figure 8.4a. 5m x 5m grid cells.
$$\frac{\text{variance}}{\text{mean}} = \frac{1.00}{.096} = 10.3925$$

Figure 8.4a-f. The derivation of variance-to-mean ratios (VMR) of item distribution in successively larger grid cells or "samples" of Seedskadee Unit 28. Each of the composite figures has two components: (1) a map of chert and quartzite debitage in the Unit with superposed grids of varying size, (2) a histogram of the number of grids containing chert debitage and the number of items of quartzite debitage.

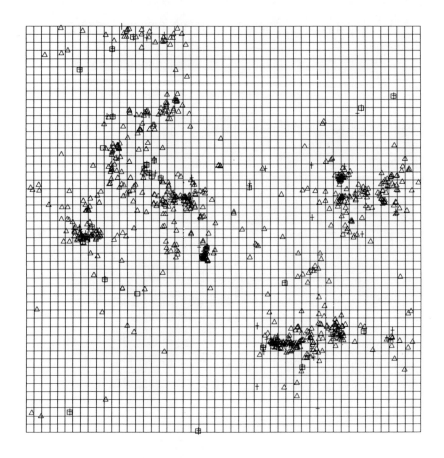

Debitage: 10m Grid Cells

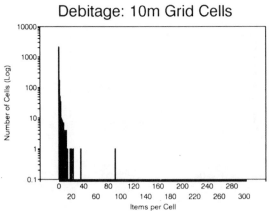

Figure 8.4b. 10m x 10m grid cells.
$$\frac{\text{variance}}{\text{mean}} = \frac{5.70}{.384} = 14.8407$$

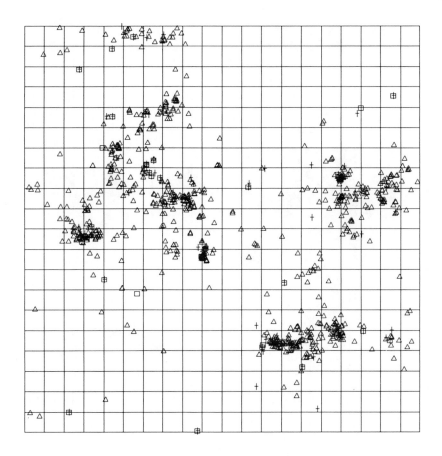

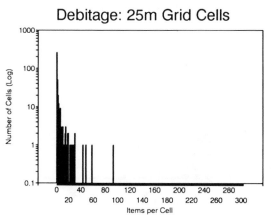

Debitage: 25m Grid Cells

Figure 8.4c. 25m x 25m grid cells.
$$\frac{\text{variance}}{\text{mean}} = \frac{59.53}{2.400} = 24.8058$$

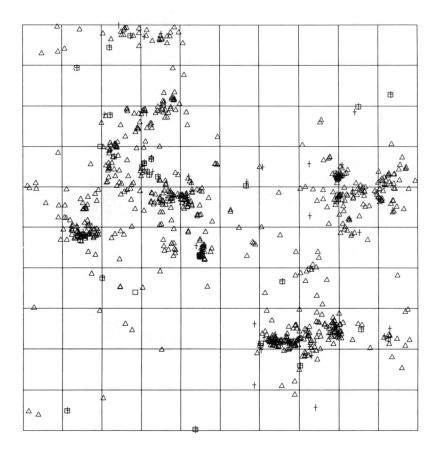

Debitage: 50m Grid Cells

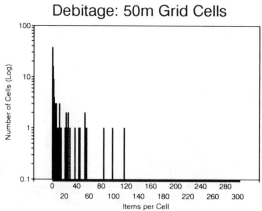

Figure 8.4d. 50m x 50m grid cells.

$$\frac{\text{variance}}{\text{mean}} = \frac{415.27}{9.600} = 43.2576$$

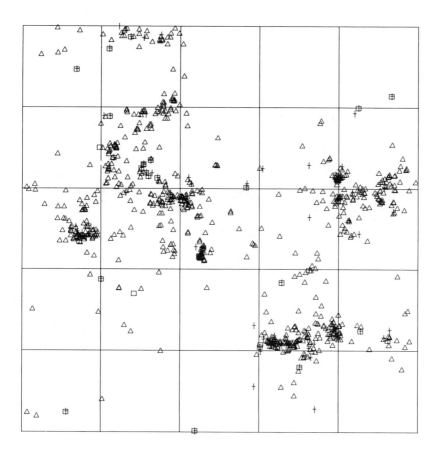

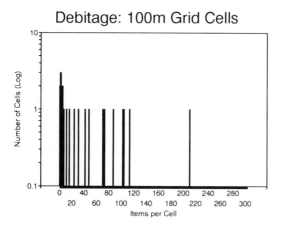

Debitage: 100m Grid Cells

Figure 8.4e. 100m x 100m grid cells. $\dfrac{\text{variance}}{\text{mean}} = \dfrac{2713.67}{38.400} = 70.6684$

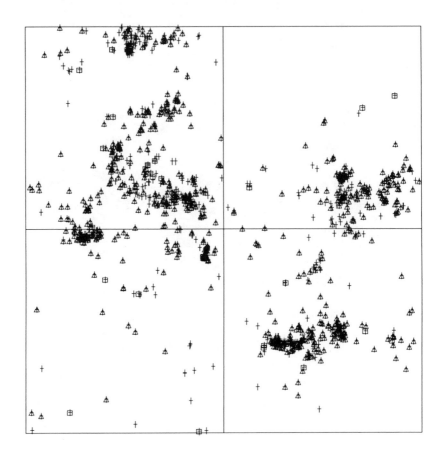

Debitage: 250m Grid Cells

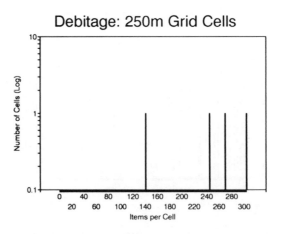

Figure 8.4f. 250m x 250m grid cells. $\dfrac{\text{variance}}{\text{mean}} = \dfrac{4940.67}{240.000} = 20.5861$

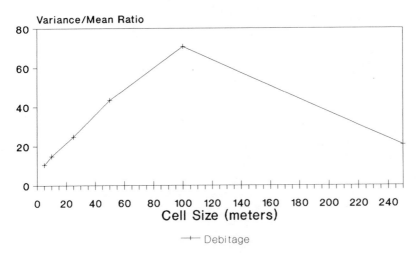

Figure 8.4g. Grid cell sizes (x axis) plotted against VMR (y axis). Comparison of such graphs provides the basis for analysis of scales of distribution in the archaeological record.

Chert Artifacts

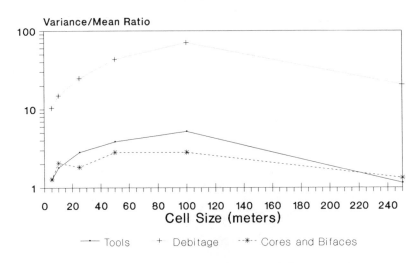

Figure 8.5a. VMR at varying scales for chert debitage, tools and cores/bifaces, Seedskadee Unit 28. This composite graph allows direct comparison of differences in distributional scales among artifact classes, but it also masks the VMR peaks exhibited by single artifact types. Such peaks can be more clearly interpreted in single-type VMR graphs with equalized scales (Figs. 8.5b–d).

Chert Debitage

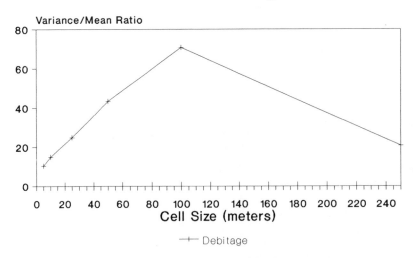

Figure 8.5b. VMR for chert debitage, Seedskadee Unit 28.

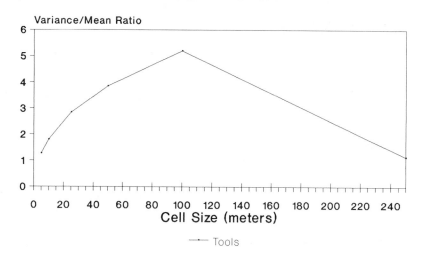

Figure 8.5c. VMR for chert tools, Seedskadee Unit 28.

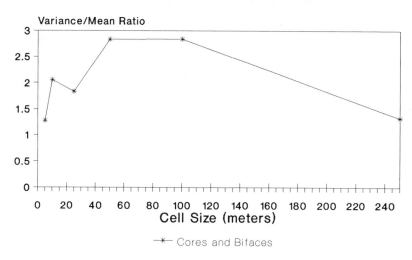

Figure 8.5d. VMR for chert cores and bifaces, Seedskadee Unit 28.

Quartzite Artifacts

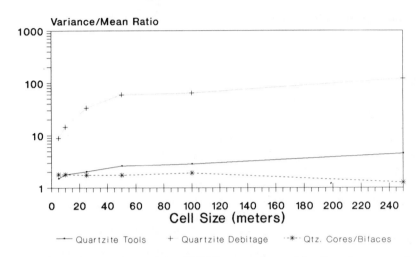

Figure 8.5e. Composite graph of VMR at varying grid cell scales, quartzite debitage, tools, and cores/bifaces, Seedskadee Unit 28.

Quartzite Debitage

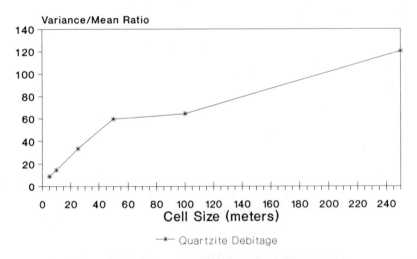

Figure 8.5f. VMR for quartzite debitage, Seedskadee Unit 28.

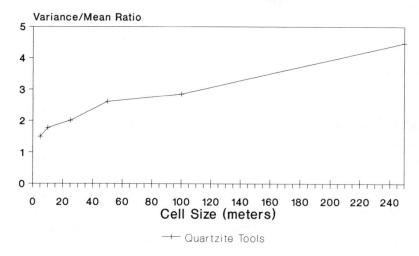

Figure 8.5g. VMR for quartzite tools, Seedskadee Unit 28.

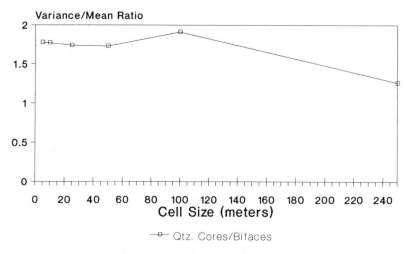

Figure 8.5h. VMR for quartzite cores and bifaces, Seedskadee Unit 28.

COMPUTER METHODS USED IN THE ANALYSES

One of the most common objections to the distributional archaeological approach I advocate is that it is surely too difficult to collect large amounts of information on the locations and characteristics of all of the artifacts and other archaeological materials found in the field. As illustrated by the Seedskadee data base, this is simply not true. Using systematic, partitioned, intensive field methods, such data were collected in large survey units in the southwestern Wyoming study area.

A better argument, perhaps, would be that dealing with such a body of data analytically is extremely difficult. Even using computers, which one obviously must, handling this sort of data is time-intensive. In the course of the Seedskadee project, data were recorded by hand in the field. Locational information was recorded by a mapping team, and information on the intrinsic characteristics of each artifact was coded by another team on Fortran forms. These two data sets then had to be entered into computer files and merged with one another.

Simply entering the data was time-consuming and expensive, and the resulting files were filled with errors introduced during both field coding and data punching. The first step in dealing with the data was to clean the files. This was facilitated by the fact that there are many data combinations that are simply impossible—for instance, an unutilized flake with retouched edges, a flake with total dorsal cortex cover as well as dorsal flake scars, or objects recorded as outside the field survey units. Using the University of New Mexico computer system, short programs were written to flag such impossible combinations, which were then inspected. When the correct attributes could be figured out the data were changed; when they could not be reconciled, data had to be discarded.

While the dimensional analyses described here are based on a simple idea, the resampling of distributional data using different sample grid sizes, they require a large number of computations. Data sets from all sample units must be merged, and the subcategories of data that are to be examined entered into other files. These files are then further divided into groups at each sample grid size. Means and statistics for characteristics at each sample grid size are calculated. These are then presented in graphic form.

CONTROLLING FOR DEPOSITIONAL AND POST-DEPOSITIONAL FACTORS

I have emphasized that there are many factors intervening between past episodic behavior and archaeological interpretation. Some of the most important of these are occasioned by natural depositional and postdepositional processes. That natural processes act upon the discarded archaeological record is an intuitively simple concept and is recognized by all archaeologists to different degrees. Defining and quantifying the action of natural processes on the archaeological record, however, is a complex problem. The geomorphological processes involved are multitude, are in many cases poorly understood, and probably often operate on spatial and temporal scales that are similar to and beat against those at which episodic discard takes place.

Collecting data on the nature of geomorphological processes at a wide range of spatial scales would obviously be as difficult or more so than collecting distributional archaeological data. It is my understanding, in fact, that geomorphologists may presently be at roughly the same stage in their science that we are in ours: that of just beginning to consider how to record and analyze such data over large continuous areas.

Nonetheless, in recognition of the belief that it is necessary to attempt to control for these processes in some way in order to interpret archaeological distributions, I shall make use of a simple four-part taxonomy of landscape surface types or geomorphological zones within which each of the Seedskadee survey areas fall.

Zones photointerpreted during the experiment described in Chapter 6 were modified somewhat for purposes of the data analyses discussed here. The four general geomorphological zones used in the analyses described here are dunes, sandsheets, terraces, and mesatops.

While these analyses of spatial scale do not depend on the visual inspection of pictures of artifact patterns within the areas surveyed, I present four examples as illustrations of what typical distributions in these zones look like.

In **dune** areas (Fig. 8.6) the surface is partially covered by active or inactive sand dunes, between which interdunal areas or flats occur. **Sandsheet** areas (Fig. 8.7) are also covered with a sand mantle, but it

Unit 28

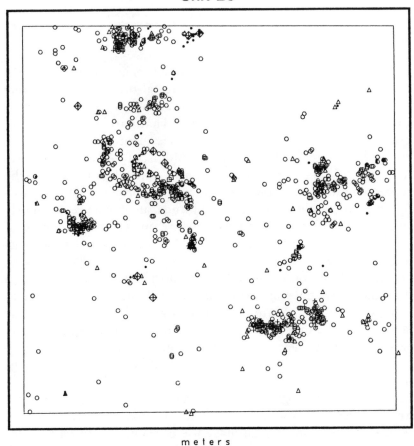

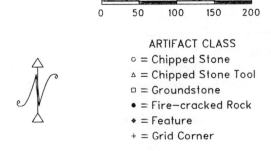

meters

0   50   100   150   200

ARTIFACT CLASS
o = Chipped Stone
△ = Chipped Stone Tool
□ = Groundstone
● = Fire—cracked Rock
◆ = Feature
+ = Grid Corner

Figure 8.6. Artifact distribution, typical dune area.

Unit 6

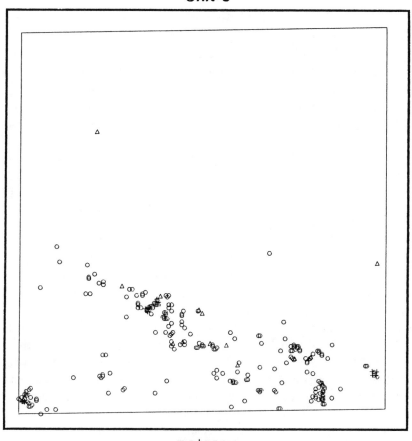

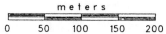

ARTIFACT CLASS
o = Chipped Stone
△ = Chipped Stone Tool
+ = Grid Corner

Figure 8.7. Artifact distribution, typical sandsheet area.

is more or less continuous. Dominant geomorphological surface processes in dune and sandsheet areas are relatively low-energy aeolian transport of fine sediments, localized gravitational processes occurring as dunes shift their boundaries, and localized, low-energy water flows in small internal drainages.

Terraces (Fig. 8.8) are those of the Green River and its tributaries and have been shaped and affected at different times by higher-energy fluvial processes, as well as erosion and deposition caused by more localized drainage, sheetwash, and overbank flooding. Mesatops (Fig. 8.9) occupy the highest portions of the study area and consist of remnant, relatively level surfaces. They are usually capped with resistant gravels and subject to little discernible fluvial erosion except at their margins. Aeolian processes may be important in some places on mesatops, too.

A total of 19 of the Seedskadee survey units are used in the analyses that follow. Five of these (Units 4, 8, 10, 19 and 28) have been classified as dune units, four (3, 6, 17, 25) as sandsheets, three (16, 22, and 24) as terrace units, and seven (2, 7, 12, 15, 20, 21, and 26) as mesatops.

I will not go into greater detail on archaeologically relevant natural processes in these four landform type areas, primarily because there may well be a complex interplay between natural and cultural processes determining the nature of the contemporary archaeological record there. Artifacts may be differentially covered and hidden by sediments in each area, or exposed there; and each area hosts its own characteristic vegetation, which may greatly affect visibility and discovery of archaeological materials.

In addition there are of course probable cultural reasons determining why and how each type of area was occupied. These reasons could be simple—for instance, people may have been seeking specific plant or animal resources, shelter from winds, or lookouts. Reasons why people used these zones differentially may have been more complex, however, involving an interplay with natural processes rather than simply occurrences. Perhaps, for instance, useful lithic materials were exposed in dunes in the summer and on mesatops during the winter. Natural processes may have been very real parts of ongoing cultural systems, just as they are part of our ongoing archaeological endeavors.

My approach to controlling for natural surface processes is to examine patterning in the spatial scales of portions of the archaeological record not only within the universe of the data collected during the Seedskadee survey but also within each of the zones. I shall then explore

Unit 22

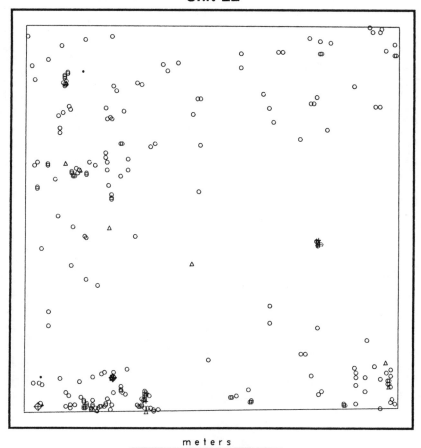

meters

0   50   100   150   200

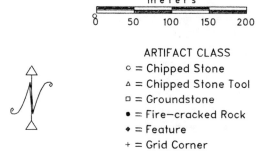

ARTIFACT CLASS
○ = Chipped Stone
△ = Chipped Stone Tool
□ = Groundstone
● = Fire-cracked Rock
◆ = Feature
+ = Grid Corner

Figure 8.8. Artifact distribution, typical terrace area.

Unit 12

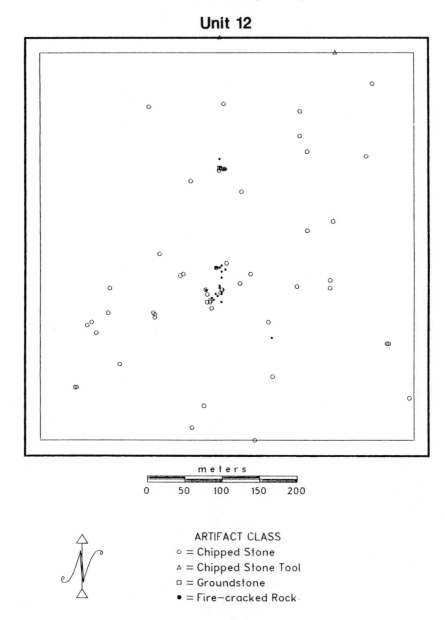

meters

0   50   100   150   200

ARTIFACT CLASS
o = Chipped Stone
△ = Chipped Stone Tool
□ = Groundstone
● = Fire—cracked Rock

Figure 8.9. Artifact distribution, typical mesatop area.

contrasts among these distributions and their possible natural and cultural interpretations.

SPATIAL SCALES OF THE MANUFACTURE AND USE OF STONE ARTIFACTS

My first example of the interpretive potential of distributional archaeological data is largely inductive, proceeding from looking at spatial distributions to interpreting them in systemic terms. It focusses on the differential scales of the manufacture, use, and discard of the chipped stone artifacts that make up most of the archaeological record in the Seedskadee survey area.

A basic distinction between technological strategies or parts of these strategies was made in earlier chapters in terms of expedience as opposed to curation. Empirically, the differences between the use of stone tools expediently and in a curated manner are the loci of manufacture, use, and discard. In the most expedient case things are manufactured, used, and then discarded at one place during one episode. Curation is evidenced when items are manufactured at one place (or more than one, in the case of staged manufacture) and discarded at another. Use of the items at some point away from the place of manufacture is assumed; it may be where the item is discarded, or elsewhere, or in some cases there may be no such use at all. Curation is the result of planning for the unavailability of raw materials at distant places or, probably more often, results from time stress that places a premium on specialized, multipurpose tool kits.

The reason I have tiptoed around using the terms "curated systems" and "expedient systems" above is that these are not systems but ways that implements participate in systems. A technological strategy of total expedience is unlikely but imaginable; one with curated components would always have also to have expedient components, for the more specialized a carried tool kit is the more often it must be supplemented when unforeseen contingencies arise.

Another expectation that has been made much of—probably too much—is that expedient tools, being the result of situational manufacture and use, should have minimal energy input and be crude-looking, while curated implements should be complex and refined. Curation and expedience, however, are not formal properties of individual tools, but rather are organizational properties of technology. Neither curation nor expedience exists at any one place or time, either in the past or in the archaeological record. They are dynamic properties of things within systems. One cannot look at an implement and pronounce it curated or expedient. Neither can one look at a site and determine whether the things there are curated or expedient. Instead, the differential locations of manufacture, use, and discard must be examined.

Given the composite nature of the archaeological record, this is not necessarily a straightforward task. Only rarely are many different sources of lithic materials precisely identifiable in an area, and while core-refitting approaches over large regions have been suggested they are, practically speaking, impossible.

Using distributional data, however, spatial scales of lithic manufacture, use, and discard may be explored over areas large enough to inform us about some aspects of lithic technology. While it is unnecessary to inspect whole regions or whole systems, the windows through which we see systems must be relatively large to allow discrimination of large scales.

To illustrate such an approach, let us look at scales in the spatial patterning of three classes of artifacts—debris, utilized and retouched flakes, and formal tools—using the Seedskadee distributional data base. I have differentiated these classes according to whether they are composed of one of the two major discernible lithic material types there, quartzite and chert. I have plotted variance-to-mean ratio (VMR) graphs using simple counts of occurrence of each artifact and material type within each grid cell along a grid size axis of 5 through 500m. The VMR lines in each graph are further broken down by the geomorphic or landscape zone types discussed earlier in this chapter (dunes, sandsheets, terraces, mesatops, and an additional category containing observations for all zones). I regret that these graphs (Figs. 8.10, 8.11, 8.12), which contrast 210 different values, are somewhat difficult to look at and compare.

Only the variance-to-mean ratio is examined in this analysis, as simple counts of items in sample grids are used in its definition. We have no interpretive guidelines for determining the meaning of greater or lesser quantities of debris, flakes, or tools. In fact, if the archaeological record is cumulative simple counts are quite uninterpretable until much that we do not presently understand is known.

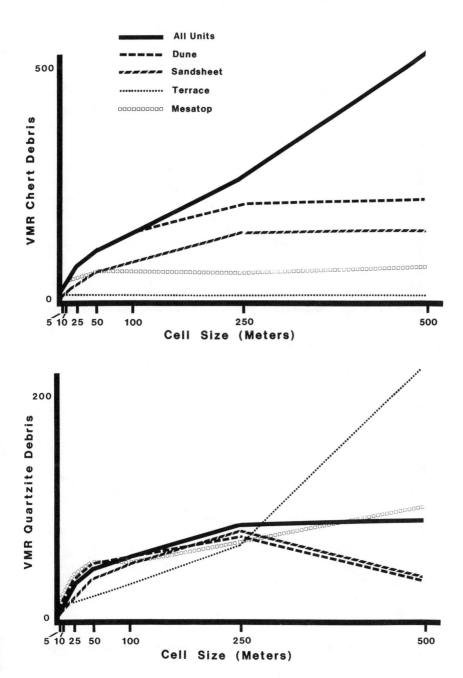

Figure 8.10. Variance-to-mean ratios (VMR) at varying sample grid cell scales for chert and quartzite debris, Seedskadee Project survey units, by geomorphological zone.

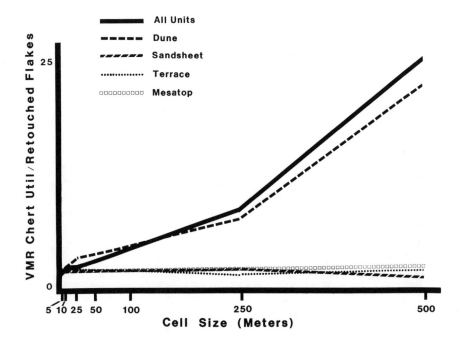

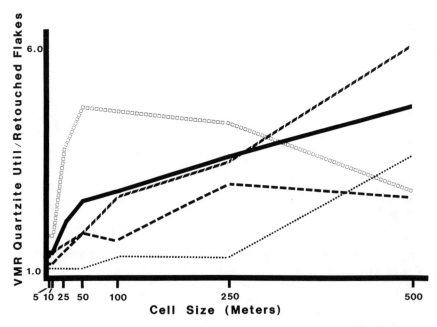

Figure 8.11. Variance-to-mean ratios (VMR) at varying sample grid cell scales for chert and quartzite utilized/retouched flakes, Seedskadee Project survey units, by geomorphological zone.

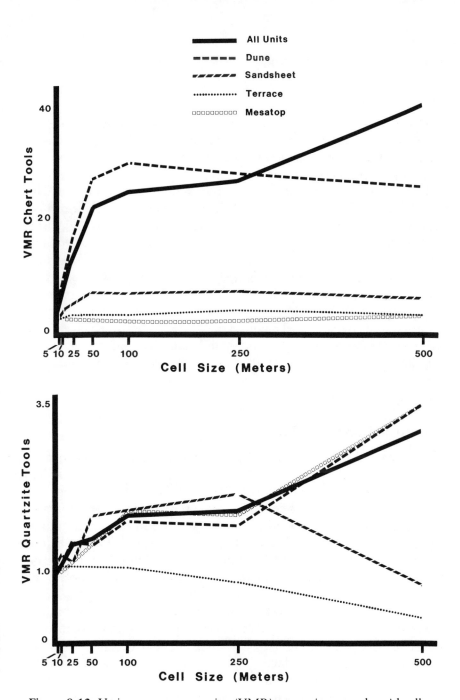

Figure 8.12. Variance-to-mean ratios (VMR) at varying sample grid cell scales for chert and quartzite tools, Seedskadee Project survey units, by geomorphological zone.

Debris

Debris consists of unbroken and broken unutilized flakes with no discernible use wear or retouching, and of angular debris, cores, and tested cobbles. It is assumed that unutilized debris is discarded in the immediate context of manufacture.

In general, from an examination of the amplitudes of the curves in the VMR graphs for quartzite and chert debris (Fig. 8.10), it can be seen that quartzite debris is far less strongly clustered at any scale than is chert debris. The peaks and inflections of the lines show that in dune and sandsheet areas quartzite and chert manufacturing debris is clustered, or recurs across the landscape, in similar ways, with peaks at 250m. This is not the case for the VMR lines for terraces and mesatops. Chert manufacturing debris on terraces and mesatops is not clustered at any spatial frequency. The quartzite VMR curves in terrace areas increase constantly, which probably indicates that quartzite cobbles are clustered at a scale greater than 500m, as in mesa areas also, with very slight clustering at 25 to 50m scales. This might be the scale at which cobble exposures occur.

Utilized and Retouched Flakes

Utilized and retouched flakes are implements, and are assumed to have been used for some purpose, but are in all probability discarded where they were used. They may, however, be made from material carried in raw form, or as cores, or from immediate sources, or made from other tools. There is much more variation in the VMR graphs for utilized and retouched quartzite flakes (Fig. 8.11) at scales below 250m than in the corresponding graphs for chert. This patterning seems to indicate that, at small scales at least, informal quartzite tools were used at a wide variety of functionally specific sorts of locations, while informal chert tools were used at places that repeat themselves at much lower frequencies across the landscape. This may simply mean that informal chert tools were used less often, or that they were used in more restricted or fewer places. More probably, it means that quartzite tools were manufactured for many specific and unique purposes—that is, they are manufactured and used expediently. Chert tools may be used in as many places, but they were probably discarded during less frequent episodes of refurbishing at more widely spaced locations.

Also, making informal chert tools may be more expensive than making informal quartzite tools, if informal and expedient chert tools were made from carried, prepared, and possibly heat-treated cores, or from formal chert tools used as raw material. An inspection of some statistics for lithic artifacts in dune areas shows that while 73 percent of the utilized and retouched flakes are chert, only 27 percent of all cores are of that material, the rest, of course, being quartzite.

Tools

Comparison of the VMR graphs for utilized and retouched flakes (Fig. 8.11) and formal tools (unifaces and bifaces, Fig. 8.12) shows that retouched quartzite flakes and quartzite tools are used or discarded in the same ways—that is, they have similar spatial scales of patterning—up to 250m scales. Beyond 250m the trend in spatial patterning of quartzite tools increases in dunes and mesatops and decreases in sandsheet and terrace areas. For utilized and retouched quartzite flakes a mirror image is seen: tool VMR decreases after 250m for dunes and mesatops and increases for sandsheets and terraces. Perhaps the context of quartzite tool and flake tool discard is most similar in dunes and mesatops and a different pattern of discard takes place on sandsheet and terraces.

As in the VMR graphs for utilized and retouched flakes, quartzite tool patterning scales are quite complex at higher spatial frequencies (that is, at smaller scales, in this case below 100m). Below these frequencies sandsheet and terrace patterning is similar, and dunes and mesatops seem somewhat alike. These are the same pairs of areas that corresponded in the VMRs for utilized and retouched quartzite flakes, but the two sets of curves are reciprocal in the direction of their inflections: in particular, the VMRs in dunes and mesatops go up after 250m, indicating low frequencies (that is, large scales) of clustering or repetition for quartzite tools. VMRs for sandsheet and terrace quartzite tools, in contrast, are lower at larger scales (above 250m). In fact, at scales over 100m in terrace areas and at about 500m in sandsheets quartzite VMRs are below 1.

A VMR of 1 indicates that spatial distributions are random, and below 1 they are more even than random, at each scale. Even distributions are archaeologically unexpected and remarkable, and indicate that the placement of each item is dependent on the placement of the other items of that type. Such distributions are found among Chinese agricultural villages, anthills, and other competitive parts of cultural and biological systems.

Chert tools, by comparison, are highly clustered in dunes at 100m scales, and slightly clustered at about 50m scales in sandsheet areas. On terraces and mesatops chert tools are relatively unclustered.

Interpretations

Interpretations of different portions of the technological system or systems in different places across the landscape can be approached by comparing similarities or disjunctions in scales of patterning among the three preceding sets of VMR graphs.

Similar scales of patterning, as suggested by the VMR graphs, in debris as opposed to utilized and retouched flakes may indicate an expedient component in which utilized and retouched flakes are generally manufactured from raw materials, used, and discarded during single episodes. This expedient component of the system or systems appears in quartzite use at all scales in dunes and on terraces, at up to 250m scales in sandsheet areas, and is not found on mesatops. This may indicate that quartzite was brought to mesatop areas in the form of prepared cores. A quartzite flake manufacture and use disjuncture in sandsheet areas is less pronounced, but present.

The same expedience indicator for chert appears only in dune areas, and there only relatively weakly. This may be the result of discarded formal chert tools being recycled as cores for the manufacture of expediently used flakes. Formal tools, probably manufactured in distant places, thus became local raw material for expedient implements. Such recycling may well have taken place long after the original tool discard, and as mentioned previously may be largely responsible for the nature of the eventual archaeological record in such places, playing havoc with traditional interpretations of local as opposed to nonlocal materials.

The debris (Fig. 8.10) and tool (Fig. 8.12) VMR graphs show that the patterns of quartzite VMR scales are similar in sandsheet areas and somewhat similar on mesatops, which may indicate that quartzite tools are not very curated in these places. In dunes there is a marked disjunction of debris and tool VMRs after 250m scales, possibly because quartzite materials were carried into these areas to specific places in unprepared form, cached, and then "quarried" there for tool manufacture. This would probably take place only at locations used for some period of time or reused often, perhaps multifamily bases.

On terraces the debris and tool VMR picture is quite different. Some quartzite tools manufactured there may have been taken away to other areas, and some of the things classified as tools, mostly large early bifaces (biface 1s and biface 2s) remain there, evenly distributed. Are these bifacial cores "competing" with one another?

One possible way this could happen is if these cores were used as furniture—that is, they remained and were reused at specific places rather than being carried about. An ethnographically derived example of site furniture is mongongo cracking stones used at wet-season camps by Basarwa (Bushmen) in northwestern Botswana. Upon camping the Basarwa look for stones. People may remember leaving nutcracking stones at a camp where they previously stayed, or they may have no such knowledge but the expectation that if someone else camped there in a past mongongo season they left stones. Only if no stones are found is someone sent to find a new nutcracking stone. When the camp is abandoned the stones remain, "cached" for a future use.

There are no mongongo nuts, nor, to my knowledge, any other nuts in the Green River Basin. Nonetheless, early bifacial quartzite cores may reflect a strategy of search and reuse similar to that of the Basarwa nutcracking stones. It may be that in terrace areas, where it is my impression that large quartzite cobbles are ubiquitous, already chipped cobbles are more attractive, in that they are much easier to use as sources of expedient nonformal flake tools than are raw cobbles. If one finds a bifacial core within a reasonable distance, one uses it rather than making a new core. If one does not, one manufactures a new core and then leaves it there, adding to the even distribution of tools on terraces.

Chert debris and tool VMRs are similar in terrace and mesatop areas, possibly due to the expedient manufacture and use of chert tools there, or more probably the expedient reuse of previously discarded formal chert tools. The VMR graphs for dune and sandsheet areas are similar to one another and very different from the terrace and mesatop graphs. In dune areas especially, formal chert tools are clustered at much higher spatial scale frequencies than debris. This is somewhat surprising. One interpretation of this patterning is that the staged manufacture of chert tools takes place in dune areas at much more specific places than does discard (and perhaps use) of those tools. Chert tools are part of a curated technological strategy in dune areas. Debris VMR patterning in dunes is somewhat similar to utilized and retouched flake patterning, possibly the result of recycling of curated formal tools for unforeseen purposes, and then discarding (not always, of course, but at slightly elevated frequencies over time) the ruined tools.

There are also some interesting general interpretations to be drawn from looking at all of the VMR graphs in Figures 8.10, 8.11, and 8.12 together. These conclusions show that the analysis of scales, accomplished though the examination of distributional data, can help archaeologists to think about archaeology rather than simply to reconstruct systems and their components. One of these is that one cannot always identify quartzite—which is intuitively crude and of low quality—as expedient, or attractive fine-grained chert as curated. Another is that the VMR traces resulting from examining all landscape types together often mask important variation.

In order to examine the spatial patterns resulting from technological patterning further, it would be ideal to have information on the scales of spatial patterning of the natural occurrence of quartzite and chert to compare with their culturally modified products. Collecting the distributional data for this purpose would require inventorying and point-plotting perhaps millions of quartzite cobbles or other raw material nodules across landscapes, and would be very difficult. It is, nonetheless, an important direction for future technological inquiry.

Although my interpretations here have been about behavior, it is more than likely that there is a visibility component, controlled by natural geomorphological processes, responsible for some of the spatial variation indicated by the VMR graphs. The importance of these processes may be profound. Most taphonomic studies and analyses in archaeology have been directed toward demonstrating that postdepositional natural processes distort the archaeological record, making it worthless or at least difficult to interpret in many situations. A few studies have suggested ways of correcting for or filtering out postdepositional processes so that the underlying, Pompeiilike archaeological record can be read correctly.

I suspect that the natural processes of surface disturbance are just as important in forming the archaeological record predepositionally as postdepositionally. There is undoubtedly a complex interplay between the visibility and availability of local raw materials: unused materials or just as often previously used and discarded implements, cores, or flakes, which are modified and reused. There is no reason to think that natural processes affected past people, who depended on the visibility of lithic materials for their very livelihoods, to any lesser extent than they affect our archaeological perceptions today. It will not be easy to deal with the implications of such intertwined natural and cultural formation processes. Nonetheless, it is something that archaeology must address, and when future researchers do so it may well qualitatively alter our interpretations of the archaeological record almost everywhere.

A DEDUCTIVE APPROACH TO INDICATORS OF SYSTEMS COMPONENTS

A second illustration of some ways in which distributional archaeological survey data may be used is deductive in the sense that it is based not simply on an initial inspection of patterning followed by its interpretation, but rather on formulating expectations before inspecting patterns. In the investigative framework of archaeology illustrated in Figure 2.2 and the accompanying discussion I indicated that the theory-to-method flow of deductive explanation is probably the most efficient way to go about doing science. This is not to say that it will always be the most immediately satisfying logical direction. In fact, the case might be made that it will not be. Deductive reasoning, if honestly approached, holds great potential for falsifying itself—that is, it is far more likely that expectations will not be completely fulfilled than that they will be.

The example presented here identifies some or all of the seven types of occupations that were suggested in Chapter 6 following summaries of the archaeological and ethnographic literature on southwestern Wyoming and the Great Basin and Plains in general. As stated, these types of occupations were identified in an attempt to assess what was "going on" in the Green River Basin study area in prehistory. An additional purpose was to explore the question of what scales these different sorts of activities are represented at in the archaeological record. It is obvious that this kind of interpretive effort is not entirely deductive, and in fact I can think of no way to test the occupation types that are identified.

As will become apparent, those occupation types also may be somewhat inappropriate analytical units in the light of the composite, overlapping nature of the archaeological record in the study area and perhaps in most places. Nonetheless, I characterize this experiment as at least somewhat deductive. Expectations about alternative technological strategies in different locational components of a past system or systems were developed on the basis of technological arguments found in the current archaeological literature (Table 6.2). Next, a series of indices was designed to allow the measurement and recognition of these strategies using distributional archaeological data from the Seedskadee survey. The indices were then inspected, using variance-to-mean ratios plotted against cell sizes. Finally, patterns appearing in the VMR graphs were summarized. The results are not as clean, as easily interpretable, or as satisfying as the conclusions reached in the inductive exploration of chert and quartzite manufacturing and tool use above.

TECHNOLOGICAL STRATEGIES IN SYSTEMS COMPONENTS

Table 6.2 (p. 154) lists a wide range of expectations about assemblage contents for systems components. These expectations were drawn from discussions of different aspects of technological strategies and their relationship to overall systemic organization appearing in the recent archaeological literature. In order to examine these properties of technology they must be translated into measurable terms that are comparable from place to place. For this reason, rather than relying on functional artifact or assemblage typologies I formulated indices that can be applied across artifact types to compare the archaeological record as it appears at different spatial scales within the study area. I chose these indices because I felt they would be sensitive to the variation in technological strategies outlined in Table 6.2, and also because values for each of these could be measured using the distributional data collected during the survey. These indices and their associated expectations fall into two general categories.

Reduction Stages

Within this general category I have used three indices designed to allow discrimination among occupation types. The first of these is **reduction stage diversity**, which should be high where a complete range of manufacturing or gearing-up activities takes place (different sorts of base camps) and low where large amounts of expedient implement manufacture occurs (foraging locations) or where portable tool kits and staged manufacture are important (logistic and traveling locations).

Two additional indicators of differences in reduction stage, the proportion of high reduction stage flakes and that of low reduction stage flakes, were also derived. **Proportions of high reduction stage flakes** should be high where carried tools are used as raw materials for situational implement manufacture, and moderate where more formal tool manufacture takes place. **Proportions of low reduction stage flakes** should be high where expedient implements are manufactured from relatively unprepared cores or raw material, and particularly low where time stress is an important factor in shaping lithic strategies.

Assemblage Composition

Six indices of the kinds and proportions of tools in assemblages, and their relationship with debris and other technological products, were defined.

The values of a **tool-to-debris ratio** should be low where manufacturing or gearing-up is taking place and the tools manufactured are subsequently taken away—that is, at base camps. It should also be low where expedient materials are manufactured, or where carried tools are not used so intensively that they must either be refurbished or discarded (foraging locations). In places where staged manufacture or the refurbishment of personal gear takes place, the tool-to-debris ratio should be moderate but probably not high.

A ratio of **utilized flakes to tools,** that is, of informal and probably more expedient tools to formal tools, should be high at places where expedient tool manufacture and use takes place either alone (foraging locations) or in concert with more planned manufacture (bases). It should be moderate when expedient tools are produced from portable, curated personal tool kits (at foraging or traveling locations) because these curated materials are more valuable, particularly under time stress.

The **percentage of biface thinning flakes** in an assemblage is an indication of late stages of flake removal. This might be occasioned by the removal of flakes for expedient uses from formal, personal gear. It could also occur in the late stages of staged manufacture. Proportions of biface thinning flakes in assemblages should be high, then, at logistic locations and traveling locations, as well as at foraging locations. At bases, where all stages of manufacture take place, the proportion of biface thinning flakes should not be high compared with other flakes.

Biface 3s, or late stage bifaces, are probably the most curated of tools, and should thus be found more often where they were maintained or replaced than where they were used. A greater **percentage of biface 3s to other formal tools** should occur in base camps, with low proportions at foraging locations and only moderate proportions at logistic and traveling locations.

The **number of edges per tool** is probably an indicator of portability of tools and the inclusion of a constellation of specific edges in implements manufactured for planned uses under time constraints. The highest numbers of edges per tool should be the consequence of logistic strategies.

Assemblage diversity, a measure of the variety and equability of the distribution of tool types within an assemblage, should be high in situations where relatively general tools are used together in a nonmobile context (base camps) and lower where a portable, specific tool kit is important (foraging and logistic locations).

PUTTING THE INDICES INTO OPERATION

In order to be useful, of course, these indices had to be measured using the attributes of artifacts.

Reduction stage measures were based on a composite reduction stage index derived by using the properties of flakes discussed in Chapter 5. The attributes of whole flakes used in the reduction stage index were cortex cover, platform characteristics, dorsal scar count density, and a thinness measure. Cortex cover was characterized in the Seedskadee field data as ranging from 0 to 3 (no cover to total cortex cover); this measure was transformed for the purposes of the reduction stage index to a range of 0.875 (total cortex) through 9.125 (no cortex). Flake platform characteristics taken as indicative of progressively higher reduction stages were cortical platforms, single-facet platforms, and multiple-facet platforms; these states were transformed to a scale of 1.5 through 8.5. A dorsal scar density value, calculated by the dorsal scar count divided by the flake's length, was standardized to a range of 0 through 10. Finally, a thinness measure calculated as the length of the flake divided by its thickness was standardized to range from 0 through 10. The stage index was calculated from these four measures, and then adjusted to a range of 1 through 10: [(cortex + platform + dorsal scar density + thinness) x 0.417308] - 1.036714 = stage. Lower values represent earlier reduction stages.

The stage index values were rounded to the nearest integer value. The Shannon diversity index (Odum 1975:222–23) was used to calculate reduction stage diversity. Measures of high reduction stage were based on counting flakes of reduction stages greater than or equal to 5; the low reduction stage measure was determined by counting flakes with reduction stage less than 5.

The tool-to-debris ratio consists of the number of formal tools (biface 1, biface 2, biface 3, and unifaces) divided by total cores, angular debris, undifferentiated flakes, biface thinning flakes, and pressure flakes. The ratio of utilized flakes to tools consists of utilized flakes divided by formal tools (bifaces 1–3 and unifaces), and is high where there are relatively few tools. The percentage of biface thinning flakes is measured in terms of their variation with all other flakes, multiplied by 100; the percentage of biface 3s is relative to other bifaces and unifaces in a sample unit. The edge-to-tool ratio was the number of edges coded in the field divided by the number of formal tools.

An overall assemblage diversity measure was based on proportions of cores, debris (chunks and angular debris), tested cobbles, undifferentiated flakes, biface thinning flakes, utilized and retouched flakes, pressure flakes, biface 1s, biface 2s, biface 3s, and unifaces. These taxa served as the class types for calculation of diversity using the Shannon diversity index.

PATTERNING IN INDICES

Integer counts of items per sample cell can be inspected using a simple variance-mean ratio (VMR), as was done for chert and quartzite debris earlier in this chapter, to examine scales of patterning in such data. For continuous data such as densities or the values of the indices operationalized above, where no specific values can be expected, it is desirable to use a slightly different VMR calculation, in which the continuous mean values are corrected for. Grieg-Smith (1983:94) has suggested using the formula (variance - mean)/(mean)^2, which was employed in the graphs of index versus cell size that appear below.

While no specific index values are to be expected, index values are meaningful in a way that simple counts are not. High, moderate, and low values of each index are to be expected (Table 8.1) for different occupation types. For this reason, in addition to the modified VMR measure for each index, the mean values were also graphed at each cell size. Figures 8.13 through 20 illustrate the VMRs and means of the index values at cell sizes of 5, 10, 25, 50, 100, 250, and 500m.

The examination of these graphs entails searching first for clustering or lack thereof using the upper graphs in each figure. When differential patterning at various scales is identified, the mean values at those scales are then referred to. The mean values have been taken as

Table 8.1. Expectations for values of seven technical indices for postulated Green River Basin occupation types.

Technical Indices	Short-term Foraging Base	Foraging Location	Semi permanent Multi-family Base	Permanent Multi-family Base	Logistic Location #1	Logistic Location #2	Travelling Camp
Stage Diversity	high	low	high	high	low-mod	low	low
High Reduction Stages	high	high	mod	mod	mod	high	high
Low Reduction Stages	high	high	mod	mod	mod	low	low
Tool/Debris Ratio	low	low	low	low	mod	mod	mod
Utilized Flakes/Tools Ratio	high	high	high	high	mod	mod	mod
Proportion Biface Thinning Flakes	low	high	low	low	high	high	high
Proportion Biface 3s	high	low	high	high	mod	mod	mod
Edge/Tool Ratio	low	low	low	low	high	high	mod
Assemblage Diversity	high	low	high	high	low	low	low

identifiers—as diagnostic, in a way, of the presence or absence of expected values for each occupation type.

I would like to emphasize that the interpretation of these values is intuitive, that they are relative, and that another interpreter might explain the results differently. The important point is that such an exercise provides a way of thinking about the scales of spatial properties of portions of the archaeological record. A summary of my interpretations of the scales at which differential patterning appears in the indices, and the significance of these interpretations in terms of the expectations listed in Table 8.1 appears in Table 8.2.

These interpretations could be discussed and debated at far greater length than is appropriate here. There are several general things that can be said about them, however. First, some encouraging overall patterning is apparent in the scales of distribution of the occupation types. Indications of foraging locations seem to cluster more at high spatial frequencies, logistic and traveling locations at lower spatial frequencies, and base camps between these two extremes. This pattern may indicate simply that there are far more foraging locations and also more bases than logistic and traveling locations. It may be that the frequency of creation of different occupation types accounts for this—there are more temporary foraging loci, fewer logistic and traveling loci, and an intermediate number of base locations represented in the archaeological record. In addition, these results support the proposition that appropriate places for different sorts of occupations are restricted to different degrees. If, as discussed in earlier chapters, logistic mobility strategies involve the reuse of specific places, then there should appear to be fewer of these than places that would not necessarily be reused purposely.

A less encouraging observation, however, is that some of the indices seem to indicate counterintuitive scales of clustering of the different occupation types. The graph of the ratio of utilized flakes to tools, for instance, identifies foraging and multifamily bases at relatively large scales (250m), as do the proportion of biface 3s (500m or higher) and the type diversity measure (up to 250m). Some indicators show logistic and traveling locations at very high spatial frequencies (the biface thinning flake, biface 3, and edge-to-tool indices at 5m). Part of the problem undoubtedly lies in my expectations for each index, and in the fact that the indices are undoubtedly measuring a number of real variables or indicators that do not correlate perfectly. These are problems that will be present with any deductive indicators; given compa-

Table 8.2. Observations of variance-to-mean ratios and means at varying cell sizes, summarized from Figs. 8.8–8.15, and interpretations concerning occupation types and scales. Abbreviations used in this table are: D, dune areas; S, sandsheet areas; T, terrace areas; and M, mesatop areas.

Index	5m	10m	25m	50m	100m	250m	500m
Reduction Stage Diversity			M:Clustered at low mean values *Foraging or Logistic Locations*	D:Clustered low means S:Clustered at 50m+, low means *Foraging/Logistic Locations*		T:Clustered moderate means *Logistic Location 1*	
High Reduction Stages						D:Clustered S:Clustered	T:Clustered 500m+ M:Clustered 500m+
Low Reduction Stages						D:Clustered S:Clustered	T:Clustered 500m+ M:Unclustered
						Logistic or Travelling Locations	

Index	5m	10m	25m	50m	100m	250m	500m
Tool/Debris Ratio	D:Clustered low means S:Clustered low means T: Clustered low means *Foraging Bases, Multifamily Bases or Foraging Locations*	T:Unclustered low mean	S:Clustered low means *Foraging Base, Multifamily Base, For. Location*	D:Clustered high means *Logistic Travelling Locations* M:Clustered low means	S:Clustered moderate means T: Clustered moderate means *Logistic, Travelling Locations* M:Unclustered low means *Foraging Location, Base or Multifamily Bases*	D:Unclustered low mean *Foraging Locations or Bases* T:Unclustered high means *Logistic, Travelling Locations*	M:Unclustered high means *Locations, Travelling Locations*
Utilized Flake/ Tool Ratio			D:Clustered low means S:Clustered low means M:Clustered moderate means ?		D:mod clustering, high means S:same, low means *Logistic Locations*	S:Unclustered high means *Foraging or Multifamily Bases*	

Table 8.2. (*continued*)

Index	5m	10m	25m	50m	100m	250m	500m
Proportion of Biface Thinning Flakes	D:Clustered high means *Foraging Base/Loc or Multifamily Base* T:Clustered low means *Logistic or Traveling Locations*			D,M:Clustered low means S:Clustered moderate means *Logistic, Traveling Locations*			T,M: Unclustered high means *Logistic or Foraging Locations*
Proportion of Bifaces 3s	D:Clustered moderate means *Logistic Locations*	T:Clustered low means *Foraging Locations*	T:Clustered low means *Foraging Locations*	S:Clustered low means *Foraging Locations*	S:Clustered low means *Foraging Locations*		M:Unclustered high means *Foraging, Multifamily Bases*

Table 8.2. (*continued*)

Index	5m	10m	25m	50m	100m	250m	500m
Edge/Tool Ratio	D:Clustered high means S:Clustered high means *Logistic Locations?*	D,S:Mod. clustered low means T:Clustered low means *Foraging Locations, Bases, Multi-family Bases*		M:Clustered high means *Logistic Locations*	T:Clustered moderate means ?		D:Unclustered low means S,T:Unclustered high means *Logistic Locations*
Type Diversity				T:Inflection, low means *Logistic or Foraging Locations*	D:moderate means S:low means *Permanent Multifamily Base?*	M:Inflection, mod. means *Multifamily Bases or Foraging Bases?*	

rable survey data from other places, better indices and expectations could certainly be devised.

Some of the indices are, in addition, difficult to interpret in an unambiguous way from the VMR graphs. One problem is the scales at which the graph traces themselves can be resolved only by visual inspection. The graphed lines vary in a complex manner at high frequencies, but graphing them at appropriate scales at these frequencies would make it impossible to see the variation at lower frequencies. I have compromised in order to allow the presentation of each of the graphs on a single scale. I have cut off my examination of scales at 5m, although far higher frequencies of patterning could be examined using these data. These would also be more difficult to interpret in terms consistent with larger scales. Certainly, clustering at scales larger than those detected by the 25m square sample grids cannot be interpreted as being due to an episode of occupation—they are simply too large for hunter-gatherer "sites." The diversity indices, probably as a result of the general nature of diversity measures, all produce graph traces that are quite similar. Diversity indices may not be particularly good measures to inspect by using VMR graphs.

There is another important lesson to be taken. It may be that the occupation types—base camps, foraging locations, logistic locations, and the like—that archaeologists have suggested as things to be identified in the archaeological record are inappropriate analytical categories at this logical level. It is difficult, however, to suggest better entities to be sought among the complex patterning resulting from a continuous and overlapping archaeological landscape. I shall address this topic further in the concluding chapter. The archaeological record may be a qualitatively different phenomenon than ongoing human behavior—or its patterning in ethnographic time.

Figures 8.13 through 8.20 follow, text resumes on page 243.

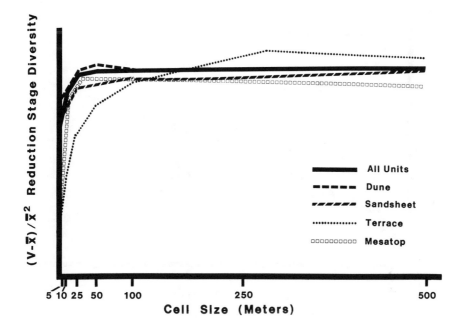

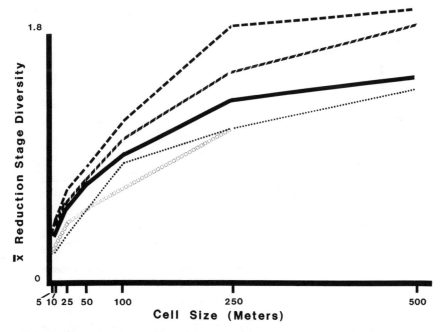

Figure 8.13. Variance-to-mean ratios (VMR) at varying sample grid cell scales for Reduction Stage Diversity Index, Seedskadee Project survey units, by geomorphological zone.

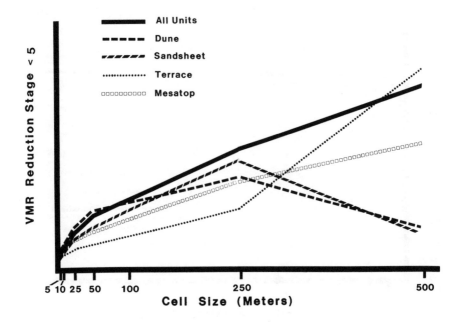

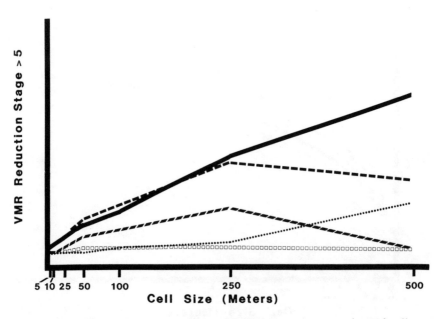

Figure 8.14. Variance-to-mean ratios (VMR) at varying sample grid cell scales for reduction stages less than and greater than 5, Seedskadee Project survey units, by geomorphological zone.

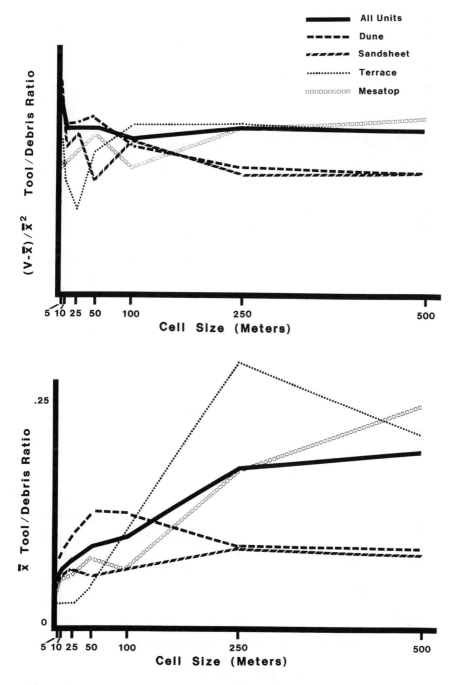

Figure 8.15. Variance-to-mean ratios (VMR) at varying sample grid cell scales for the Tool/Debris Ratio Index, Seedskadee Project survey units, by geomorphological zone.

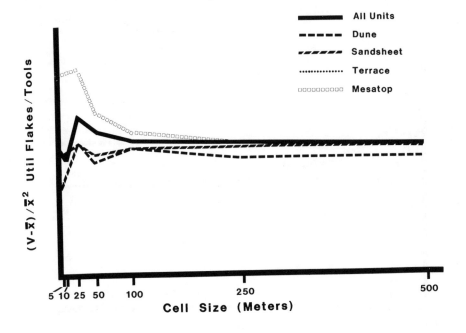

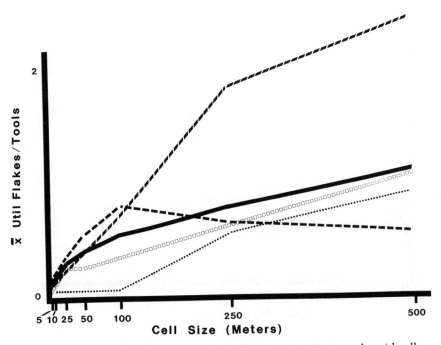

Figure 8.16. Variance-to-mean ratios (VMR) at varying sample grid cell scales for the Utilized Flakes/ToolsTool Ratio Index, Seedskadee Project survey units, by geomorphological zone.

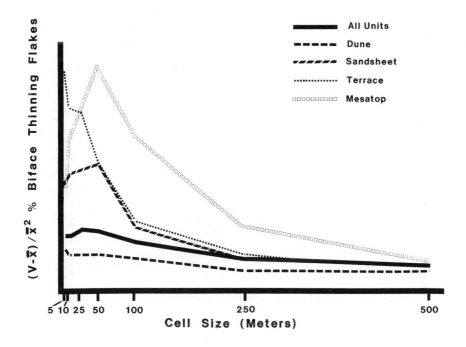

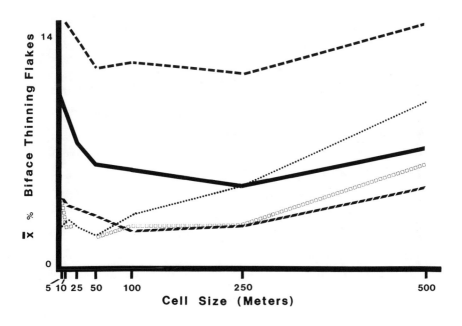

Figure 8.17. Variance-to-mean ratios (VMR) at varying sample grid cell scales for the Percentage of Biface Thinning Index, Seedskadee Project survey units, by geomorphological zone.

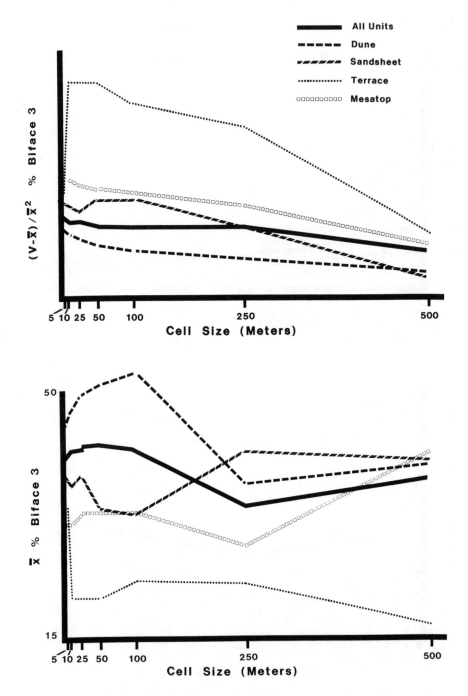

Figure 8.18. Variance-to-mean ratios (VMR) at varying sample grid cell scales for the Percentage of Biface 3s Index, Seedskadee Project survey units, by geomorphological zone.

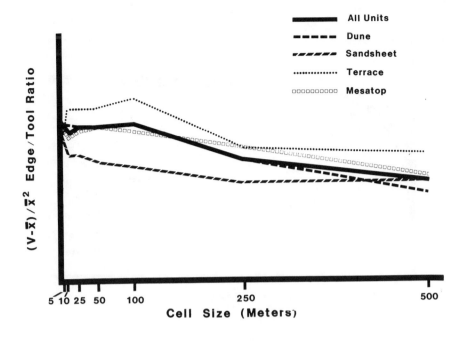

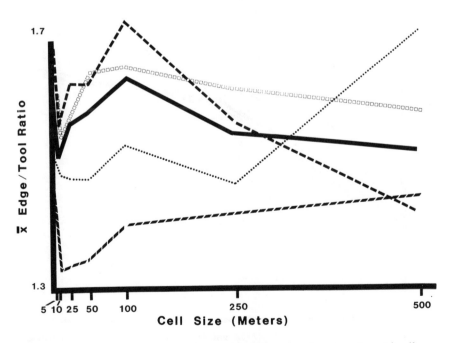

Figure 8.19. Variance-to-mean ratios (VMR) at varying sample grid cell scales for the Edge/Tool Ratio Index, Seedskadee Project survey units, by geomorphological zone.

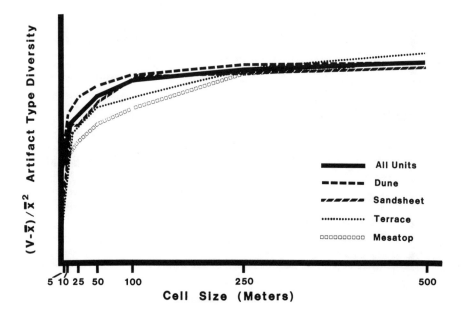

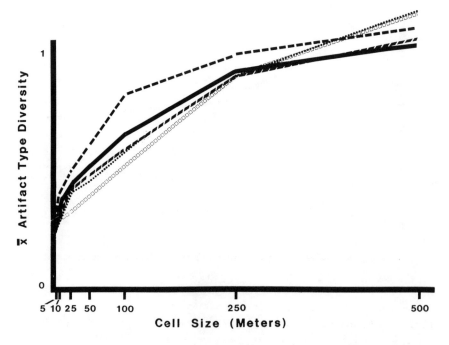

Figure 8.20. Variance-to-mean ratios (VMR) at varying sample grid cell scales for the Artifact Type Diversity Index, Seedskadee Project survey units, by geomorphological zone.

SCALES OF PATTERNING IN THE ARCHAEOLOGICAL RECORD, AND THEIR IMPLICATIONS FOR THE ARCHAEOLOGY AND THE PREHISTORY OF THE GREEN RIVER BASIN

The interpretations I have made above have been in terms of scales of clustering or repetition of indicators of different strategies or components of strategies across the landscape. How are these scales related to what was happening prehistorically in the Green River Basin and how archaeologists perceive it?

First, it appears that all of the occupation types projected as possible in the Green River Basin on the basis of the archaeological and ethnohistoric literature may well have taken place there. This includes the components of both foraging and more logistically organized adaptations. What is more, to judge from the wide range of scales at which the different indices cluster or are repeated, the places at which the activities that participated in these systems happened may have been of many different sizes, or in varying densities. To me, this indicates that many different strategies are responsible for the archaeological record in the Green River Basin.

This, in fact, is to be expected for all hunter-gatherers. If there is one thing characteristic of hunter-gatherer adaptations, it is constant and almost instantaneous change in the face of changing environmental and other conditions. Group sizes, locations, labor organization, strategies of resource procurement, and technological strategies are, then, predictably of many different types over even relatively short time spans. In one sense all hunter-gatherers are part of one big adaptive system, while in another sense there is probably always a number of adaptations in operation among even a single group over a period of months or days. When complexities of this sort occur, broad cultural chronologies are probably out of place. Not only could portions of, say, Palaeoindian adaptations be identical to those of the "Late Plains Archaic people," but given an overlapping and dynamic archaeological record, they are physically indistinguishable as well.

The analysis of scales of contrast between the use of quartzite and chert points up some methodological problems in southwestern Wyoming archaeology, and probably in the methodologies used in other places as well. On mesatops and terraces lithic materials (particularly quartzite) are ubiquitous but relatively sparsely (though evenly) exposed. The distributions of culturally modified materials may in fact be dependent upon the locations of other cores or implements over large areas.

If, during the course of fieldwork, archaeologists single out small portions of this continuous archaeological record as "sites," important patterning will be missed. Nonetheless, the whole area is not a "site" either, in any episodic way.

Even if one records sites, then, in order to detect such patterning one must also record the entirety of the surface archaeological record, including that within as well as outside of the sites, at uniformly high resolution.

In dune areas, and to a somewhat lesser extent in sandsheet landscapes, the patterning of scales of the index indicators is quite different. Areas where tools were refurbished or manufactured, especially chert tools, are highly clustered at moderate to large scales, while places where they were used and occasionally sharpened, or where flakes were removed from chert tools for more expedient use, are also clustered but at much smaller scales. Some clusters of materials that score high in terms of the index indicators are uniformly in clusters of 5m diameter, and probably smaller. Archaeologists working in southwestern Wyoming and interpreting its archaeology have for the most part viewed sand dune areas as preferred settlement areas for large groups, mostly because of the large numbers of artifacts there. If extensive areas in dunes are labelled as sites, and sampled using quadrats or other less-than-intensive methods, or, worse yet, by simply collecting diagnostic artifacts, well-defined patterning will also be missed.

The most important positive implications of the patterning observed in the course of these scalar analyses probably have to do with how to use sampling frames. While assigning specific site sizes in all of the areas inspected would be difficult—in fact unrealistic on the basis of my analyses—the differences in patterning across the landscape might be used to determine differential "window" sizes one needs to look at. In mesatop and terrace areas these need to be relatively large. Many of the index indicators in such areas exhibited their highest VMR peaks at 500m scales; the windows necessary to gauge whether these are true peaks there should probably be larger than 500m square. In the dune areas, considerably smaller survey unit sizes may yield the distributional archaeological data necessary to see the scales of patterning relevant to the operation of past systems.

9

BEYOND SURVEY ARCHAEOLOGY

-- -- -- -- -- -- -- -- -- -- -- -- --

In the spirit of archaeology's current state of critical self-consciousness, I have suggested that one important area on which we should concentrate lies in consistency of theory and method. One symptom of inconsistency between what we want to know about the past and our interpretations of the archaeological record is the uncritical use of the concept of the "site." Sites are employed variously as units of pattern recognition in the archaeological record, as analytical entities, and as units of behavioral interpretation. In my view, the site concept is inappropriate at each of these levels.

While there are obviously specific places at which people did things, they are but one component of what we really want to know about: systems of human organization. The archaeological record is the product of material items exiting and reentering organizational systems during the repetitive repositioning of these systems across the landscape over long periods. Before and after the discard of materials, their nature and placement is affected by a complex interplay of cultural and natural processes.

The resultant archaeological record can be expected to be a compound, overlapping document more like a time exposure than a series of snapshots. The image apparent in this time exposure is brighter in some places than in others, but is continuous to some extent almost everywhere due to the long time over which it has been exposed. This seems obvious for the surface archaeological record, but disjunctures between discard and depositional events ensure that it is also the case for most sealed deposits.

In recognition of the existence of a compound and continuous archaeological record, some archaeologists have suggested methods based on artifacts rather than sites as units of discovery, pattern recognition, and analysis. Building on these suggestions, I have advanced and operationalized an approach I have called distributional archaeology. Distributional archaeology is based on the intensive discovery of individual artifacts in the field and the high-resolution recording of their locations and attributes over relatively large contiguous survey areas. A distributional archaeological survey carried out in the Green River Basin of southwestern Wyoming illustrates the practicality and possibility of this method.

Distributional archaeological data can be subjected to virtually any sort of analysis suggested by archaeologists; they can also be the basis for new interpretations of archaeological patterning not available or even possible using site, intersite, or intrasite data collection and analysis strategies. In the analyses presented here the unique potential of distributional data has been explored. Analytical methods suggested by archaeologists working with spatially restricted excavation data, and by plant ecologists, have been adapted to facilitate the examination of the spatial scales of patterning inherent in the archaeological record of my Wyoming study area. I have examined these scales of patterning both in the light of previous archaeological and ethnological interpretations and in terms of their potential for allowing the recognition of overlapping past systems and their component technological and mobility strategies.

I devised a series of technological indices I thought would be diagnostic of possible past occupation types in the Green River Basin, and examined their spatial variation at successively smaller sample grid sizes (from 500 to 5m) using variance-to-mean ratio graphs. This method, also called dimensional analysis of variance, allows the assessment of the characteristic size and degree of clustering, or lack thereof, in spatial data. The patterning thus revealed suggests that a wide variety of different settlement or occupation types, including foraging locations, foraging bases, multifamily base camps, logistic locations, and traveling locations, can be supported in the study area. These settlement or occupation types overlap in space, something that is entirely

predictable and which reinforces some of the more theoretical propositions discussed in earlier chapters. What is more, different technological indices indicate patterning of the same occupation types at
different scales in areas defined as being of different environmental
types, a conclusion consistent with the flexible nature of hunter-gatherer
adaptations even over short periods.

Almost all modern hunter-gatherers exhibit considerable planning
and tactical depth, in the terms of Binford (1986). Members of such
groups obtain raw materials as much as a year or more before using
them. Planning, however, does not always work out—in fact, the more
planning that takes place, the more likely it is that unplanned activities will require the use of expedient answers to unforseen contingencies. The result of these situational deviations from the anticipated is
that the materials left by groups of people may appear in the technological record very differently when they are in "base camps" than when
they are "in the field." This technological reflection of planning
disjunctures results in "interesting and complicated archaeological
patterns" (Binford 1986:5)—exactly what is seen in the Seedskadee
data. Especially in areas exhibiting greater seasonal stress, or greater
efficiency demands for obtaining food (both of which are important
in Wyoming),

> rarely is there strong patterning of a 'categorical' type . . . instead,
> assemblages are reticulated compounds of numerous subsets of the
> technology. Rarely is there a strong set of 'categorical' differences
> recognizable among 'types' of places occupied by a single system.
> Likewise, when independent measures of the conditions being coped
> with at the time of archaeological deposition can be monitored at
> different places and at different times (e.g., environmental indicators and
> faunal remains), rarely is there any categorical associational patterning
> such that some tools always go with a given species or a particular
> activity. The ability to shift tactics to accommodate unanticipated
> conditions ensures against such robust and simple patterning.

Binford refers to robust and simple patterning in the contents of
assemblages. While he cautions against seeking robust patterning
associationally—that is, between tool types—there is no reason that
more robust patterning should not be seen in examining the scales of
indices constructed deductively, with some reference to their causes.
Robust patterning may in fact be visible in the scalar distribution of
some of the Seedskadee technological indices, which allow the mea-

surement of the spatial scales of strategies, rather than simply proximal associations of types of artifacts, which is the primary objective of site-oriented studies.

FUTURE DIRECTIONS IN DISTRIBUTIONAL ARCHAEOLOGY

In the fieldwork, analysis, and interpretation of my Seedskadee research I have attempted a methodological approach that is at least partly new. In the course of such an attempt one naturally reaches conclusions about better ways to do things and other directions to pursue in the future.

The results of the dimensional analyses of variance show patterning at almost all scales between the 5 and 500m square limits imposed by survey unit sizes, and also suggest that patterning at larger scales exists in the data. Larger survey units are necessary to examine larger-scale patterning, however. In future distributional archaeological efforts much larger contiguous areas should be surveyed and their contents measured. In order to explore the potential of distributional archaeology further, it would also be advantageous to compare large areas from other parts of the world. Surveys based on the recognition of variously defined "sites" and the regionally specific diagnostic items they contain can never be compared with one another; surveys done in the distributional manner advocated here—with all artifacts recorded—can always be compared at some level. This is not a call for standardization of research designs, nor really of data collection. It is, rather, a plea for data to be collected in a consistent manner, with the artifact as the unit of discovery, measurement, and recording. Discovery must be intensive, all artifacts that can be found must be treated equally by being mapped at high resolution, and coverage must extend over large areas, perhaps thousands of times the size of sites observed by ethnographers.

This recommendation seems antithetical to most of the current precepts of cultural resource management archaeology. The values many of its practitioners and advocates continually voice are pragmatic: cultural resource management is done with the taxpayers' money, and it should be done as cheaply as possible. How can we go out and record everything found on the surface, treating it equally, and be cost-effective? The answer is simple. Once distributional archaeology has been done in an area, the surface archaeological record has been, effectively, "mitigated." There is no value to the distinction between Phase II and

Phase III survey in an area so treated. Not only will distributional archaeological fieldwork and analysis in an area to be evaluated allow the identification of properties eligible for the National Register as well or better than a Phase II survey, but in many ways most of these manifestations have already been recorded, their research potential realized, and land-disturbing activities can progress.

The great promise of distributional archaeology for cultural resource management archaeologists is that once it is accepted archaeology will slowly begin to become comparable on both a regional and trans-regional basis.

In order to make a distributional archaeological survey approach demonstrably workable, which is probably the only way it can gain acceptance, it will be necessary to streamline the field methods I have described in Chapter 7. Fortunately, this may be largely a hardware and software problem. Portable computers and efficiently designed coding programs should allow faster and more error-free coding of artifact attributes; data-logging devices attached to electronic distance measurement theodolites will accomplish the same for locational recording.

Incorporating the noncultural aspects of the environment into interpretations of the archaeological record may pose a far greater problem. It is not enough to have high-resolution information for large areas on the patterning of cultural materials; environmental patterning relevant to depositional and postdepositional processes must be recorded in a comparable manner. In addition, as I have stressed, predepositional natural distributions—for instance patterning in cobbles and other stones, and perhaps in their exposure and availability over very short, perhaps seasonal, periods—may be even more important for the interpretation of the archaeological record.

Also, it must be remembered that predepositional and postdepositional resource distributions and availability are not strictly separable; they are a feedback system. "Behavioral archaeologists" (cf. Schiffer 1976, 1987) are almost correct in saying that the archaeological record is the record of discard processes. The other process that the archaeological record very directly reflects, however, is the "un-discard" of artifacts—that is, the removal, modification, and recycling of existing artifacts. I suspect that recycling and reusing things is every bit as prevalent as throwing things away, and that when archaeology finally reaches some sort of qualitative revolution, as we all hope it will, this observation may well be the basis of it. At any rate, recording data relevant to the ubiquitous recycling and reuse of artifacts is overlooked by almost all archaeological data collection strategies today, and doing so may add immensely to the effort we may have to expend in the future.

Once high-resolution distributional data are collected they must be analyzed. The variance-to-mean ratio methods I have used in the demonstrations in Chapter 8 have yielded interesting and informative results, but far more efficient and more easily interpretable methods can probably be devised. These might include power spectrum analysis, digital filtering, and pattern recognition methods, all of which require computer-intensive matrix operations. Fortunately, dedicated systems that can economically perform such calculations on enormous matrices are now available, and are currently in use for processing digital images taken from airborne and satellite multispectral scanners. We may find geographical information systems (GISs) increasingly useful in archaeological analysis, once we have appropriate data to use with them (beyond a few dots representing sites within each square mile). I feel such systems can be adapted profitably for analyses of distributional archaeological data.

BEYOND SURFACE SURVEY ARCHAEOLOGY

What of the implications of a distributional approach that may go beyond survey archaeology? I hope I have demonstrated the value of distributional archaeology for meshing method and theory in archaeological survey by suggesting that the assumptions of this sort of approach are probably just as applicable to interpreting site excavation data.

Archaeological and Anthropological Methodology and Translations at a Site Level

Consider the correspondence between the archaeological record and the ethnographic record at a methodological level. Archaeologists have worried about making archaeology anthropological, most recently under the rubric of ethnoarchaeology. Most ethnoarchaeology involves a rather direct translation between observations of living peoples' behavior and the nature and placement of the materials they leave in the archaeological record.

While thinking about how to compare ethnographic situations to the archaeological record in a distributional way, it occurred to me that perhaps one could place a camouflaged or at least armored camera in an occupied, ongoing hunter-gatherer camp to provide an analogue to the "time exposure" sample of behavior that results in artifact distributions. The shutter could be left open—but in a very short time, the emulsion would be filled, and the image would be hopelessly continuous. I recently saw a time exposure of thousands of automobiles crossing the Brooklyn Bridge (the shutter probably having been left open for only a few minutes). One could never separate one set of headlights from another, or tell whether one vehicle stopped and another accelerated. Very luckily for archaeology, this is not the kind of "time exposure" represented by the archaeological record. The physical archaeological record is composed not of a continuous flow of events but the discard of discrete physical evidence (artifacts) that can "reflect" only instants.

A better way to approximate such discrete instants would be to set our ethnoarchaeological camera to take pictures at intervals for time-lapse photographs. Time-lapse photographs are usually played back as a motion picture, producing sequences in which flowers seem to bloom, then wither and die, all in a few seconds; or in which clouds race across the sky. One probably wouldn't want to do this with ethnographic time-lapse frames; locations and types of behavior, and perhaps the names of participants, would instead be noted frame by frame.

But what interval between frames would be best for mapping human activities? What kind of chronology or temporal resolution would let us separate activities from other activities and yet document the progression from one to another? My conclusion—based in part upon actually having attempted ethnographic observations of Bushman behavior using pencil and paper—is that intervals of an hour, or even possibly of ten or fifteen minutes, would show behavior as hopelessly discontinuous, with patterning from frame to frame difficult or impossible to interpret. The human actors would appear to jump from one place to another, with no clue to where they had been between frames. Objects would suddenly appear, remain for a few or many frames, and then disappear without apparent human agency. It is hard enough to make any sense out of what is going on or even to record its sequence when the ethnographer is actually there; it would be impossible to do so with time-lapse ethnoarchaeological camera frames.

Yet this is exactly the sort of sample that the archaeological record affords of past behavior, or more properly speaking, the discard behavior from which archaeological distributions partially derive. It is like opening the shutter again and again, but not changing the film. Discard events associated with the continuous flow of human activities may take place at intervals far greater than ten minutes or an hour. Over short periods (days or even weeks), their results may be almost invisible and the constituents of patterning in them difficult or impossible to separate and associate. Behavioral events or episodes, on the other hand, take place continually. The behavioral instants that result in the archaeological record—the discard of discrete physical artifacts—are just that: instants. Instants have spatial location but no temporal content or dimension. The time at which these instants take place is not at all obvious or transparent from looking at the film.

It is also interesting to think about the similarities between the difficulty of translating from instantaneous behavior to the archaeological record, and from this same sort of behavior to the things that ethnologists record and use as data. The ethnographic record is composed of material things just as is the archaeological record—not just objects and places, but songs, uttered justifications, and stated reasons for doing things. Translating between the ethnographic record and instantaneous behavior requires, if not a distributional approach, "distributional thinking" about overlapping and continuous distributions. Ultimately, both ethnographic and archaeological translations and interpretations of the flow of instantaneous human behavior—the anthropological laws we seek but have not yet found—may have to be reached in the same way, through a behavioral calculus that would unite the two. Such a calculus will use sampled instants, both ethnographic and archaeological, to reconstitute both and to compare them. Once we devise such a calculus the structuralist/reconstructionist double bind will be no more.

Archaeology and Anthropology on a Theoretical Level: Sites and Cultures

It has often been argued that sites and site types are necessary adjuncts to translating the archaeological record into a synthesis of the activities of and relationships among different peoples or cultures. Both "sites" and "cultures," I feel, are primitive terms in a developing science.

A useful analogy is afforded by "the ether," which was the response of physicists in the late nineteenth century to questions about the medium through which radio signals and light were propagated. Physicists of the period believed that electromagnetic radiation existed in the form of waves, like sound waves. Sound wave propagation required a medium such as air or water for the waves to travel through; radio and light waves, however, could also be demonstrated to travel through the vacuum of space, through nothingness. To avoid the apparent contradiction, it was reasoned that space must be filled with something—ether—through which certain waves could travel. The advent of the wave-particle theory of electromagnetic radiation early in this century made the existence of ether a rather laughable nonproblem.

The concept of culture might well be considered another primitive term, intimately related to the beginning of anthropology more than a century ago, and still very much in use today. In 1931 Alfred Kroeber advanced the culture-area concept, justifying it as a "community product of nearly the whole school of American anthropologists" (Harris 1968:374). People predictably did different sorts of things in order to adapt to different sorts of environments. Kroeber's formulations were based largely upon Clark Wissler's (1917) correlations of "food areas" with "culture areas." Kroeber and his colleagues amassed lists of many thousands of culture traits, both material and ideological, in an attempt to define culture areas in North America empirically.

Kroeber's assumption was that "on the one hand culture can be understood primarily only in terms of cultural factors, but . . . on the other hand no culture is wholly intelligible without reference to the noncultural or so-called environmental factors with which it is in relation and which condition it" (Kroeber 1939, cited in Vayda 1969:350). Attempting to correlate ethnic distinctions with culture trait lists, however, proved frustrating: "the interactions of culture and environment become exceedingly complex when followed out. And this complexity makes generalization unprofitable, on the whole. In each situation or area different natural factors are likely to be impinging on culture with different intensity" (Vayda 1969:351). Kroeber was unable to operationalize the relationship between environments and cultures.

Kroeber apparently felt, at least to some extent, that the problem lay in his delineation or understanding of what culture was, and throughout his professional career he continued to explore the concept "to assist other investigators in reaching greater precision in [its] definition" (Kroeber and Kluckhohn 1952:4). As Leslie White has shown, however, in a review of Kroeber and Kluckhohn's (1952) last major work on this subject (White 1954), there are two levels at which terms can be defined. One of these is empirical, involving questions of precision of measurement, while the other is semantic—simply deciding how we shall use words. White concluded, essentially, that "culture" is and will continue to be the latter sort of concept in anthropology, a primitive, undefinable term for the subject matter of the science.

Yet archaeologists traditionally translate different sorts of associations of formally similar materials into "cultures," and continue to do so today. The places at which these materials are associated are "sites." From associations of materials at sites, culture histories and sequences are fabricated, and the ways that culturally distinct groups interacted with their environments are definitionally explained.

In this book I have tried to illustrate that whether one takes an ethnographic or an archaeological perspective, reasoning either from theory or from the empirical facts of the archaeological record, "sites" may not just be difficult to define precisely or interpret easily. *They are very likely not there at all.* We can continue to use this time-honored, primitive term seriously and keep trying to define something that is undefinable, unmeasurable, and even antithetical to the development of archaeological science. Or we can relegate it to an interesting phase in the history of our science and get on with the business of investigating what we are really interested in, the composite and overlapping use of the landscape by human systems, using realistic terms of discovery, measurement, and analysis. I sincerely hope I have provided some impetus here toward the latter course.

APPENDIX A:

LITHIC DATA CODING FORM,

SEEDSKADEE SURVEY

-- -- -- -- -- -- -- -- -- -- -- -- --

1–5   Shot Number: consisting of a flag color (orange or red), and an artifact number

7–8   Material Type:
  1. cryptocrystalline
  2. glassy volcanic
  3. crystalline volcanic
  4. sandstone
  5. other sedimentary
  6. metamorphic
  7. other
  9. indeterminate

10–12   Length: maximum dimension (for flakes, maximum length of axis perpendicular platform) measured to nearest 5mm

14–16   Width: largest dimension perpendicular to the width measurement, to the nearest 5mm

18–20   Thickness: maximum thickness, measured to nearest 5mm

22   Completeness: estimated completeness of artifact
  1. greater than half
  2. less than half
  3. whole
  9. indeterminate

23   Illustration: whether artifact was illustrated, type of illustration, and whether collected
  1. drawn

2. photographed

3. collected

25–29   Weight: to the nearest 0.5g

31–32   Type:

10. Core—artifacts bearing no positive bulb of percussion, and bearing at least two or more negative scars at least two centimeters long originating from one or more surfaces

11. Bipolar Core—a core with platform remnants on opposing ends and with opposing negative scars and/or bulbs of percussion resulting from force rebounding from two directions

12. Single-platform Core—a core with flakes removed from only one platform plane

13. Multiplatform Core—a core with flakes removed from more than one platform plane

14. Blade Core—a core with blades (flakes more than twice as long as they are wide) removed from one platform plane

20. Angular Debris—debitage upon which no ventral surface can be defined but which exhibits unquestionable negative scars characteristic of the percussion technique

30. Flake—a lithic artifact that exhibits a dorsal and ventral side. Whole flakes exhibit a recognizable bulb of force and a platform

31. Biface Thinning Flake—a long, thin curved flake with many dorsal scars, ventral lipping, a multifaceted platform resulting from removal from a worked edge, and no cortex

32. Bipolar Flake—defined by the presence of two positive bulbs of percussion on the same or different surfaces, or the existence of one positive bulb of percussion at one end of the artifact and a negative scar originating from the opposite end of the same or a different surface. Crushing at opposite ends of the item is often evident. Flakes often exhibit a conical bulb of percussion. A lateral strip of cortex often separates opposing platforms, thus differentiating bipolar flakes from bipolar cores.

40. Tested Cobble—a cobble from which a single flake or multiple flakes have been removed as if the material had been tested for suitability as a tool medium, and cobbles that appear to have been intentionally broken in half

41. Chunk—a cobble or other stone with an unmodified surface

42. Uniface—any artifact that has flake scars which extend over one-third or more of only one surface of the artifact

50. Biface—any artifact that has flake scars extending over one-third or more of both the dorsal and ventral sides. Bifaces undergo changes in morphology from the bifacial core or roughout stage through the preform stage to a finished tool (after Camilli and Nelson 1983).
51. Biface 1—a biface exhibiting primary thinning (a bifacially worked edge, irregular outline, or widely and variably spaced flake scars)
52. Biface 2—a biface exhibiting secondary trimming (a bifacially worked, semi-irregular outline, and closely spaced and/or semiregularly spaced flake scars)
53. Biface 3—a shaped piece, bifacially worked, with a regular outline and closely and/or quite regularly spaced flake scars
80. Other

34   Cortical covering
       1. over 50 percent
       2. under 50 percent
       3. total
       9. indeterminate

35   Dorsal scar count: 0–9, with more than 9 coded as 9

36   Platform characteristics
       0. missing
       1. cortical (cortex present on platform)
       2. crushed
       3. noncortical single facet
       4. noncortical multiple facet
       5. ground
       8. other
       9. indeterminate

Record for Tools:

38   Breakage:
       0. whole
       1. tip
       2. base
       3. midsection
       4. whole, tip crushed/battered
       5. whole, tip broken
       6. whole, base broken
       7. reworked
       9. broken, indeterminate fragment

Note: for tools with more than one modified edge, each edge was coded on a separate line on the coding form, in columns 39–44.

39   Modification:
        1. utilization (systemic scarring up to 2mm from tool edge)
        2. unifacial marginal retouch (less than 1/3 of surface)
        3. bifacial marginal retouch (more than 1/3 of surface)
        4. unifacially flaked (more than 1/3 of surface)
        5. bifacially flaked (more than 1/3 of surface)
        6. ground edge

40   Location of modification:
        1. side
        2. end
        3. end and side
        4. entire surface
        9. indeterminate

41   Edge shape: for formally shaped tools
        1. point
        2. spur
        3. notch
        4. denticulate
        5. concave
        6. convex
        7. straight
        8. irregular
        9. indeterminate

42   Edge angle (original): angular measure of the cross-section of the edge prior to retouch or utilization
        1. less than $45°$
        2. greater than $45°$

43   Edge angle (modified): angular measure of the cross-section of the edge after retouch or modification
        1. less than $45°$
        2. more than $45°$

44   Percent postdetachment edge modification: the amount of total linear edge modification on a tool compared with the total quantity of edge line; postmodification breaks are not included
        0. none
        1. less than 5 percent
        2. 5–25 percent
        3. 26–50 percent
        4. 51–75 percent
        5. 75–100 percent
        9. indeterminate

45   Percent of postdetachment surface modification: percentage of the total area of modified surface of a tool compared to the total area of the surface

0. none
1. less than 5 percent
2. 5–25 percent
3. 26–50 percent
4. 51–75 percent
5. 75–100 percent
9. indeterminate

Record for Ground Stone:

51–52   Type:

10. Metate—oval or rectangular sandstone slabs which are sometimes intentionally shaped by flaking, grinding, or pecking
11. slab
12. basin
13. bedrock
14. trough
18. other
20. mano—an artifact with at least one surface characterized by one or more smooth facets produced through grinding
21. ovate hand stone (whole, 15 cm long or less)
22. subrectangular hand stone
23. two hand (whole, over 15 cm long)
24. other
30. mortar—steep-sided milling basin designed as a vessel for mashing, pounding, or grinding
31. bedrock
40. pestle—a cylindrical milling stone over twice as long as its diameter, with grinding or battering scars on one or both ends produced by grinding or pounding in a mortar
41. worked slab—a thin, flat block of material intentionally shaped but with no apparent milling surface
42. abrader—an object generally made of an abrasive material such as sandstone, with a grooved surface for dulling edges of chipped stone tools, presumably to facilitate hafting
43. polishing stone—smooth-surfaced cobble or pebble less than 10 cm long
44. pecking stone—a whole or partial cobble exhibiting a surface or surfaces that show crushing wear characteristic of pecking or striking blows
50. hammerstone—artifacts exhibiting battering with accompanying scars on surface edge margins (the intersections of two plane surfaces) or on convex surfaces; may not be prepared by unifacial or bifacial reduction

        51. sphere
        52. disk
        53. oblong
        54. irregular
        58. other
        60. other, specify

54   Preparation:
        0. none
        1. pecking on ground surface
        2. edges flaked/pecked
        3. grooved
        4. other
        9. indeterminate

55   Worn surfaces
        1. unifacial
        2. bifacial
        3. edge margins
        4. other
        9. indeterminate

56–57   Cross section of utilized face(s)
        1. flat
        2. concave
        3. concave
        4. convex
        5. ends polished/bevelled
        6. other
        9. indeterminate

58   Wear
        1. ground
        2. battered
        3. polished
        4. other
        9. indeterminate

Dimensions of interior grinding surface (in centimeters)
60–62   Length
64–66   Width
68–70   Depth
71–80   Comments

REFERENCES

— — — — — — — — — — — — —

AHLER, STANLEY A.
1975   *Pattern and variety in Extended Coalescent technology.* Ph.D. disserta-
        tion, Department of Anthropology, University of Missouri, Columbia.

AIKENS, C. MELVIN
1976   Cultural hiatus in the eastern Great Basin? *American Antiquity*
        41(4):543–50.

ALLCHIN, BRIDGET
1966   *The Stone-Tipped Arrow: Late Stone-age Hunters of the Tropical
        Old World.* New York: Barnes and Noble.

AMMERMAN, ALBERT J.
1981   Surveys and archaeological research. *Annual Review of Anthropology*
        10:63–88.

AMMERMAN, ALBERT J., AND M.W. FELDMAN
1978   Replicated collection site site surfaces. *American Antiquity* 43:734–40.

ARMITAGE, C.L., S.D. CREASMAN, AND J.C. MACKEY
1982   The Deadman Wash Site: a multi-component (Palaeo-Indian, Archaic,
        Late Prehistoric) site in southwestern Wyoming. *Journal of Inter-
        mountain Archaeology* 1(1):1–10. Rock Springs, Wyo.

ASCH, DAVID L.
1975   On sample size problems and the uses of nonprobabilistic sampling.
        In *Sampling in Archaeology,* edited by James W. Mueller, pp. 170–91.

BAMFORTH, DOUGLAS B.
1986   Technological efficiency and tool curation. *American Antiquity* 51(1):38–50.

BAUMHOFF, MARTIN A.
1958   History of Great Basin ethnography. *University of California Archaeological Survey Reports* 42:1–6. Berkeley.

BEHRENSMEYER, ANNA K., AND ANDREW P. HILL
1980   *Fossils in the Making.* Chicago: University of Chicago Press.

BETTINGER, ROBERT L.
1977   Predicting the archaeological potential of the Inyo–Mono region of eastern California. In *Conservation Archaeology,* edited by Michael B. Schiffer and George J. Gumerman, pp. 217–26. New York: Academic Press.

BINFORD, LEWIS R.
1964   A consideration of archaeological research design. *American Antiquity* 29:425–41.
1965   Archaeological systematics and the study of culture process. *American Antiquity* 31(2):203–10.
1976   Forty-seven trips: a case study in the character of some formation processes. In *Contributions to Anthropology: The Interior Peoples of Northern Alaska,* edited by Edwin S. Hall, pp. 299–351. National Museums of Man, Mercury Series, Paper No. 49. National Museum of Man, Ottawa.
1978   *Nunamiut Ethnoarchaeology.* New York: Academic Press.
1979   Organization and formation processes: looking at curated technologies. *Journal of Anthropological Research* 35:255–73.
1980   Willow smoke and dog's tails: hunter-gatherer settlement systems and archaeological site formation. *American Antiquity* 45:4–20.
1981   Behavioral Archaeology and the "Pompeii Premise." *Journal of Anthropological Research* 37(3):195–208.
1982   The archaeology of place. *Journal of Anthropological Archaeology* 1:5–31.
1985   In pursuit of the future. Plenary address, 50th annual meeting of the Society for American Archaeology, Denver, 3 May 1985.
1986   Isolating the transition to cultural adaptations: an organizational approach. Paper presented to the Advanced Seminar on "The Origins of Modern Human Adaptations," School of American Research, Santa Fe, N.M., April 20–26, 1986. First draft.

BINFORD, LEWIS R., AND SALLY R. BINFORD
1966   A preliminary analysis of functional variability in the Mousterian of Levallois facies. In *Recent Studies in Palaeoanthropology,* edited

by J.D. Clark and F.C. Howell. *American Anthropologist* 68(2): 238–95.

BINFORD, LEWIS R., AND JEREMY A. SABLOFF
1982   Paradigms, systematics, and archaeology. *Journal of Anthropological Research* 38(2):137–53.

BINFORD, LEWIS R., AND NANCY M. STONE
1985   'Righteous Rocks' and Richard Gould: some observations on misguided 'debate.' *American Antiquity* 50(1):151–53.

BOWERS, PETER M., ROBSON BONNICHSEN, AND DAVID M. HOCK
1983   Flake dispersal experiments: non-cultural transformation of the archaeological record. *American Antiquity* 48:553–72.

BRAIN, C.K.
1967a   Bone weathering and the problem of bone pseudo-tools. *South African Journal of Science* 63:97–99.
1967b   Hottentot food remains and their bearing on the interpretation of fossil bone assemblages. *Scientific Papers of the Namib Desert Research Station* 32:1–11.
1969   The contribution of Namib Desert Hottentots to an understanding of Australopithecine bone accumulations. *Scientific Papers of the Namib Desert Research Station* 39:13–22.
1981   *The Hunters or the Hunted? An Introduction to African Cave Taphonomy.* Chicago: University of Chicago Press.

BROOKS, ALISON S., AND JOHN E. YELLEN
1987   The preservation of activity areas in the archaeological record: ethnoarchaeological and archaeological work in northwest Ngamiland, Botswana. In *Method and Theory for Activity Area Research: An Ethnoarchaeological Perspective*, edited by Susan Kent, pp. 63–106. New York: Columbia University Press.

BUTLER, B.M., AND N.H. LOPINOT
1982   Debitage variation in Archaic Period sites in the Lower Ohio Valley. Paper presented at the 47th annual meeting of the Society for American Archaeology, Minneapolis.

BUTZER, KARL W.
1977   Geo-archaeology in practice. *Reviews in Archaeology* 4:125–31.
1982   *Archaeology as Human Ecology: Method and Theory for a Contextual Approach.* Cambridge: Cambridge University Press.

CAMILLI, EILEEN L.
1983a   Site occupational history and lithic assemblage structure: an example from southeastern Utah. Ph.D. dissertation, Department of Anthropology, University of New Mexico.

1983b   Flake assemblage variability on Cedar Mesa, southwestern Utah. Paper presented at the XIth International Congress of Anthropological and Ethnological Science, Vancouver, August 1983.

1984a   Scatters: stone tools in the archaeological record and people in the past. Fourth annual Ruth E. Kennedy Memorial Lecture, Maxwell Museum, University of New Mexico, April 27, 1984.

1985   Prehistoric use of landscapes and the archaeological surface distribution. Paper presented at the 50th annual meeting of the Society for American Archaeology, Denver, 3 May 1985.

1988   Chapter 7: Settlement components in the moderate production area. In *San Augustine Coal Project archaeological investigations in west-central New Mexico: report of the first field season,* by Eileen L. Camilli, Dabney Ford, and Signa L. Larralde; edited by Barbara L. Daniels. New Mexico Bureau of Land Management Cultural Resource Series No. 3.

1989   The occupational history of sites and the interpretation of prehistoric technological systems: an example from Cedar Mesa, Utah. In *Time, Energy and Stone Tools,* edited by Robin Torrence. Cambridge: Cambridge University Press, pp. 17–26.

CAMILLI, EILEEN L., SIGNA L. LARRALDE, AND JOHN RONEY
1985   Navajo-Hopi Land Exchange Archaeological Project interim report. New Mexico Bureau of Land Management, Santa Fe.

CAMILLI, EILEEN L. AND MARGARET NELSON
1983   In-field lithic analysis codes, Ladder Ranch Field School. Department of Anthropology, University of New Mexico, Albuquerque.

CARR, CHRISTOPHER
1984   The nature of organization of intrasite archaeological records and spatial analytic approaches to their investigation. In *Advances in Archaeological Theory and Method,* vol. 7, edited by Michael B. Schiffer, pp. 103–222. New York: Academic Press.

CHAPMAN, RICHARD C.
1977   Analysis of lithic assemblages. In *Settlement and Subsistence Along the Lower Chaco River: The CGP Survey,* edited by Charles A. Reher, pp. 371–452. Albuquerque: University of Mew Mexico Press.

CLARKE, DAVID L.
1973   Archaeology: loss of innocence. *Antiquity* 47:1–18.

COLLINS, MICHAEL B.
1975   Lithic technology as a means of processual inference. In *Lithic Technology: Making and Using Stone Tools,* edited by Earl H. Swanson, Jr., pp. 15–34. Chicago: Aldine.

CONKEY, MARGARET W.
1980   The identification of prehistoric hunter-gatherer aggregation sites: the case of Altamira. *Current Anthropology* 21(5):609–20.

CREASMAN, STEVEN D.
1986   The altithermal: palaeoenvironmental reconstruction and subsistence change in southwest Wyoming. In *Archaeological Resource Management on the Great Plains,* edited by Alan J. Osborne and Robert C. Hassler. Lincoln: University of Nebraska Press.

CREASMAN, STEVEN D., JANICE C. NEWBERRY, PATRICIA A. TREAT, HERBERT RODRIGUEZ, AND RONALD E. KAINER
1981   Cultural resource investigations of the Desert Springs West Loop (5B) pipeline. Archaeological Services, Western Wyoming College, Rock Springs.

DANCEY, WILLIAM S.
1973   Prehistoric land use and settlement patterns in the Priest Rapids area, Washington. Ph.D. dissertation, University of Washington, Seattle.
1974   The archaeological survey: a re-orientation. *Man in the Northeast* 8:98–112.

DAVIS, E.L.
1975   The "exposed archaeology" of China Lake, California. *American Antiquity* 40:39–53.

DAVIS, E. MOTT
1956   Archaeological survey of the Big Sandy Reservoir area, southwestern Wyoming. *Notebook No. 2, Laboratory of Anthropology.* Lincoln: University of Nebraska Press.

DAY, KENT C.
1961   Preliminary archaeological survey of the Flaming Gorge Reservoir, Utah–Wyoming. Manuscript, Department of Anthropology, University of Utah, Salt Lake City.

DAY, KENT C., AND DAVID S. DIBBLE
1963   Archaeological survey of Flaming Gorge Reservoir Area, Wyoming–Utah. *University of Utah Anthropological Papers* No. 65, *Upper Colorado Series* No. 9. Salt Lake City.

DEETZ, JAMES
1967   *Invitation to Archaeology.* Garden City, N.J.: Natural History Press.

DIBBLE, DAVID S. AND KENT C. DAY
1962   A preliminary survey of the Fontenelle Reservoir, Wyoming. *University of Utah Anthropological Papers* No. 58, *Upper Colorado Series* No. 7.

DILLEHAY, T.D.
1973   Small archaeological site investigations for interpretation of site activities. *Bulletin of the Texas Archeological Society* 44:169–77.

DOELLE, WILLIAM HARPER
1976   Desert resources and Hohokam subsistence: the CONOCO Florence Project. *Arizona State Museum, Archaeological Series* 103. Tucson.
1977   The multiple survey strategy for cultural resource management studies. In *Conservation Archaeology*, edited by Michael B. Schiffer and George J. Gumerman, pp. 201–11. New York: Academic Press.

DOMINICK, DAVID
1936   The Sheepeaters. *Annals of Wyoming* 36:131–68.

DRUCKER, PHILIP
1937   Cultural element distributions: V. Southern California. *University of California Publications: Anthropological Records* 1(1). Berkeley.

DUNNELL, ROBERT C.
1971   *Systematics in Prehistory*. New York: Free Press.
1985   The interpretation of low density archaeological records from plowed surfaces. Paper presented at the 50th annual meeting of the Society for American Archaeology, Denver, 3 May 1985.

DUNNELL, ROBERT C. AND WILLIAM S. DANCEY
1983   The siteless survey: a regional scale data collection strategy. In *Advances in Archaeological Method and Theory,* vol. 5, edited by Michael B. Schiffer, pp. 267–87. New York: Academic Press.

EBERT, JAMES I.
1982   Seedskadee Project: proposal for remote sensing and class I survey. Branch of Remote Sensing, National Park Service, Albuquerque.
1983   Distributional archaeology: nonsite discovery, recording, and spatial analytical methods for application to the surface archaeological record. Dissertation proposal, Department of Anthropology, University of New Mexico, Albuquerque.
1985   Modeling human systems and "predicting" the archaeological record: the unavoidable relationship between theory and method. Paper presented at the 50th annual meeting of the Society for American Archaeology, Denver, 3 May 1985.

EBERT, JAMES I., AND TIMOTHY A. KOHLER
1986   The theoretical and methodological basis of archaeological pre dictive modeling. In *Predicting the Past,* edited by Lynne Sebastian and W.J. Judge, Bureau of Land Management, Denver Area Office. In press.

EBERT, JAMES I., SIGNA LARRALDE, AND LUANN WANDSNIDER
1983   Distributional archaeology: survey, mapping, and analysis of sur-
        face archaeological materials and their landform associations in the
        Green River Basin, Wyoming. Paper delivered at the 1983 Plains
        Conference, Rapid City, South Dakota, November 2–5, 1983.
1984   Predictive modeling: current abuses of the archaeological record and
        prospects for explanation. Paper presented at the 49th annual meet-
        ings of the Society for American Archaeology, Portland, April 14,
        1984.

EULER, ROBERT C.
1964   Southern Paiute archaeology. *American Antiquity* 29(3):379–81.

EULER, ROBERT C., AND CATHERINE S. FOWLER
1966   Southern Paiute ethnohistory. *University of Utah Anthropological
        Papers* No. 78, *Glen Canyon Series* No. 28. Salt Lake City.

FISH, P.R.
1976a   Patterns of prehistoric site distribution in Effingham and Screven
        Counties, Georgia. *University of Georgia, Laboratory of Anthro-
        pology Series* Report 11.
1976b   The interpretive potential of Mousterian debitage. Ph.D. disserta-
        tion, Department of Anthropology, Arizona State University, Tempe.
1978   Consistency in archaeological measurement and classification. *Amer-
        ican Antiquity* 43:86–89.
1979   The interpretive potential of Mousterian debitage. *Arizona State Uni-
        versity Anthropological Research Papers* 16.

FLANNERY, KENT V.
1966   The postglacial "readaptation" as viewed from Meso-america. *Ameri-
        can Antiquity* 31(6):800–05.

FOLEY, ROBERT A.
1977   Space and energy: a method for analysing habitat value and utiliza-
        tion in relation to archaeological sites. In *Spatial Archaeology,* edited
        by David L. Clarke, pp. 163–87. London: Academic Press.
1978   Incorporating sampling into initial research design: some aspects of
        spatial archaeology. In *Sampling in Contemporary British Archae-
        ology,* edited by J. Cherry, C. Gamble and S. Shennan, pp. 49–65.
        British Archaeological Reports (British Series) 50. London.
1980   The spatial component of archaeological data: off-site methods and
        some preliminary results from the Amboseli Basin, southern Kenya.
        *Proceedings of the VIII Pan-African Congress in Prehistory and Qua-
        ternary Studies,* 39–40.
1981a   A model of regional archaeological structure. *Proceedings of the Pre-
        historic Society* 47:1–17.

1981b   Off-site archaeology and human adaptation in eastern Africa: an analysis of regional artefact density in the Amboseli, southern Kenya. *British Archaeological Reports International Series 97, Cambridge Monographs in African Archaeology 3.*

1981c   Aspects of variability in palaeoecological studies. In *Economic Archaeology: Towards an Integrated Approach,* edited by G. Bailer and A. Sheridan, pp. 66–75. *British Archaeological Reports (International Series) 96.*

1981d   Off-site archaeology: an alternative approach for the short-sited. In *Patterns of the Past: Essays in Honor of David L. Clarke,* edited by I. Hodder, G. Isaac, and N. Hammond, pp. 157–83. Cambridge: Cambridge University Press.

FOWLER, CATHERINE S.

1982   Settlement patterns and subsistence systems in the Great Basin: the ethnographic record. In *Man and Environment in the Great Basin,* edited by David B. Madsen and James F. O'Connell. Society for American Archaeology Papers 2.

FOWLER, D.D., AND C.S. FOWLER

1971   Anthropology of the Numa: John Wesley Powell's manuscripts on the Numic Peoples of western North America. *Smithsonian Contributions to Anthropology 14.*

FRANCIS, JULIE E.

1980   Lithic raw material procurement and utilization as an indicator of changes in hunter-gatherer subsistence and settlement systems. In *Wyoming Contributions to Anthropology,* edited by L.C. Shaw and W.B. Fawcett, Jr., pp. 1–15. Department of Anthropology, University of Wyoming, Laramie.

FRISON, GEORGE C.

1973   The Wardell Buffalo Trap 48SU301: communal procurement in the Upper Green River Basin, Wyoming. *Anthropological Papers of the Museum of Anthropology, University of Michigan 48:1–111.* Ann Arbor.

1978   *Prehistoric Hunters of the High Plains.* New York: Academic Press.

GIFFORD, DIANE P.

1977a   Observations of modern human settlements as an aid to archaeological interpretation. Ph.D. dissertation, Department of Anthropology, University of California, Berkeley.

1977b   Ethnoarchaeological observations on natural processes affecting cultural materials. In *Explorations in Ethnoarchaeology,* edited by Richard A. Gould, pp. 77–102. Albuquerque: University of New Mexico Press.

1980   Ethnoarchaeological contributions to the taphonomy of human sites. In *Fossils in the Making*, edited by A.K. Behrensmeyer and A.P. Hill, pp. 94–107. Berkeley: University of California Press.

1981   Taphonomy and palaeoecology: a critical review of archaeology's sister discipline. In *Advances in Archaeological Method and Theory*, vol. 4, edited by Michael B. Schiffer, pp. 365–438. New York: Academic Press.

GIFFORD, DIANE P., AND ANNA K. BEHRENSMEYER

1977   Observed formation and burial of a recent human occupation site in Kenya. *Quaternary Research* 8:245–66.

GLADFELTER, B.G.

1977   Geoarchaeology: the geomorphologist and archaeology. *American Antiquity* 42:519–38.

GONZALES, RAFAEL C., AND PAUL WINTZ

1977   *Digital Image Processing*. Reading, Mass.: Addison-Wesley.

GOODYEAR, ALBERT C.

1975   Hecla I and II: an interpretive study of archaeological remains from the Lakeshore Project, Papago Reservation, south central Arizona. *Arizona State University, Anthropological Research Paper 9*. Tempe.

1979   A hypothesis for the use of cryptocrystalline raw materials among Palaeo-Indian groups of North America. *Institute for Archaeology and Anthropology, Research Manuscript Series 56*. University of South Carolina, Columbia.

GOULD, RICHARD A.

1968   Living archaeology: the Ngatatjara of western Australia. *Southwestern Journal of Anthropology* 24:101–22.

1978   The anthropology of human residues. *American Anthropologist* 80(4):815–35.

1980   *Living Archaeology*. Cambridge: Cambridge University Press.

GOULD, RICHARD A., AND S. SAGGERS

1985   Lithic procurement in central Australia: a closer look at Binford's idea of embeddedness in archaeology. *American Antiquity* 50:117–36.

GOULD, RICHARD A., D.A. KOSTER, AND A.H.L. SONTZ

1971   The lithic assemblage of the Western Desert Aborigines of Australia. *American Antiquity* 36:149–69.

GRIEG–SMITH, P.

1952   The use of random and contiguous quadrats in the study of the structure of plant communities. *Annals of Botany* 16:293–316.

1964   *Quantitative Plant Ecology*. London: E. Arnold.
1983   *Quantitative Plant Ecology*. Second edition. Oxford: Blackwell Scientific Publications.

HARAKO, REIZO
1978   Patterns of mobility among hunting and gathering people—an ecological comparative study of Bushmen and Pygmies. *Reports for "Mobility for Man and Society," IATSS Symposium on Traffic Science*, pp. 111–18. Tokyo.

HARPENDING, HENRY, AND HERBERT DAVIS
1977   Some implications for hunter-gatherer ecology derived from the spatial structure of resources. *World Archaeology* 8(3):277–86.

HARRIS, MARVIN
1968   *The Rise of Anthropological Theory*. New York: Columbia University Press.

HEIZER, ROBERT F.
1970   Ethnographic notes on the Northern Paiute of the Humboldt Sink, west central Nevada. In *Languages and Cultures of Western North America*, edited by Earl H. Swanson, Jr., pp. 232–45. Pocatello: Idaho State University Press.

HITCHCOCK, ROBERT KARL
1982   The ethnoarchaeology of sedentism: mobility strategies and site structure among foraging and food producing populations in the Eastern Kalahari Desert, Botswana. Ph.D. dissertation, Department of Anthropology, University of New Mexico, Albuquerque.

HULTKRANTZ, AKE
1970   The source literature on the "Tukudika" Indians in Wyoming: facts and fancies. In *Languages and Cultures of Western North America*, edited by Earl H. Swanson, Jr., pp. 246–64. Pocatello: Idaho State University Press.
1974   The Shoshones in the Rocky Mountain area. In *Shoshone Indians*, pp. 173–214. New York: Garland Publishing Co.

HUSCHER, BETTY H., AND HAROLD A. HUSCHER
1942   Athapaskan migration via the intermontane region. *American Antiquity* 8(1):80–88.

IRWIN-WILLIAMS, CYNTHIA
1967   Picosa: the elementary Southwestern culture. *American Antiquity* 32(4):441–57.

ISAAC, GLYNN Ll.
1966   New evidence for Olorgesailie relating to the character of Acheulian

occupation sites. In *Actas del V Congreso Panafricano de Prehistoria y de Estudio del Cuaternario II. Publicaciones del Museo Arqueologico Santa Cruz de Tenerife* 6, edited by L.D. Cuscoy, pp. 135–45.

1967   Towards the interpretation of occupation debris: some experiments and observations. *Kroeber Anthropological Society Papers* 37:31–57.

1976   Plio-Pleistocene artifact assemblages from East Rudolf, Kenya. In *Earliest Man and Environments in the Lake Rudolf Basin*, edited by Y. Coppens, F.C. Howell, G.Ll. Isaac, and R.E. Leakey, pp. 552–64. Chicago: University of Chicago Press.

1978   Casting the net wide: a review of archaeological evidence for early hominid land-use and ecological relations. In *Current Arguments on Early Man*, edited by Lars-Konig Konigsson, pp. 226–51. Oxford: Pergamon Press.

1981   Stone age visiting cards: approaches to the study of early land use patterns. In *Pattern of the Past: Studies in Honor of David Clarke*, edited by I. Hodder, G. Isaac, and N. Hammond, pp. 131–56. Cambridge: Cambridge University Press.

ISAAC, GLYNN Ll. AND J.W.K. HARRIS
1975   The scatter between the patches. Paper presented to the Kroeber Anthropological Society, May 1975.

ISAAC, GLYNN Ll., JOHN W.K. HARRIS, AND FIONA MARSHALL
1981   Small is informative: the application of the study of mini–sites and least effort criteria in the interpretation of the early Pleistocene archaeological record at Koobi Fora, Kenya. *Union Internacional de Ciencias Prehistoricas y Protohistoricas, X Congreso*, pp. 102–19. Mexico City: UNESCO.

JEFFERSON, JAMES, R.W. DELANEY, AND G.C. THOMPSON
1972   *The southern Utes: a tribal history.* Edited by Floyd A. O'Neill. The Southern Ute Tribe, Ignacio, California.

JEFFRIES, R.W.
1976   The Lookout Valley research project: a micro-regional approach to location analysis in settlement archaeology. *Southeastern Archaeological Conference, Bulletin* 19:14–18.

1982   Debitage as an indicator of interregional activity diversity in northwest Georgia. *Midcontinental Journal of Archaeology* 7(1):99–132.

1983   Intraregional behavior variability: a regional approach to lithic analysis. Paper presented at the XI International Congress of Anthropological and Ethnological Science, Vancouver.

JENNINGS, JESSE D.
1956   The American Southwest, a problem in cultural isolation. Society for American Archaeology *Memoirs* 11. Salt Lake City.

1957   Danger Cave. Society for American Archaeology *Memoirs* 14. Salt Lake City.

1964   The Desert West. In *Prehistoric Man in the New World,* edited by J.D. Jennings and E. Norbeck, pp. 149–74. Chicago: University of Chicago Press.

1974   *Prehistory of North America.* Second edition. New York: McGraw Hill.

JOCHIM, MICHAEL A.

1976   *Hunter-Gatherer Subsistence and Settlement: A Predictive Model.* New York: Academic Press.

JOHNSON, JAY K.

1983   Biface production trajectories in Mississippi: a regional perspective. Paper presented at the XI International Congress of Anthropological and Ethnological Sciences, Vancouver.

JONES, GEORGE THOMAS

1984   Prehistoric land use in the Steens Mountain area, southeastern Oregon. Ph.D. dissertation, Department of anthropology, University of Washington, Seattle.

JONES, GEORGE T., DONALD K. GRAYSON, AND CHARLOTTE BECK

1983   Artifact class richness and sample size in archaeological surface assemblages. In *Lulu Linear Punctated: Essays in Honor of George Irving Quimby,* edited by Robert C. Dunnell and Donald K. Grayson, pp. 55–73. *Anthropological Papers of the Museum of Anthropology, University of Michigan* 72. Ann Arbor.

JUDGE, W. JAMES

1973   *PalaeoIndian Occupation of the Central Rio Grande Valley in New Mexico.* Albuquerque: University of New Mexico Press.

1981   Transect sampling in Chaco Canyon—evaluation of a survey technique. In *Archaeological Surveys of Chaco Canyon, New Mexico,* by Alden W. Hayes, David M. Brugge, and W. James Judge, pp. 1–68. Washington, D.C.: National Park Service.

KAINER, RONALD E.

1980   Task I: base data and research design for the Class II cultural resource inventory of the overthrust belt area in southwestern Wyoming. Report to Bureau of Land Managmeent (Contract YA-512-CT9-201), Western Wyoming College, Rock Springs.

KATZ, P.

1976   A technological analysis of the Kansas City Hopewell chipped stone industry. Ph.D. dissertation, University of Kansas.

KELLY, ISABEL T.

1934   Ethnography of the Surprise Valley Paiute. *University of California Publications in American Archaeology and Ethnology* 31(3):67–210. Berkeley.

1964   Southern Paiute ethnography. *Anthropological Papers of the University of Utah* 69. Salt Lake City.

KELLY, ROBERT L.

1985   Hunter-gatherer mobility and lithic technology. Paper presented at the 50th annual meeting of the Society for American Archaeology, Denver, 3 May 1985.

KERSHAW, KENNETH A.

1964   *Quantitative and Dynamic Ecology.* New York: American Elsevier.

KERSHAW, KENNETH A., AND JOHN HENRY H. LOONEY

1985   *Quantitative and Dynamic Plant Ecology.* London: Edward Arnold.

KIRKBY, A., AND M.J. KIRKBY

1976   Geomorphological processes and the surface survey of archaeological sites in semi-arid areas. In *Geoarchaeology: Earth Sciences and the Past,* edited by D.A. Davidson and M.L. Shackley, pp. 229–53. London: Duckworth.

KLINGER, T.C.

1976   The problem of site definition in cultural resource management. *Arkansas Academy of Science, Proceedings* 30:54–56.

KNIGHT, S.H.

1950   Physical aspects of the Green River Basin and adjacent mountain ranges. *Wyoming Geological Association Guidebook,* Fifth Annual Field Conference, 1950. Casper.

KNUDSON, RUTH ANN

1973   Organizational variability in late Palaeo-Indian assemblages. Ph.D. dissertation, Department of Anthropology, Washington State University, Pullman.

KORNFELD, MARCEL

1982   Down the hill without a site. *Wyoming Contributions to anthropology* 3:91–104. University of Wyoming, Laramie.

KRIEGER, ALEX D.

1944   The typological concept. *American Antiquity* 9:271–88.

KROEBER, A.L.

1939   *Cultural and Natural Areas of Native North America. University of California Publications in American Archaeology and Ethnology* 38.

KROEBER, A.L., AND C. KLUCKHOHN

1952   *Culture: A Critical Review of Concepts and Definitions. Papers of the Peabody Museum of American Archaeology and Ethnology 47.* Harvard University.

LAIRD, CAROBETH

1976   *The Chemehuevis.* Banning, Calif.: Malaki Museum Press.

LARRALDE, SIGNA L.

1984   Quality control in lithics analysis: a test of precision. *Haliksai'i: UNM Contributions to Anthropology* 3:1–21.

1988   Chapter 6: Lithic Analysis. In *San Augustine Coal Project archaeological investigations in west-central New Mexico: report of the first field season,* by Eileen L. Camilli, Klara B. Kelley, Dabney Ford, and Signa L. Larralde; edited Barbara L. Daniels. Cultural Resource Series No. 3. Bureau of Land Management, Socorro Resource Area, New Mexico.

LEWARCH, DENNIS E., AND MICHAEL J. O'BRIEN

1981   The expanding role of surface assemblages in archaeological research. In *Advances in Archaeological Method and theory,* 4, edited by Michael B. Schiffer, pp. 297–342. New York: Academic Press.

LOVIS, WILLIAM A.

1976   Quarter sections and forests: an example of probability sampling in the northeastern woodlands. *American Antiquity* 41:364–72.

LYMAN, ALBERT R.

1930   Pahute Biscuits. *Utah Historical Quarterly* 3:118–20. Utah Historical Society, Salt Lake City.

MACKEY, J.C., DOUGLAS KULLEN, S.D. CREASMAN, JILL E. SALL, KATHY HARVEY, AND C.L. ARMITAGE

1982   Palaeoenvironmental reconstruction and subsistence change at the Deadman Wash Site in southwestern Wyoming. *Journal of Intermountain Archeology* 1(1):11–65. Rock Springs, Wyo.

MACNEISH, RICHARD S.

1964   Ancient Mesoamerican civilization. *Science* 143(3606):531–37.

MADSEN, DAVID B.

1975   Dating Paiute-Shoshoni expansion in the Great Basin. *American Antiquity* 40(1):80–86.

1978   Recent data bearing on the question of a hiatus in the eastern Great Basin. *American Antiquity* 43:508–09.

MADSEN, D.B., AND M.S. BERRY

1975   A reassessment of northeastern Great Basin prehistory. *American Antiquity* 40(4):391–405.

MAGNE, MARTIN P.R.

1981 Controlled lithic reduction experiments towards an understanding of lithic utilization in large scale settlement-subsistence systems of the Interior Plateau. Paper presented at the 46th annual meeting of the Society for American Archaeology, San Diego.

1983 Lithics and livelihood: stone tool technologies of central and southern interior B.C. Ph.D. dissertation, Department of Anthropology and Sociology, University of British Columbia, Vancouver.

MALOUF, CARLINE

1974 The Gosiute Indians. In *Shoshone Indians,* pp. 25–172. New York: Garland.

MANNERS, ROBERT A.

1974 Southern Paiute and Chemehuevi: an ethnohistoric report. In *Paiute Indians I,* edited by D.A. Horr, pp. 29–300. New York: Garland.

MASON, R.D.

1979 Regional, zonal, and site-intensive surveys in highland Mesoamerica. In *Recent Approaches to Surface Data and Sampling,* edited by M.J. O'Brien and D.E. Lewarch, pp. 89–105. *Western Canadian Journal of Anthropology* 8(3).

McANANY, PATRICIA

1986 Lithic Technology and Exchange Among Swamp Cultivators of the Eastern Maya Lowlands. Ph.D. Dissertation, Department of Anthropology, University of New Mexico, Albuquerque. In preparation.

McMANAMON, FRANCIS P.

1981 Probability sampling and archaeological survey in the Northeast: an estimation approach. In *Foundations of Northeast Archaeology,* edited by D.R. Snow, pp. 195–227. New York: Academic Press.

1984 Discovering sites unseen. In *Advances in Archaeological Method and Theory,* vol. 7, edited by Michael B. Schiffer, pp. 223–92. New York: Academic Press.

MEIGHAN, CLEMENT W.

1959 Varieties of prehistoric cultures in the Great Basin region. *Southwestern Museum Masterkey* 33:46–58.

METCALF, MICHAEL D.

1986 Contributions to the Prehistoric Chronology of the Wyoming Basin. In *Archaeological Resources Management on the Great Plains,* edited by Alan J. Osborne and Robert C. Hassler. Lincoln: University of Nebraska Press.

MORENON, E.P., M. HENDERSON, AND J. NIELSEN

1976 The development of conservation techniques and a land use study conducted near Ranchos de Taos, New Mexico. Fort Burgwin Research Center, Southwestern Methodist University, Dallas.

MORISITA, M.
1959   Measuring the dispersion of individuals and analysis of the distribution patterns. Kyushu University, *Memoires of the Faculty of Science, Series E (Biology)* 2:215–35.

MORROW, C.A.
1982   Late Middle Archaic chipped stone technologies at Carrier Mills. In *Prehistoric Cultural Adaptations in the Carrier Mills Archaeological District, Saline County, Illinois,* vol. 2, edited by R.W. Jeffries and Brian M. Butler. *Center for Archaeological Investigations, Research Paper* 33:1289–346. Southern Illinois University, Carbondale.

MOSELEY, M.E., AND C. J. MACKEY
1972   Peruvian settlement pattern studies and small site methodology. *American Antiquity* 37:67–81.

MOSS, JOHN H.
1951   Early Man in the Eden Valley. *The University Museum, Museum Monographs*. University of Pennsylvania, Philadelphia.

MUELLER, JAMES W.
1974   The use of sampling in archaeological survey. *Memoirs of the Society for American Archaeology* 28. *American Antiquity* 39(2), part 2.

MUELLER-DOMBOIS, D., AND H. EHRENBERG
1975   *Aims and Methods of Vegetation Ecology*. New York: John Wiley.

MURDOCK, GEORGE PETER
1967   *Ethnographic Atlas*. Pittsburgh: University of Pittsburgh Press.

MURPHY, ROBERT F., AND YOLANDA MURPHY
1960   Shoshone-Bannock Subsistence and Society. *University of California, Anthropological Records* 16:293–338.

MUTO, GUY
1971a   A technological analysis of the early stages in the manufacture of lithic artifacts. M.A. thesis, Department of Anthropology, Idaho State University.
1971b   A stage analysis of the manufacture of chipped stone implements. In *Great Basin Anthropological Conference 1970: Selected Papers,* edited by C. Melvin Aikens, pp. 109–17. *Oregon Anthropological Papers* 1.

NANCE, JACK D.
1980   Non-site sampling in the lower Cumberland River Valley, Kentucky. *Mid-Continental Journal of Archaeology* 5(2):169–91.

O'BRIEN, MICHAEL J. AND DAVID E. LEWARCH
1981   Plowzone archaeology: contributions to theory and technique. *Vanderbilt University Publications in Anthropology* 27.

O'BRIEN, MICHAEL J., D.E. LEWARCH, AND R.D. MASON
1979   The use of archaeological sampling and survey strategies on an irrigation community in the Valley of Oaxaca, Mexico. In *Recent Approaches to Surface Data and Sampling*, edited by M.J. O'Brien and D.E. Lewarch, pp. 89–105. *Western Canadian Journal of Anthropology* 8(3).

ODUM, EUGENE P.
1975   *Ecology*. Second edition. New York: Holt, Rinehart and Winston.

OSBORNE, ALAN J., AND ROBERT C. HASSLER, EDS.
1986   *Archaeological Resources Management on the Great Plains*. Lincoln: University of Nebraska Press.

OSWALT, WENDELL H.
1973   *Habitat and Technology: The Evolution of Hunting*. New York: Holt, Rinehart and Winston.
1976   *An Anthropological Analysis of Food-Getting Technology*. New York: John Wiley.

PHAGAN, CARL
1976   A method for the analysis of flakes in archaeological assemblages: a Peruvian example. Ph.D. dissertation, Department of Anthropology, Ohio State University.

PIELOU, E.C.
1961   Segregation and symmetry in two-species populations as studied by nearest neighbor relations. *Journal of Ecology* 49:255–69.

PLOG, F., AND J.N. HILL
1971   Explaining variability in the distribution of sites. In *The Distribution of Prehistoric Population Aggregates*, edited by G.J. Gumerman, pp. 7–36. *Prescott College Anthropological Reports* 1.

PLOG, S., F. PLOG, AND W. WAIT
1978   Decision making in modern surveys. In *Advances in Archaeological Method and Theory*, vol. 1, edited by Michael B. Schiffer, pp. 383–421. New York: Academic Press.

POKOTYLO, DAVID L.
1978   Lithic technology and settlement patterns in Upper Hat Creek

Valley, B.C. Ph.D. dissertation, University of British Columbia, Vancouver.

1982   Towards an understanding of prehistoric upland settlement behavior in the British Columbia southern interior plateau. In *Networks of the Past: Regional Interaction in Archaeology*, edited by P.D. Frances, F.J. Kense, and P.G. Duke, pp. 119–20. The Anthropological Association of the University of Calgary.

POWELL, SHIRLEY L.
1980   Material cultural and behavior: a prehistoric example for the American Southwest. Ph.D. dissertation, Department of Anthropology, Arizona State University, Tempe.

PRICE, T.D.
1979   Mesolithic systems in the Netherlands. In *The Early Post-Glacial Settlement of Northern Europe: an Ecological Perspective*, edited by P. Mellars, pp. 81–114. London: Duckworth.

RAAB, L. MARK, ROBERT F. CANDE, AND DAVID W. STAHLE
1979   Debitage graphs and Archaic settlement patterns in the Arkansas Ozarks. *Mid-Continental Journal of Archaeology* 4(2):167–82.

REAGAN, A.B.
1934   The Gosiute (Goshute), or Shoshoni-Goship Indians of the Deep Creek Region in western Utah. *Proceedings of the Utah Academy of Science, Arts and Letters* 11:43–54.

READ, DWIGHT W.
1975   Regional sampling. In *Sampling in Archaeology*, edited by James W. Mueller, pp. 45–60. Tucson: University of Arizona Press.

REDMAN, CHARLES L.
1974   Archaeological sampling strategies. *Addison-Wesley Module in Anthropology 55*. Reading, Mass.: Addison-Wesley.

REID, LESLIE WAYNE
1972   A history of the education of the Ute Indians, 1847–1905. Ph.D. dissertation, Department of Educational Administration, University of Utah, Salt Lake City.

RENAUD, ETIENNE B.
1932   Yuma and Folsom artifacts. *Proceedings of the Colorado Museum of Natural History* 11(2).

1936   *The archaeological survey of the high western plains. 7th report. Southern Wyoming and southwestern South Dakota, summer 1935.* Department of Anthropology, University of Denver.

1938   The Black's Fork Culture of southwest Wyoming. *The Archaeolog-*

ical Survey of the Western Plains, 10th report. Department of Anthropology, University of Denver.

1940   Further research work in the Black's Fork Basin, southwest Wyoming. *The Archaeological Survey of the High Western Plains,* 12th report. Department of Anthropology, University of Denver.

REHER, CHARLES A., AND GEORGE C. FRISON
1977   Territorial inference from source analysis of lithic assemblages. Manuscript, Department of Anthropology, University of Wyoming, Laramie.

REYNOLDS, WILLIAM E.
1983   The archaeology and history of the LaBarge area, southwestern Wyoming: a class II cultural resources inventory. Report prepared for the Bureau of Land Management, Rock Springs District, by Chambers Consultants and Planners, Albuquerque.

RICK, J.W.
1976   Downslope movement and archaeological intrasite spatial analysis. *American Antiquity* 41:133–44.

RIDDELL, FRANCIS A.
1960   *Honey Lake Paiute ethnography. Nevada State Museum Anthropology Papers* 4. Carson City.

RIORDAN, R.V.
1982   The controlled surface collection of a multicomponent site in southwestern Ohio: a replication experiment. *Midcontinental Journal of Archaeology* 7:45–59.

RODGERS, J.B.
1974   An archaeological survey of the Cave Buttes Dam alternative site and reservoir, Arizona. *Arizona State University, Anthropological Research Paper* 8.

ROTH, GEORGE
1981   Incorporation and changes in ethnic structure: the Chemehuevi Indians. Ph.D. dissertation, Department of Anthropology, Northwestern University, Evanston, Ill.

SAS, INC.
1982   *SAS User's Guide: Basics, 1982 Edition.* Cary, N.C.: SAS Institute, Inc.

SCHIFFER, MICHAEL B.
1976   *Behavioral Archaeology.* New York: Academic Press.
1987   *Formation Processes of the Archaeological Record.* Albuquerque: University of New Mexico Press.

SCHIFFER, MICHAEL B., AND GEORGE J. GUMERMAN
1977   *Conservation Archaeology.* New York: Academic Press.

SCHIFFER, MICHAEL B., AND JOHN H. HOUSE
1977a   Archaeological research and cultural resource management: the Cache River Project. *Current Anthropology* 18:43–68.
1977b   The Cache River survey design. In *Conservation Archaeology,* edited by Michael B. Schiffer and George J. Gumerman, pp. 191–200. New York: Academic Press.

SCHIFFER, MICHAEL B., A.P. SULLIVAN, AND T.C. KLINGER
1978   The design of archaeological surveys. *World Archaeology* 10:1–28.

SCHIFFER, MICHAEL B., AND SUSAN J. WELLS
1982   Chapter 9: Archaeological surveys, past and future. In *Hohokam and Patayan: Prehistory of Southwestern Arizona,* edited by R.H. McGuire and Michael B. Schiffer, pp. 345–83. New York: Academic Press.

SCHLANGER, SARAH H.
1981   Tool caching behavior and the archaeological record. Paper presented at the 46th annual meeting of the Society for American Archaeology, San Diego.

SCHOCK, SUSAN, IAN VON ESSEN, STEVEN D. CREASMAN, JANICE NEWBERRY-CREASMAN, A. DUDLEY GARDNER, LINDA SCOTT, AND DOUGLAS KULLEN
1982   The Cow Hollow Creek Site: a multi-component campsite in the Green River Basin, Wyoming. *Journal of Intermountain Archaeology* 1(2):100–21. Rock Springs, Wyo.

SHARROCK, FLOYD W.
1966   *Prehistoric occupation patterns in southwest Wyoming and cultural relationships with the Great Basin and Plains culture areas. University of Utah Anthropological Papers* 77. Salt Lake City.

SHIMKIN, D.B.
1940   Shoshone-Comanche origins and migrations. *Proceedings of the Sixth Pacific Science Conference of the Pacific Science Association* 4:17–25. 1947 *Wind River Shoshone ethnography. University of California, Anthropological Records* 5(4). Berkeley.

SHIMKIN, DEMITRI B., AND RUSSELL M. REID
1970   Socio-cultural persistence among Shoshoneans of the Carson River Basin (Nevada). In *Languages and Cultures of Western North America,* edited by Early H. Swanson, Jr., pp. 172–200. Pocatello: Idaho State University Press.

SMITH, ANNE M.

1974 Ethnography of the northern Utes. *Papers in Anthropology* 17. Albuquerque: Museum of New Mexico Press.

SPAULDING, ALBERT C.

1948 Review of "Archaeology of the High Western Plains. Seventeen Years of Archaeological Research," by Etienne Renaud. *American Antiquity* 13(3):262–63.

STAFFORD, C. RUSSELL

1985 Hunter-gatherer settlement strategies: a regional perspective on intrasite spatial analysis. Paper presented at the 50th annual meeting of the Society for American Archaeology, Denver, 1–5 May 1985.

STAHLE, DAVID W., AND JAMES E. DUNN

1982 An analysis and application of the size distribution of waste flakes from the manufacture of bifacial stone tools. *World Archaeology* 14(1):84–95.

STEWARD, JULIAN H.

1933 Ethnography of the Owens Valley Paiute. *University of California Publications in American Archaeology and Ethnology* 33(3):233–350.

1938 Basin-plateau aboriginal sociopolitical groups. *Bureau of American Ethnology Bulletin* 120. Washington, D.C.: U.S. Government Publishing Office.

1940a Native Cultures of the Intermontane (Great Basin) area. In "Essays in Historical Anthropology," pp. 445–502. *Smithsonian Miscellaneous Collections* 100. Washington, D.C.

1940b The foundations of Basin-Plateau Shoshonean society. In *Languages and Cultures of Western North America,* edited by Earl H. Swanson, Jr., pp. 113–51. Pocatello: Idaho State University Press.

STEWART, OMER C.

1970 The question of Bannock territory. In *Languages and Cultures of Western North America,* edited by Earl H. Swanson, Jr., pp. 201–31. Pocatello: Idaho State University Press.

SWANSON, EARL H., JR.

1972 *Birch Creek: human ecology in the northern Rocky Mountains 9000 B.C.–A.D. 1850.* Pocatello: Idaho State University Press.

SWANSON, EARL H., JR., CHESTER KING, AND JAMES CHATTERS

1969 A settlement pattern in the foothills of east central Idaho. *Tebiwa* 12(1):31–38.

TALMADGE, V., O. CHESTER, AND I.A. STOFF

1977   The importance of small, surface, and disturbed sites as sources of significant archaeological data. *Cultural Resource Management Series,* NTIS PB-270939. National Park Service, Department of the Interior, Washington, D.C.

TANAKA, JIRO

1976   Subsistence ecology of the central Kalahari San. In *Kalahari Hunter-Gatherers: Studies of the !Kung and their Neighbors,* edited by Richard B. Lee and Irven DeVore, pp. 98–119. Cambridge, Mass.: Harvard University Press.

TAYLOR, WALTER

1948   *A Study of Archaeology.* Memoir No. 69, American Anthropological Association. Reprinted 1965, 1967 by Southern Illinois University Press, Carbondale.

THOMAS, DAVID HURST

1971   Prehistoric subsistence-settlement patterns of the Reese River Valley, central Nevada. Ph.D. dissertation, University of California, Davis.

1972   A computer simulation model of Great Basin Shoshonean settlement patterns. In *Models in Archaeology,* edited by David L. Clarke, pp. 671–704. London: Methuen.

1973   An empirical test of Steward's model of Great Basin settlement patterns. *American Antiquity* 38:155–76.

1974   *Predicting the Past: An Introduction to Anthropological Archaeology.* Basic Anthropology Units. New York: Holt, Rinehart and Winston.

1975   Nonsite sampling in archaeology: up the creek without a site? In *Sampling in Archaeology,* edited by James W. Mueller, pp. 61–81. Tucson: University of Arizona Press.

1983   *The archaeology of Monitor Valley, 1. Epistomology. Anthropological Papers of the American Museum of Natural History,* vol. 58, part 1. New York.

TODD, LAWRENCE C., DAVID J. RAPSON, AND ERIC E. INGBAR

1985   Glimpses of organization: integrating site structure with analysis of assemblage content. Paper presented at the 50th annual meeting of the Society for American Archaeology, Denver, 1–5 May 1985.

TORRANCE, ROBIN

1983   Time budgeting and hunter-gatherer technology. In *Hunter-Gatherer Economy in Prehistory,* edited by Geoff Bailey, pp. 11–22. Cambridge: Cambridge University Press.

TREAT, PATRICIA A., BARBARA HICKMAN, ALAN ALPERT, AND DONALD J. WEIR
1982   Class I Cultural Resources Overview for the Proposed Frontier Pipeline. Submitted to Frontier Pipeline Co., Chicago, Ill., by Commonwealth Associates, Inc., Jackson, Mich.

TRUBOWITZ, N.L.
1978   The persistence of settlement pattern in a cultivated field. In *Essays in Memory of Marian E. White,* edited by W. Engelbrecht and D. Grayson, pp. 41–66. *Occasional Papers in Anthropology 5.* Department of Anthropology, Franklin Pearce College, Rindge, N.H.

UNIVERSITY OF UTAH
1983   *IMACS Users Guide.* Intermountain Antiquities Computer System. Archeological Center, Department of Anthropology, University of Utah, Salt Lake City.

VAYDA, ANDREW P., ED.
1969   *Environment and Cultural Behavior: Ecological Studies in Cultural Anthropology.* Garden City, N.Y.: Natural History Press.

VITA-FINZI, C., AND E.S. HIGGS
1970   Prehistoric economy in the Mount Carmel area of Palestine: site catchment analysis. *Proceedings of the Prehistoric Society* 36:1–37.

WAIT, WALTER
1977   Identification and analysis of the "non-sedentary" archaeological site in northwestern New Mexico. Ph.D. dissertation, Department of Anthropology, State University of New York, Binghamton.

WANDSNIDER, LUANN
1984   Assessing the impact of select geomorphological processes on the integrity of the surface archaeological record. Dissertation prospectus, Department of Anthropology, University of New Mexico, Albuquerque.
1989   Long-term land use, formation processes, and the structure of the archaeological landscape: a case study from southwestern Wyoming. Ph.D. Dissertation, Department of Anthropology, University of New Mexico.

WANDSNIDER, LUANN, AND JAMES I. EBERT
1983a   Modeling climatic and landform features affecting the character of the archaeological record in arid lands: a remote sensing approach in southwestern Wyoming. Paper presented at the Silver Anniversary Meetings of the Western Social Science Association and the Association of Arid Lands Studies, April 27–30, Albuquerque.
1983b   Accuracy and precision of nonsite archaeological survey methods in the Seedskadee area, southwestern Wyoming. Paper delivered at the

1983 meetings of the Society of Independent Anthropologists, Albuquerque.

1985   Geomorphological processes and the integrity of archaeological remains in dune fields. Paper presented at the 50th annual meeting of the Society for American Archaeology, Denver, 1–5 May 1985.

WANDSNIDER, LUANN AND SIGNA LARRALDE

1984   Seedskadee Cultural Resource Assessment Project: Report to the Branch of Remote Sensing. Branch of Remote Sensing, National Park Service, Albuquerque.

WEDEL, WALDO R.

1963   The High Plains and their utilization by the Indians. *American Antiquity* 29(1):1–16.

1968   Mummy Cave: prehistoric record from the Rocky Mountains of Wyoming. *Science* 160:184–85.

WHALLON, ROBERT, JR.

1973   Spatial analysis of occupation floors I: Application of dimensional analysis of variance. *American Antiquity* 38:320–28.

1974   Spatial analysis of occupation floors II: The application of nearest neighbor analysis. *American Antiquity* 39:16–34.

WHITE, J. PETER

1967   Ethno-archaeology in New Guinea: two examples. *Mankind* 6(9):409–14.

WHITE, J. PETER, AND DAVID HURST THOMAS

1972   What mean these stones? Ethno-taxonomic models and archaeological interpretations in the New Guinea highlands. In *Models in Archaeology,* edited by David L. Clarke, pp. 275–308. London: Methuen.

WHITE, LESLIE A.

1954   Review of "Culture: A Critical Review of Concepts and Definitions," by A.L. Kroeber and C. Kluckhohn. *American Anthropologist* 56:461–86.

WHITING, BEATRICE BLYTH

1950   Paiute sorcery. *Viking Fund Publications in Anthropology* 15. New York: Viking Fund.

WIESSNER, POLLY

1974   A functional estimator of population from floor area. *American Antiquity* 39(2):343–350.

WILKE, S.C., AND G.T. THOMPSON

1977   *Archaeological Survey of western Kent County, Maryland.* Report submitted to the Division of Archaeology, Maryland Geological Survey.

WILLEY, GORDON R., AND JEREMY A. SABLOFF
1974   *A History of American Archaeology*. San Francisco: W.H. Freeman.

WILLS, WIRT H.
1980   Ethnographic observation and archaeological interpretation: the Wikmunkan of Cape York Peninsula, Austraila. In *The Archaeological Correlates of Hunter-Gatherer Societies: Studies from the Ethnographic Record*, edited by F.E. Smiley, C.M. Sinopoli, H.E. Jackson, W.H. Wills, and S.A. Gregg, pp. 79–99. Michigan Discussions in Anthropology 5(1/2). University of Michigan, Ann Arbor.

WILMSEN, EDWIN N.
1970   Lithic analysis and cultural inference: a Palaeo-Indian case. *Anthropological Papers of the University of Arizona* 16.

WISSLER, CLARK
1917   *The American Indian; An Introduction to the Anthropology of the New World*. New York: D.C. McMurtie.

WOOD, W. RAYMOND, AND D.L. JOHNSON
1978   A survey of disturbance processes in archaeological site formation. In *Advances in Archaeological Method and Theory*, vol. 1, edited by Michael B. Schiffer, pp. 315–81. New York: Academic Press.

WOODBURN, JAMES
1972   Ecology, nomadic movement and the composition of the local group among hunters and gatherers: an east African example and its implications. In *Man, Settlement, and Urbanism*, edited by P.J. Ucko, R. Tringham, and G.W. Dimbleby, pp. 193-206. London: Duckworth.

YELLEN, JOHN E.
1976   Settlement patterns of the !Kung: an archaeological perspective. In *Kalahari Hunter-Gatherers*, edited by Richard B. Lee and Irven DeVore, pp. 47–72. Cambridge, Mass.: Harvard University Press.

ZIER, ANNE H., AND T.C. PEEBLES
1982   Report on the Kemmerer Resources Area Class II cultural resource inventory, Lincoln and Uinta Counties, Wyoming. Report Submitted by Metcalf-Zier Archaeologists, Inc. to the Bureau of Land Management (Contract No. YA-553-RFP-1-35).

INDEX

-- -- -- -- -- -- -- -- -- -- -- -- --

287